D1712474

Corrective Reading

▶Concept Applications

Comprehension C
Student Book

Siegfried Engelmann • Susan Hanner • Phyllis Haddox

SRA
McGraw-Hill

Columbus, Ohio

A Division of The McGraw·Hill Companies

Table of Contents

Photo Credits Cover Photo: KS Studios

SRA/McGraw-Hill

A Division of The **McGraw·Hill** *Companies*

Imprint 2002
Copyright © 1999 by SRA/McGraw-Hill.

Send all inquiries to:
SRA/McGraw-Hill
8787 Orion Place
Columbus, OH 43240-4027

Printed in the United States of America.

ISBN 0-02-674818-5

12 13 VHJ 07 06

A

When you combine two sentences with the word **but,**
what do you do with the period of the first sentence?
What word follows the comma?
When you combine two sentences with the word **however,**
what do you do with the period of the first sentence?
What follows the semicolon?
What follows the word **however?**

B

Here's a rule about contradictions:

> **If a statement is true, a contradiction of that statement is false.**

- Here's a statement:
  He was in Chicago at 5 A.M. on July 1.
  If that statement is true, these statements are false:
  He was in New Orleans at 5 A.M. on July 1.
  He was in St. Louis at 5 A.M. on July 1.
  He was in Milwaukee at 5 A.M. on July 1.
  These statements contradict the statement about being in Chicago, because he couldn't be in Chicago and in any of the other places at the same time.

- If this statement is true,
  Yesterday she was fifteen years old,
  then these statements contradict it:
  Yesterday she was twelve years old.
  Yesterday she was twenty years old.
  Yesterday she was eighteen years old.
  These statements contradict the true statement, because she can't be fifteen years old and any other age at the same time.

- Assume that this statement is true:
  Elmer is taller than everybody else in his family—his father, his mother, his sister Jane, and his brother Ted.
  Make up three statements that contradict the true statement about how tall Elmer is.

- Let's say that this statement is true:
  Mrs. Kaplan had one green eye and one brown eye.
  Make up three statements that contradict the true statement about Mrs. Kaplan's eyes.

- Let's say that this statement is true:

  Dan couldn't drive any kind of vehicle.

  Make up three statements that contradict the true statement.

Draw a conclusion about the Eiffel Tower.
Here's the evidence:

> **The Eiffel Tower is in Paris.**
> **Part of Paris is on a hill.**

What's the conclusion about the Eiffel Tower?
We aren't sure that the Eiffel Tower is on a hill.
Which piece of evidence explains why we can't be sure?

- Draw a conclusion about a cup.
  Here's the evidence:

> **Some containers are made of glass.**
> **A cup is a container.**

What's the conclusion about a cup?
We aren't sure that a cup is made of glass.
Which piece of evidence explains why we can't be sure?

On a sheet of lined paper, write **Part D** in the left margin. You have two minutes to copy the paragraph below.

> **When you apply for a loan, you usually have to fill out a form. You may be asked to indicate your marital status: are you married, single, divorced, or widowed?**

• Assume that this statement is true:

Tom could not drive a car.

Then this statement is a contradiction:

Tom was driving a station wagon down Fifth Street.

Here is why the statement is a contradiction. If Tom could not drive a car, then he could not drive a station wagon down Fifth Street.

• Assume that this statement is true:

Abby swam all morning.

Then this statement is a contradiction:

Abby rode her bike at 10 A.M.

Here is why the statement is a contradiction. If Abby swam all morning, then she could not have ridden her bike at 10 A.M.

• Assume that this statement is true:

Gina loved to eat all vegetables.

Then this statement is a contradiction:

Gina hated to eat broccoli.

Tell why the statement is a contradiction.

    If _____ , then _____ .

To fill in the blanks, start by saying the true statement. Then tell what couldn't also be true.

• Assume that this statement is true:

Jason always sleeps until 9 A.M.

Then this statement is a contradiction:

Jason went fishing today at 6 A.M.

Fill in the blanks to tell why the statement is a contradiction.

    If _____ , then _____ .

When you combine two sentences with the word **but,**
what do you do with the period of the first sentence?
What word follows the comma?
When you combine two sentences with the word **however,**
what do you do with the period of the first sentence?
What follows the semicolon?
What follows the word **however?**

Draw a conclusion about carrots.
Here's the evidence:

> **Carrots are vegetables.**
> **Some vegetables contain vitamin A.**

Here's the conclusion:

> **So, maybe carrots contain vitamin A.**

We aren't sure that carrots contain vitamin A. Which piece of evidence explains why we can't be sure?

- Here's some new evidence:

> **Carrots are vegetables.**
> **All vegetables are food.**

What's the conclusion about carrots?

On a sheet of lined paper, write **Part D** in the left margin. You have two minutes to copy the paragraph below.

> **If you go to college, you may get to choose where you live. Some colleges may require younger students to live in student housing, dormitories run by the school.**

A

Remember, the word **each** tells about one thing, not more than one thing.
So **each** goes with the verb **is** or the verb **was.**
   This is correct: **The soldiers are tired.**
   But this is not correct: **Each of the soldiers are tired.**
   This is correct: **Each of the soldiers is tired.**

Say each sentence below with the verb **is** or the verb **are.**

1. The girls _____ hungry.
2. The dogs _____ running.
3. The men _____ happy.
4. Each of the girls _____ hungry.
5. Each of the dogs _____ running.
6. Each of the men _____ happy.

B

Draw a conclusion about wombats.
Here's the evidence:

   Some living things have red blood.
   Wombats are living things.

Here's the conclusion:
   So, maybe wombats have red blood.
We aren't sure that wombats have red blood. Which piece of evidence
explains why we can't be sure?

• Here's some new evidence:

   All living things breathe.
   Wombats are living things.

What's the conclusion about wombats?

C

Assume that this statement is true:
   Libby loved all vehicles.
Then this statement is a contradiction:
   Libby hated motor scooters.
Fill in the blanks to tell why the statement is a contradiction.
   If _____ , then _____ .

• Assume that this statement is true:

   At 6 A.M. yesterday, I was in Paris, France.
Then this statement is a contradiction:
   At 6 A.M. yesterday, I was in London, England.
Tell why the statement is a contradiction.
   If _____ , then _____ .

What kind of sentence tells something we don't expect to happen?
Sentences that tell something we expect to happen are called **consistent.**

Here's what we know:

> **Dan has six children.**

The next sentence seems consistent with the sentence in the box:

> **He has a large house.**

Make up other sentences that seem consistent with the sentence in the box.
One of the sentences below seems consistent with the sentence in the box.
Find that sentence.

- His grocery bill is big.
- He believes in small families.
- He doesn't like children.

Here's what we know:

> **Marvin is a gardener.**

Tell whether each sentence below seems **consistent** or **inconsistent** with the sentence in the box.

1. He doesn't like to be outside.
2. He buys lots of fertilizer.
3. He grows prizewinning roses.
4. His clothes often get dirty.
5. He is allergic to grass.
6. He owns three lawn mowers.

On a sheet of lined paper, write **Part E** in the left margin. You have two
minutes to copy the paragraph below.

> **If you go to college, you may have to pay a fee. The fee is called
> tuition. Sometimes people who can't afford tuition can get
> financial aid from various organizations.**

A

What do we call sentences that tell something we expect to happen?
What do we call sentences that tell something we don't expect to happen?

Here's what we know:

> **Maureen goes to a weight-loss clinic.**

Tell whether each sentence below seems **consistent** or **inconsistent** with the sentence in the box.

1. She is often hungry.
2. She is always eating.
3. She has cake or pie after every dinner.
4. She is buying a whole wardrobe in a larger size.
5. Her friends tell her she looks better already.
6. She has gained three pounds in the last two weeks.

B

Here's how to find a contradiction in a passage:

1. Start out assuming that what the speaker says first is true.
2. Read until you find a contradiction.
3. Make up an if-then statement that explains the contradiction.

Here's a passage:

> The name of our organization is the Fair-Minded
> Organization. As the name says, <u>we're fair-minded.</u>
> We work hard. We take on difficult community projects.
> We keep women out of our organization because the work
> is too hard for them.

We assume that the underlined statement is true. If that statement is true, then it can't be true that they keep women out of their organization. Here's how we explain the contradiction:

If they are fair-minded, **then** they can't keep women out of their organization.

Remember, the word **each** tells about one thing, not more than one thing. So the word **each** goes with the verb **is** or the verb **was.**

Say each sentence below with the verb **was** or the verb **were.**

1. The cups _____ broken.
2. The players _____ resting.
3. The older lions _____ sleeping.
4. Each of the older lions _____ sleeping.
5. Each of the cups _____ broken.
6. Each of the players _____ resting.

Write **Part D** in the left margin of your paper. You have two minutes to copy the paragraph below.

> **Here's a rule about contradictions. If a statement is true, a contradiction of that statement is false. Most statements have many contradictions. You can have fun making up contradictions.**

Here's how to find a contradiction in a passage:

1. Start out assuming that what the speaker says first is true.
2. Read until you find a contradiction.
3. Make up an if-then statement that explains the contradiction.

Here's a passage:

> **The Baseball Hall of Fame is in Cooperstown, New York.** The exhibits there show the equipment that was used in famous games or by great players. Each year many people visit California, where they see the exhibits in the Baseball Hall of Fame.

We assume that the underlined statement is true. If that statement is true, then it can't be true that people visit the Baseball Hall of Fame in California. Here's how we explain the contradiction:

If the Baseball Hall of Fame is in New York, **then** people can't visit it in California.

What do we call sentences that tell something we don't expect to happen? What do we call sentences that tell something we expect to happen?

Here's what we know:

> **Diana plays the piano at a fancy restaurant.**

Tell whether each sentence below seems **consistent** or **inconsistent** with the sentence in the box.

1. She doesn't like to be around people.
2. She can play selections from memory.
3. She is six years old.
4. She wears jeans and heavy boots at work.
5. She stands up while she works.
6. She doesn't start work until 4 P.M.

Write **Part C** in the left margin of your paper. Then number it from 1 to 4. Read the story and answer the questions.

Mr. Nelson was a nice old fellow, but he had one problem. He got his words mixed up. When he wanted to say **boar,** he said **sore.** When he wanted to say **sanded,** he said **banded.**

Mr. Nelson loved to make little statues of animals. He made statues of geese, frogs, elephants, and dogs. One day he was working on a little wooden statue of a boar. (A boar is a wild pig with large tusks.) Mr. Nelson's granddaughter was watching him as he carved the boar and then sanded it. "Oh, it's starting to look really good," she said.

"Yes," Mr. Nelson replied. "This sore will soon be banded."

His granddaughter frowned. Then she smiled as she realized what he had meant to say.

1. What did Mr. Nelson mean when he said, "This sore will soon be banded"?
2. How would Mr. Nelson say, "A sanded boar"?
3. Name three kinds of animals that Mr. Nelson made statues of.
4. What is a boar?

Write **Part D** in the left margin of your paper. You have two minutes to copy the paragraph below.

Let's say you know that something is true. Some things may happen that are consistent with what you know. Other things may happen that are inconsistent with what you know.

Write **Part A** in the left margin of your paper. Then number it from 1 to 5. Read the story and answer the questions.

> Mr. Nelson was always saying funny things because he was always getting words mixed up. When he wanted to say **boat,** he said **note.** And when he tried to say **nook,** he said **book.** (A nook is a small place. A breakfast nook is a small place next to the kitchen with just enough room for a table and a few chairs.)
>
> One day, Mr. Nelson decided to dig a nook for his rowboat, so he got a shovel and went to work. Before long, he had dug out a small channel next to his boat dock. His granddaughter watched him. Finally she asked, "Grandfather, are you making a home for some fish?"
>
> "No, no," Mr. Nelson said and laughed. "I am making a note book."
>
> His granddaughter said, "You're not very funny," and she ran away.

1. What did Mr. Nelson mean when he said, "I am making a note book"?
2. How would Mr. Nelson say, "A nook for my boat"?
3. What is a nook?
4. Where was Mr. Nelson digging the boat nook?
5. What did Mr. Nelson's granddaughter think he was doing?

 Here's how to find a contradiction in a passage:

1. Start out assuming that what the speaker says first is true.
2. Read until you find a contradiction.
3. Make up an if-then statement that explains the contradiction.

What are the three things you do to find a contradiction in a passage?

What kind of sentence tells something we don't expect to happen?
What kind of sentence tells something we expect to happen?
To combine two sentences that seem consistent, we can use
the word **and,** the word **so,** or the word **therefore.**

Here's what we know:

> **Gino loves to work outside.**

Here's a sentence that seems consistent with the sentence in the box:
He got a job as a gardener.
Here are the two sentences combined with the word **and:**
Gino loves to work outside, and he got a job as a gardener.
Here are the two sentences combined with the word **so:**
Gino loves to work outside, so he got a job as a gardener.
Here are the two sentences combined with the word **therefore:**
Gino loves to work outside; therefore, he got a job as a gardener.

Here's what we know:

> **Jolene's family is very poor.**

Read the sentence below and find the one that seems consistent with the
sentence in the box.

- **She works every day after school.**
- **She spends a lot of money on clothes.**

Use the word **and** to combine the sentence in the box with the consistent
sentence.
Use the word **so** to combine the sentence in the box with the consistent
sentence.
Use the word **therefore** to combine the sentence in the box with the
consistent sentence.

Here's what we know:

> **Cindy wants to buy a car.**

Read the sentences below and find the one that seems consistent with the sentence in the box.

- **She doesn't know how to drive.**
- **She's looking for a job.**

Use the word **and** to combine the sentence in the box with the consistent sentence.

Use the word **so** to combine the sentence in the box with the consistent sentence.

Use the word **therefore** to combine the sentence in the box with the consistent sentence.

 Write **Part D** in the left margin of your paper. You have two minutes to copy the paragraph below.

> **When you combine two sentences with the word "however," change the period of the first sentence to a semicolon. Follow the semicolon with "however." Follow "however" with a comma.**

A

Here's how to find a contradiction in a passage:

1. Start out assuming that what the speaker says first is true.
2. Read until you find a contradiction.
3. Make up an if-then statement that explains the contradiction.

What are the three things you do to find a contradiction in a passage?

B

Here's what we know:

> **Rosie wants to be a doctor.**

Read the sentences below and find the one that seems consistent with the sentence in the box.

- **She reads a lot of medical books.**
- **She can't stand the sight of blood.**

Use the word **and** to combine the sentence in the box with the consistent sentence.

Use the word **so** to combine the sentence in the box with the consistent sentence.

Use the word **therefore** to combine the sentence in the box with the consistent sentence.

> When you combine two sentences with the word **but,**
> what do you do with the period of the first sentence?
> What word follows the comma?
> When you combine two sentences with the word **however,**
> what do you do with the period of the first sentence?
> What follows the semicolon?
> What follows the word **however?**

We can combine two sentences that seem consistent by using the word **and** or the word **so.** We follow the same rules that we use to combine sentences with the word **but:**

Change the period of the first sentence to a comma.

Follow the comma with the word **and** or the word **so.**

Here are two consistent sentences:

She was happy. She smiled a lot.

Here are the sentences combined with **and:**

She was happy, and she smiled a lot.

Here are the sentences combined with **so:**

She was happy, so she smiled a lot.

We can also combine consistent sentences by using the word **therefore.** We follow the same rules that we use to combine sentences with **however:**

> Change the period of the first sentence to a semicolon.
> Follow the semicolon with the word **therefore.**
> Follow **therefore** with a comma.

Here are two consistent sentences:

She was happy. She smiled a lot.

Here are the sentences combined with **therefore:**

She was happy; therefore, she smiled a lot.

Think of how the words **and, so,** and **therefore** work. Which word follows the same sentence combination rules as the word **however?**

Which words follow the same sentence combination rules as the word **but?**

Here are two consistent sentences:

He was tired. He went to bed.

Tell how you would combine the sentences with the word **and.** Say the combined sentence and tell about the punctuation.

Tell how you would combine the sentences with the word **so.** Say the combined sentence and tell about the punctuation.

Tell how you would combine the sentences with the word **therefore.** Say the combined sentence and tell about the punctuation.

 Write **Part C** in the left margin of your paper. You have two minutes to copy the paragraph below.

> **Before you combine two sentences, decide if they are consistent or inconsistent. If the sentences are consistent, you can combine them with the word "so," the word "and," or the word "therefore."**

A When you combine two sentences with the word **but,**
what do you do with the period of the first sentence?
What word follows the comma?
When you combine two sentences with the word **however,**
what do you do with the period of the first sentence?
What follows the semicolon?
What follows the word **however?**

We can combine two sentences that seem consistent by using the word **and** or the word **so.** We follow the same rules that we use to combine sentences with the word **but:**

> Change the period of the first sentence to a comma.
> Follow the comma with the word **and** or the word **so.**

Here are two consistent sentences:
> **David doesn't eat any sweets. He has very healthy teeth.**

Here are the sentences combined with **and:**
> **David doesn't eat any sweets, and he has very healthy teeth.**

Here are the sentences combined with **so:**
> **David doesn't eat any sweets, so he has very healthy teeth.**

We can also combine consistent sentences by using the word **therefore.** We follow the same rules that we use to combine sentences with **however:**

> Change the period of the first sentence to a semicolon.
> Follow the semicolon with the word **therefore.**
> Follow **therefore** with a comma.

Here are two consistent sentences:
> **David doesn't eat sweets. He has very healthy teeth.**

Here are the sentences combined with **therefore:**
> **David doesn't eat sweets; therefore, he has very healthy teeth.**

Think of how the words **and, so,** and **therefore** work.
Which word follows the same sentence combination rules as the word **however?**
Which words follow the same sentence combination rules as the word **but?**

Here are two consistent sentences:

Nina is hungry. She is eating a lot.

Tell how you would combine the sentences with the word **and.**
Say the combined sentence and tell about the punctuation.
Tell how you would combine the sentences with the word **so.** Say the combined sentence and tell about the punctuation.
Tell how you would combine the sentences with the word **therefore.** Say the combined sentence and tell about the punctuation.

B The model sentence below contains vocabulary words that you will use in other sentences. You're going to memorize the model sentence. Make sure that you know what the words mean and how to spell them.

Here's the model sentence:

By hesitating, she lost her opportunity.

Here's what it means:

By pausing, she lost her chance.

Study the model sentence until you can say it without looking at it.
What does the word **hesitating** mean?
What does the word **opportunity** mean?
What's another way of saying, **By pausing, she lost her chance?**

For each item, say a sentence that means the same thing.

1. Although he paused, he did not give up his chance.
2. Tom had four chances to buy that house.

Write **Part C** in the left margin of your paper. Then number it from 1 to 4. Read the story and answer the questions.

> The pages of early Greek manuscripts were completely covered with writing. There were no breaks or punctuation marks to aid the reader. When writers switched from one topic to another, they would put a small mark in the margin next to the line where the new topic was introduced. The Greeks took their words **para** (by the side of) and **graphos** (writing) and named the little mark in the margin **paragraphos.** Today we indent the first line when we begin a new topic instead of putting a mark in the margin, but the word **paragraph** is still with us to indicate the switch in topics.

1. What did the pages of early Greek manuscripts look like?
2. How did writers indicate a change of topic?
3. What does the Greek word **paragraphos** mean?
4. How do we indicate a change of topic today?

 Write **Part D** in the left margin of your paper. You have two minutes to copy the paragraph below.

> **If you wish to increase your writing speed, you must not hesitate. You could lose this opportunity to improve your rate; however, you may get another chance tomorrow.**

Here's the model sentence you learned:

> **By hesitating, she lost her opportunity.**

What sentence means the same thing?
What word means **pausing?**
What word means **chance?**
What's another way of saying, **She lost her chance?**

You learned rules about using two words to combine sentences that seem inconsistent. Which two words?
You learned rules about using three words to combine sentences that seem consistent. Which three words?

Think of the words **and, so,** and **therefore.**
Two of these words follow the same sentence combination rules as the word **but.** Which two words?
One word follows the same sentence combination rules as the word **however.** Which word?

Write **Part C** in the left margin of your paper. You have two minutes to copy the paragraph below.

> **Here's the rule for combining two consistent sentences with the word "so." Change the period of the first sentence to a comma. Follow the comma with the word "so."**

You learned rules about using two words to combine sentences that seem inconsistent. Which two words?
You learned rules about using three words to combine sentences that seem consistent. Which three words?

Think of the words **and, so,** and **therefore.**
Two of these words follow the same sentence combination rules as the word **but.** Which two words?
One word follows the same sentence combination rules as the word **however.** Which word?

Write **Part B** in the left margin of your paper. You have two minutes to copy the paragraph below.

> **If a question asks about your monthly expenses, it asks how much you have to pay out each month for things like rent and food and car maintenance.**

INFORMATION TEST. Write **Part C** in the left margin of your paper. Then number it from 1 to 3, and answer each item. You have two minutes.

1. What is a boar?
2. What is a nook?
3. What does the Greek word **paragraphos** mean?

★ **D** **Write Part D** in the left margin of your paper. Then number it from 1 to 4. Read the story and answer the questions.

> Mr. Nelson's granddaughter had three rabbits—two large ones and a smaller black-and-white one. On the day before Thanksgiving, Mr. Nelson took his granddaughter with him to the pet shop. They were going to buy a treat for the rabbits. The problem was that Mr. Nelson didn't always say the words he wanted to say. For example, when he wanted to say **carrots,** he said **parrots.** When he wanted to say **pick,** he said **kick.**
>
> Mr. Nelson and his granddaughter walked up to the man behind the counter. Mr. Nelson looked at the man, smiled, and said, "We're here to kick some parrots for our rabbits."
>
> The man threw Mr. Nelson and his granddaughter out of the pet shop.

1. What did Mr. Nelson mean when he said, "We're here to kick some parrots"?
2. Did the man in the pet store know what Mr. Nelson was trying to say?
3. How do you know?
4. How would Mr. Nelson say, "We should pick carrots all day"?

A

You learned a model sentence that means this:

By pausing, she lost her chance.

Say that model sentence.

What word in the model sentence means **pausing?**

What word in the model sentence means **chance?**

B

In the passage below, the verbs **was** and **were** are used incorrectly two times. Read each sentence and tell if there is an incorrect word in the sentence. If there is, say the sentence correctly.

> Four fire engines streaked toward the burning building. Three of them was long and had ladders. All of them were red. Gallons of water was spraying from a crack in a pipe.

C

Here's a new model sentence:

His directions were ambiguous and redundant.

Read the sentence to yourself. Study the sentence until you can say it without looking at it.

Here's what the model sentence means:

His directions were unclear and repetitive.

What word in the model means **unclear?**

What word in the model means **repetitive?**

For each item, say a sentence that means the same thing.

1. Her questions were <u>unclear</u> and <u>repetitive</u>.
2. His <u>unclear</u> and <u>repetitive</u> speech made the time drag.

D

Write **Part D** in the left margin of your paper. You have two minutes to copy the paragraph below.

> **George has neat penmanship; however, he is not a very good writer. His stories are so ambiguous that it is difficult to understand what he is trying to say.**

★ **E** Write **Part E** in the left margin of your paper. Then number it from 1 to 5. Read the story and answer the questions.

> Millions of years ago, a kind of animal named eohippus lived in North America. Eohippus was a small animal, the size of a fox. It had four soft toes on its feet, a stubby mane, and a wispy tail. Although the last eohippus died over fifty million years ago, we know that it was related to the horse because its skeleton resembles the skeleton of a modern horse—especially in the way the teeth are arranged. Not only was eohippus related to the horse, it was the earliest-known close relative of the horse.

1. What is the name of the earliest-known close relative of the horse?
2. Where did eohippus live?
3. When did the last eohippus die?
4. How big was eohippus?
5. How do we know that eohippus was related to a modern horse?

LESSON 22

A

Here's the latest model sentence you learned:

His directions were ambiguous and redundant.

What sentence means the same thing?

What word means **unclear?**

What word means **repetitive?**

What's another way of saying,

His speech was unclear and repetitive?

B

In the passage below, the verbs **is** and **are** and the verbs **was** and **were** are used incorrectly three times. Read each sentence and tell if there is an incorrect word in the sentence. If there is, say the sentence correctly.

> The impression that you get from western movies are really not very accurate. Most cowboys was lonely and overworked. A person living in the Old West was sometimes forced to go without food or shelter for days at a time. As for the glamorous gunfighter, he are more a myth than a historical fact.

C

You learned a model sentence that means this:

By pausing, she lost her chance.

Say that model sentence.

What word in the model sentence means **pausing?**

What word in the model sentence means **chance?**

D

Write **Part D** in the left margin of your paper. You have two minutes to copy the paragraph below.

> **If a question asks about job qualifications, tell your job experience and why you would be good at the job. If a question asks about monthly income, tell how much money you make each month.**

★ **E** Write **Part E** in the left margin of your paper. Then number it from 1 to 5. Read the story and answer the questions.

Staying alive was difficult for eohippus. Many large meat-eating animals enjoyed eating the small horses. Eohippus was not equipped with fangs, claws, or a hard shell. The only defense eohippus had was the ability to outrun its enemies. Slow runners were caught and eaten. Fast runners escaped the teeth of the meat-eating animals that prowled North America. As centuries passed, the body of eohippus changed because only the fastest runners lived to mate and have offspring. The body of the animal became larger and its feet became better suited for running. The outside toes on each foot got smaller and smaller. At the same time, the middle toes got larger and larger. Its feet were becoming more like hooves. The animal had changed so much that scientists do not call it eohippus. The scientists named the new animal pliohippus.

1. How did eohippus defend itself?
2. What happened to slow runners?
3. Which eohippus lived to have offspring?
4. How did the feet of eohippus change over the centuries?
5. Why did the feet of eohippus change?

When you combine two sentences with the word **but,**
what do you do with the period of the first sentence?
What word follows the comma?
When you combine two sentences with the word **and,**
what do you do with the period of the first sentence?
What word follows the comma?
When you combine two sentences with the word **therefore,**
what do you do with the period of the first sentence?
What follows the semicolon?
What follows the word **therefore?**

Here are two facts:

Fact A. **Herman has lots of muscles.**
Fact B. **Herman is a vegetarian.**

Some items below are relevant to fact A.
Some items are relevant to fact B.
Some items are irrelevant to both facts.

1. **Herman lifts barbells every day.**
   Is that relevant to fact A, relevant to fact B, or irrelevant?
2. **Herman likes to go to the ballet.**
   Is that relevant to fact A, relevant to fact B, or irrelevant?
3. **Herman hasn't had a steak in twelve years.**
   Is that relevant to fact A, relevant to fact B, or irrelevant?
4. **Herman worked as a furniture mover for three years.**
   Is that relevant to fact A, relevant to fact B, or irrelevant?

You learned a model sentence that means this:
   His directions were unclear and repetitive.
Say that model sentence.
What word in the model sentence means **unclear?**
What word in the model sentence means **repetitive?**

Write **Part D** in the left margin of your paper. You have two minutes to copy the paragraph below.

> **When you combine consistent sentences with the word "therefore," change the period of the first sentence to a semicolon. Follow the semicolon with the word "therefore." Follow "therefore" with a comma.**

★

Write **Part E** in the left margin of your paper. Then number it from 1 to 4. Read the story and answer the questions.

> Mr. Nelson worked hard in the yard all day. It was autumn, and lots of leaves had fallen from the trees. Mr. Nelson raked the yard and swept the sidewalk. When he finished, he felt a sharp pain in his back. He went inside where his granddaughter Irene was reading a book. She looked up at him and said, "Oh, grandpa, you look so tired."
>
> "Sore, too," Mr. Nelson said.
>
> To appreciate the next thing that Mr. Nelson said, you have to understand that he didn't always say what he wanted to say. For instance, if Mr. Nelson wanted to say **shower,** he said **tower.** If he wanted to say **take,** he said **shake.** With one hand on his back, he stretched and said, "I think I'll go shake a tower."
>
> Irene shook her head, said, "Have fun," and went back to her book.

1. What did Mr. Nelson mean when he said, "I think I'll go shake a tower"?
2. How would Mr. Nelson say, "That shower felt good"?
3. Did this story take place in July?
4. How do you know?

A When you combine two sentences with the word **however,** what do you do with the period of the first sentence?
What follows the semicolon?
What follows the word **however?**
When you combine two sentences with the word **and,** what do you do with the period of the first sentence?
What word follows the comma?
When you combine two sentences with the word **so,** what do you do with the period of the first sentence?
What word follows the comma?

B You learned a model sentence that means this:
His directions were unclear and repetitive.
Say that model sentence.
What word in the model sentence means **unclear?**
What word in the model sentence means **repetitive?**

C Write **Part C** in the left margin of your paper. You have two minutes to copy the paragraph below.

> **As centuries passed, the body of eohippus changed because only the fastest runners lived to mate and have offspring. The body of the animal became larger, and its feet became better suited for running.**

★ **D** Write **Part D** in the left margin of your paper. Then number it from 1 to 6. Read the story and answer the questions.

> Modern horses and other similar animals belong to a group called equus. Although eohippus and pliohippus were related to modern horses, they are not called equus. The first animal named equus appeared about one million years ago. It was the size of a pony and looked a lot like a modern pony, with a long mane, a full-sized tail, and hard hooves. During the time that equus developed, it roamed to many different parts of the world. Each equus developed differently, depending on where it lived. In cold climates where there was little food, equus became an animal with a strong, stocky body, short legs, and a shaggy coat. In areas where the climate was mild and there was lots of food, equus became a big, strong animal similar to the draft horse or the work horse. In hot climates, equus became a slender, quick, and graceful animal.

1. What do we call the group of animals that modern horses belong to?
2. When did the first equus appear?
3. How big was the first equus?
4. Why did some types of equus become large and strong while others became slender and quick?
5. Why did one kind of equus develop a shaggy coat?
6. In what regions did equus become slender and quick?

A Write **Part A** in the left margin of your paper. You have two minutes to copy the paragraph below.

> The first equus appeared about one million years ago. During the time that equus developed, it roamed to many different parts of the world. Each equus developed differently, depending on where it lived.

B **VOCABULARY TEST.** Write **Part B** in the left margin of your paper. Write the model sentence that means the same thing as the sentence below. You have one minute.

> By <u>pausing</u>, she lost her <u>chance</u>.

C **INFORMATION TEST.** Write **Part C** in the left margin of your paper. Then number it from 1 to 9. Answer each item. You have seven minutes.

1. What does the Greek word **paragraphos** mean?
2. What is the name of the earliest-known close relative of the horse?
3. How do we know that eohippus was related to a modern horse?
4. What is a boar?
5. How did eohippus defend itself?
6. Why did the feet of eohippus change over the centuries?
7. What is a nook?
8. What do we call the group of animals that modern horses belong to?
9. Why did some types of equus become large and strong while others became slender and quick?

You learned rules about using two words to combine sentences that seem inconsistent. Which two words?

You learned rules about using three words to combine sentences that seem consistent. Which three words?

Think of the words **and, so,** and **therefore.** Two of these words follow the same sentence combination rules as the word **but.**

Which two words?

One word follows the same sentence combination rules as the word **however.** Which word?

Write **Part B** in the left margin of your paper. You have two minutes to copy the paragraph below.

> **Here's how to find a contradiction in a passage. Start out assuming that what the speaker says is true. Read until you find a false statement. Make up an if-then statement that explains the contradiction.**

A

Here's a new model sentence:

> **They converted their Swiss currency into Canadian currency.**

Read the sentence to yourself. Study the sentence until you can say it without looking at it.
Here's what the model sentence means:

> **They changed their Swiss money into Canadian money.**

What word in the model means **changed?**
What word in the model means **money?**

For each item, say a sentence that means the same thing.

1. We changed our Mexican money into Japanese money.
2. She needed a lot of money to change the garage into a store.

B

Write **Part B** in the left margin of your paper. You have two minutes to copy the paragraph below.

> **If you travel to a foreign country, you will probably have to convert your own currency to the currency used in the foreign country. You can convert your currency at banks, airports, and train stations.**

A

When you combine two sentences with the word **but,**
what do you do with the period of the first sentence?
What word follows the comma?
When you combine two sentences with the word **however,**
what do you do with the period of the first sentence?
What follows the semicolon?
What follows the word **however?**
When you combine two sentences with the word **so,**
what do you do with the period of the first sentence?
What word follows the comma?

B

Here's the latest model sentence you learned:
    They converted their Swiss currency into Canadian currency.
What sentence means the same thing?
What word means **changed?**
What word means **money?**
What's another way of saying,
She went to the bank to <u>change</u> her <u>money</u> into savings bonds?

C

Write **Part C** in the left margin of your paper. You have two minutes to copy the paragraph below.

    Some deductions have irrelevant words in the second piece of evidence. To help you figure out the conclusion, you should cross out the irrelevant words. Then the conclusion will be more obvious.

★ **D** Write **Part D** in the left margin of your paper. Then number it from 1 to 4. Read the story and answer the questions.

Mr. Nelson's granddaughter had quite a few pets. She had three rabbits, one dog, and a rat. For some reason, she sometimes hazed her rat. (If you are hazing something, you are tormenting it.) She would haze the rat by taking a long twig and poking the rat.

One day Mr. Nelson was painting the garage. Irene was nearby hazing her rat. Mr. Nelson put down his paintbrush and scolded her. The problem is that when Mr. Nelson tried to say **haze,** he said **raise.** And when he tried to say **rat,** he said **hat.** Here's what he said: "Irene, stop raising your hat."

Irene looked up at him and said, "All right. I'll go shake a tower."

---

1. What did Mr. Nelson mean by what he said?
2. How would Mr. Nelson say, "She's hazing her rat again"?
3. What does **hazing** mean?
4. What did Irene mean when she said, "I'll go shake a tower"?

You learned a model sentence that means this:

They changed their Swiss money into Canadian money.

Say that model sentence.
What word in the model sentence means **changed?**
What word in the model sentence means **money?**

 Write **Part B** in the left margin of your paper. You have two minutes to copy the paragraph below.

Most people have at least one sibling. Siblings are those who have at least one parent in common; however, most people think of siblings as having both parents in common. Do you have any siblings?

  Write **Part C** in the left margin of your paper. Then number it from 1 to 5. Read the story and answer the questions.

> When you are confronted with a difficult problem that you cannot solve, somebody may give you a clue. A clue is a hint that helps you find your way out of the puzzle.
>
> The word **clue** has an interesting history. It goes all the way back to a Greek myth about a monster called the Minotaur, which lived in the middle of a great maze of tunnels. Once inside the maze, a person would be hopelessly lost. Theseus, the hero of the myth, planned to kill the Minotaur. A princess helped him. She told him how to get to the center of the maze. She also gave him a ball of thread to unwind as he made his way into the maze, leaving a trail. This trail of thread ensured that he could find his way out of the maze after he killed the Minotaur.
>
> In Middle English, the word for **thread** was **clewe.** Because the clewe helped Theseus get out of the maze, **clewe** came to mean anything that helps you out of a difficult or puzzling situation. The English spell the word **c-l-e-w;** in the United States, the word is spelled **c-l-u-e.**

1. What is a clue?
2. What did **clewe** mean in Middle English?
3. Why did Theseus want to get to the center of the maze?
4. What was the Minotaur?
5. Why did Theseus unwind a ball of thread in the maze?

LESSON 30

 Write **Part A** in the left margin of your paper. You have two minutes to copy the paragraph below.

> **When you are confronted with a difficult problem that you cannot solve, somebody may give you a clue. A clue is a hint that helps you find your way out of the puzzle.**

 INFORMATION TEST. Write **Part B** in the left margin of your paper. Then number it from 1 to 12 and answer each item. You have nine minutes.

1. What is a nook?
2. What is the name of the earliest-known close relative of the horse?
3. What is a boar?
4. How do we know that eohippus was related to a modern horse?
5. What does the Greek word **paragraphos** mean?
6. How did eohippus defend itself?
7. Why did the feet of eohippus change over the centuries?
8. What do we call the group of animals that modern horses belong to?
9. Why did some types of equus become large and strong while others became slender and quick?
10. What do you do when you haze people?
11. What is a clue?
12. What did **clewe** mean in Middle English?

 VOCABULARY TEST. Write **Part C** in the left margin of your paper. Then number it 1 and 2. Write the model sentence that means the same thing as each sentence below. You have two and a half minutes.

1. His directions were unclear and repetitive.
2. By pausing, she lost her chance.

★ **D** Write **Part D** in the left margin of your paper. Then number it from 1 to 5. Read the story and answer the questions.

> When you tantalize someone, you tease that person by putting something just out of reach. You could tantalize a hungry dog by holding a bone just above its head, where the dog can't reach it. The word **tantalize** comes from an old story.
>
> A Greek king named Tantalus killed his son and served him as food to the gods. The gods punished him for his act in an unusual way. He was sent to the underworld, where he was forced to stand chin-deep in fresh, cool water. Directly over his head hung branches laden with rich, juicy fruit. Unfortunately for Tantalus, when he became thirsty and tried to drink water, the water drained away. When he reached for the inviting fruit, the branches lifted up and stayed just out of reach. As soon as Tantalus stopped reaching, the cool water rose up to his chin again and the branches bent down over his head. According to the legend, Tantalus was tormented by hunger and thirst for the rest of time.

1. How would you tantalize a thirsty horse?
2. Why was Tantalus punished?
3. What happened when Tantalus tried to drink?
4. Why couldn't Tantalus reach the fruit?
5. What do you do when you tantalize someone?

A   There are several kinds of reference books you can use to find information.

> An **atlas** gives facts about places. It shows the size of cities and countries. It shows how far it is from one place to another. It tells the number of people who live in different places.
>
> An **encyclopedia** gives facts about nearly everything. It tells about planets and plants, about animals and buildings, and about history and famous people.
>
> A **dictionary** gives facts about words. It shows how to spell a word and how to pronounce it. It tells what part of speech a word is and what the word means. A dictionary also tells the history of words.

Which reference book would you use to find each of the following pieces of information?

1. How to pronounce the word **empathy**
2. The population of China
3. How far it is from New York City to Toronto
4. Abraham Lincoln's birthplace
5. What route to take to go from Florida to Alaska
6. The history of the word **compute**

B   Read the following passage.

> The hiccup fish of Brazil swallows huge gulps of air and makes a hiccuping sound when the air is released. A fully grown fish is four meters long. Its hiccup can be heard more than a kilometer away.

Here is a conclusion based on the passage:

A mature hiccup fish is longer than you are.

The evidence that supports this conclusion is in one of the sentences. Which sentence is that?
Here is another conclusion:

The hiccup fish sometimes comes to the surface of the water.

The evidence that supports this conclusion is in one of the sentences. Which sentence is that?

C   You learned a model sentence that means this:
They changed their Swiss money into Canadian money.
Say that model sentence.
What word in the model sentence means **changed?**
What word in the model sentence means **money?**

Write **Part D** in the left margin of your paper. You have two minutes to copy the paragraph below.

> **Ted is trying to convert me into a vegetarian. He says it's healthier not to eat meat. However, the only vegetables I will eat are turnips and beets. Who can live on turnips and beets?**

★

Write **Part E** in the left margin of your paper. Then number it from 1 to 5. Read the story and answer the questions.

Mr. Nelson was driving around looking for a place to eat. It was late at night, and not many restaurants were open. Just about the time he had decided to forget his hunger and go home, he spotted a little diner. He parked in front of it, went inside, and said hello to the woman behind the counter.

"What can I do for you?" she said.

"Let me see . . ." Mr. Nelson looked up at the large menu on the wall.

The woman said, "The grill is closed, so all we've got is cold sandwiches."

That news disappointed Mr. Nelson. He wanted something hot to eat. But when he tried to explain his problem, he got his words mixed up. Instead of saying **eat,** he said **meet,** and instead of saying **meal,** he said **eel.** So here's what Mr. Nelson said:

"That's too bad. I was hoping I could meet a hot eel in here."

The woman called a cop.

---

1. What did Mr. Nelson mean when he said, "I was hoping I could meet a hot eel"?
2. How would Mr. Nelson say, "Did you eat a cold meal at lunch"?
3. Did the woman in the diner know what Mr. Nelson was trying to say?
4. How do you know?
5. Why was the diner serving only cold sandwiches?

LESSON 32

A Read the following passage.

> Parsley is an excellent source of vitamin C and of iron. It has as much vitamin C as oranges and twice as much iron as spinach. In ancient Rome, around the time Christianity began, people nibbled parsley during funeral services.

Here is a conclusion based on the passage:

Parsley was eaten centuries ago.

The evidence that supports this conclusion is in one of the sentences. Which sentence is that?

Here is another conclusion:

Parsley has lots of nutritional value.

The evidence that supports this conclusion is in one of the sentences. Which sentence is that?

B An **atlas** gives facts about places. It shows the size of cities and countries. It shows how far it is from one place to another. It tells the number of people who live in different places.

An **encyclopedia** gives facts about nearly everything. It tells about planets and plants, about animals and buildings, and about history and famous people.

A **dictionary** gives facts about words. It shows how to spell a word and how to pronounce it. It tells what part of speech a word is and what the word means. A dictionary also tells the history of words.

C Write **Part C** in the left margin of your paper. You have two minutes to copy the paragraph below.

> **An atlas is one kind of reference book you can use to find information. An atlas gives facts about places: the size of cities and countries, distances between places, and populations of places.**

★ Write **Part D** in the left margin of your paper. Then number it from 1 to 5. Read the story and answer the questions.

In Lesson 24, you read that horses descended from an animal called equus. Equus has several other descendants. One of these descendants is the donkey, which is also known as a burro or an ass. Donkeys are much smaller than horses but are good work animals. They are easy to care for; they can work long, hard hours; they are seldom sick; and they are strong enough to carry things weighing over 250 pounds.

When a male donkey and a female horse are mated, the horse gives birth to a mule. Mules are about as large as horses and very strong. They have a reputation for being stubborn, lazy, and independent. This reputation is based on some fact; however, mules are usually hardworking and intelligent animals—smarter than horses in some respects. Before the tractor was invented, mules were ideal animals for farmwork. Mules have great endurance, so they could work long hours on the farm.

The zebra is another descendant of equus. Zebras are known for their striking black and white stripes. They are very difficult to tame; therefore, they do not make good work animals.

1. Name two descendants of equus.
2. Which descendant of equus does not do work for humans?
3. What are two other names for a donkey?
4. Why are donkeys good work animals?
5. Which is larger, a donkey or a mule?

A

Here's a new model sentence:

> **The regulation restricted their parking.**

Read the sentence to yourself. Study the sentence until you can say it without looking at it.

Here's what the model means:

> **The rule limited their parking.**

Which word in the model means **rule?**
Which word in the model means **limited?**

For each item, say a sentence that means the same thing.

1. A rule limited her voting rights.
2. Lawn sprinkling was limited because of the water shortage.

B

Name three kinds of information that you can find in an encyclopedia.
Name three kinds of information that you can find in an atlas.
Name three kinds of information that you can find in a dictionary.

C

Read the following passage.

> Reptiles are cold-blooded animals. This means that their bodies take on the same temperature as the air around them. If the weather is cold, a snake or lizard will move slowly and respond sluggishly. If it is warm, they move at a normal pace. If it gets too warm (about 38 degrees Celsius) or too cold (around freezing), the reptile could die if it doesn't find shelter.

Here is a conclusion based on the passage:

> **It is easier to catch a lizard on a cold day.**

The evidence that supports this conclusion is in one of the sentences. Which sentence is that?

Here is another conclusion:

> **On a hot day, you may find a snake under a rock.**

The evidence that supports this conclusion is in one of the sentences. Which sentence is that?

Each square on the map below is one kilometer long and one kilometer wide. Look at the map and answer the following questions.

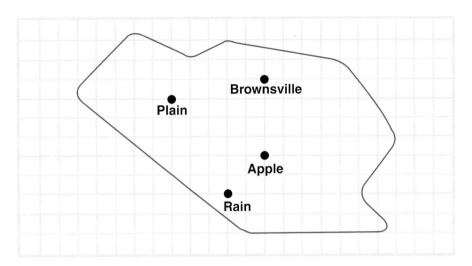

1. How far is it from Brownsville to Apple?
2. How far is it from Brownsville to Plain?
3. Is it farther from Brownsville to Apple or from Brownsville to Plain?

Write **Part E** in the left margin of your paper. You have two minutes to copy the paragraph below.

> **Donkeys are smaller than horses; however, they are good work animals. They are easy to care for, they are seldom sick, they can work long hours, and they are also quite strong.**

A Each square on the map below is ten miles long and ten miles wide.

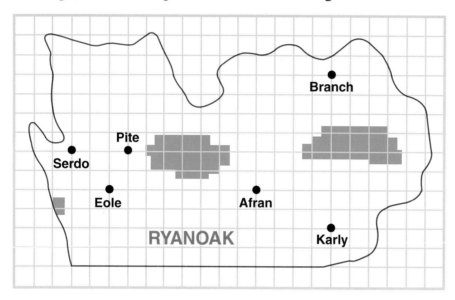

Areas that are shaded like this ▪ **are state parks.**

Look at the map and answer the following questions.

1. How far is it from Eole to Pite?
2. How far is it from Eole to Afran?
3. Is it farther from Eole to Pite or from Eole to Afran?
4. How many state parks are in the state of Ryanoak?
5. How many cities are shown in the state of Ryanoak?

B Here's the latest model sentence you learned:
   The regulation restricted their parking.
What sentence means the same thing?
What word means **rule?**
What word means **limited?**
What's another way of saying,
   To limit gasoline usage, the committee passed a rule?

Name three kinds of information that you can find in an atlas.
Name three kinds of information that you can find in an encyclopedia.
Name three kinds of information that you can find in a dictionary.

Write **Part D** in the left margin of your paper. You have two minutes to copy the paragraph below.

An encyclopedia gives facts about nearly everything. It tells about famous people and the history of countries. It also describes all kinds of animals and inventions and how people in different places live.

Here's a rule:

> **The faster something moves, the harder it is to stop it.**

Here's some additional evidence:

A car keeps going faster and faster.

By using the rule and the evidence, we can draw a conclusion.
What's that conclusion?
How do you know?

- Draw a conclusion by using this evidence with the rule:

  A truck does not go faster.

What's the conclusion?
How do you know?

- Draw a conclusion by using this evidence with the rule:

  At 4 o'clock a car is going ten kilometers an hour.
  At 5 o'clock the car is going fifty kilometers an hour.

What's the conclusion?
How do you know?

Some words usually are treated as if they name only one thing. Here are some of those words:

ice, water, grain, grass, rain, cement, and **rice**

Name some more.

Write **Part C** in the left margin of your paper. You have two minutes to copy the paragraph below.

> **A dictionary gives facts about words. It shows how to spell and pronounce words. It tells what part of speech a word is and its meaning. A dictionary also tells the history of some words.**

VOCABULARY TEST. Write **Part D** in the left margin of your paper. Then number it from 1 to 3. Write the model sentence that means the same thing as each sentence below. You have four minutes.

1. By pausing, she lost her chance.
2. They changed their Swiss money into Canadian money.
3. His directions were unclear and repetitive.

INFORMATION TEST. Write **Part E** in the left margin of your paper. Then number it from 1 to 15 and answer each item. You have eleven minutes.

1. What is a nook?
2. Name the earliest-known close relative of the horse.
3. How did eohippus defend itself?
4. What do we call the group of animals that modern horses belong to?
5. What do you do when you haze someone?
6. What did **clewe** mean in Middle English?
7. Name two descendants of equus.
8. What is a boar?
9. What does the Greek word **paragraphos** mean?
10. How do we know that eohippus was related to a modern horse?
11. Why did the feet of eohippus change over the centuries?
12. Why did some types of equus become large and strong while others became slender and quick?
13. What is a clue?
14. What do you do when you tantalize someone?
15. What are two other names for a donkey?

★ **F** Each square on the map below is two kilometers long and two kilometers wide.

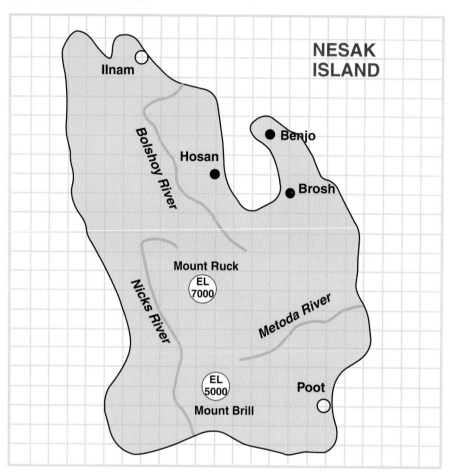

The symbol ● means that the town has between 50 and 300 people.
The symbol ◯ means that the town has between 300 and 500 people.

Write **Part F** in the left margin of your paper. Then number it from 1 to 5. Look at the map and answer the following questions.

1. How many rivers are on Nesak Island?
2. How far is it from Hosan to Ilnam?
3. Is it farther from Hosan to Ilnam or from Hosan to Poot?
4. How many towns are on Nesak Island?
5. How far is it from Brosh to Poot?

A You learned a model sentence that means this:

The rule limited their parking.

Say that model sentence.
What word in the model sentence means **rule?**
What word in the model sentence means **limited?**

B Read each argument and tell what the conclusion is.

The man speaks with a phony accent,
so he must be a complete phony.

What does the writer of this argument want us to conclude?

- Here's another argument:

It's quite clear that Anna is trying to avoid me. When she saw me
walking toward her, she crossed the street and went into the
hardware store.

What does the writer of this argument want us to conclude?

C Here's a rule:

The higher you go, the less oxygen there is in the air.

Here's some additional evidence:

Mount McKinley is higher than Mount Hood.

By using the rule and the evidence about Mount McKinley, we can draw a
conclusion. What's that conclusion?
How do you know?

- Draw a conclusion by using this evidence with the rule:

Betty is 9000 feet high and Tom is 4000 feet high.

What's the conclusion?
How do you know?

D Write **Part D** in the left margin of your paper. You have two minutes to copy the paragraph below.

> **Last summer I had the opportunity to visit France. I stayed in Paris, visiting museums and eating at fine restaurants. Since I speak only English, my opportunities to meet French people were limited.**

★ **E** Each square on the map below is ten miles long and ten miles wide.

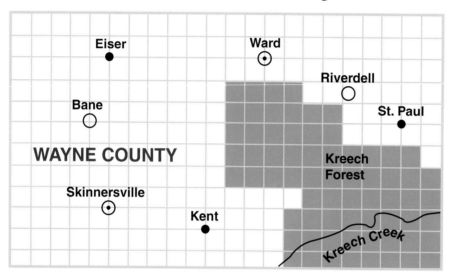

Areas that are shaded like this ▮ are state parks.
The symbol ● means that the city has between 1000 and 5000 people.
The symbol ○ means that the city has between 5000 and 10,000 people.
The symbol ⊙ means that the city has between 10,000 and 50,000 people.

Write **Part E** in the left margin of your paper. Then number it from 1 to 7. Look at the map and answer the following questions.

1. How many people live in Riverdell?
2. How many people live in Eiser?
3. Which has a greater population, Riverdell or Eiser?
4. How many cities in Wayne County have between 1000 and 5000 people?
5. How many cities have between 5000 and 10,000 people?
6. How many cities have between 10,000 and 50,000 people?
7. How many cities have more than 1000 people?

Read each argument and tell what the conclusion is.

> **I'm not voting in the presidential election this year.**
> **What's the point? The last election was rigged anyway.**

What does the writer of this argument want us to conclude?

- Here's another argument:

> **My car's been sounding funny ever since I bought gas at that new station. I don't think I'll give them any more business.**

What does the writer of this argument want us to conclude?

Here's a rule:

> **A scruple is equal to 1.296 grams.**

Here's some additional evidence:

Josie has something that weighs 1.296 grams.

How many scruples does it weigh?

Fred has something that weighs one gram.

How many scruples does it weigh?

Write **Part C** in the left margin of your paper. You have two minutes to copy the paragraph below.

> **Many regulations are designed to restrict certain kinds of behavior. During a gasoline shortage, a regulation could restrict the purchase of gas to one tank per person every week. Businesses have regulations for their employees.**

★ **D** Each square on the map below is five miles long and five miles wide.

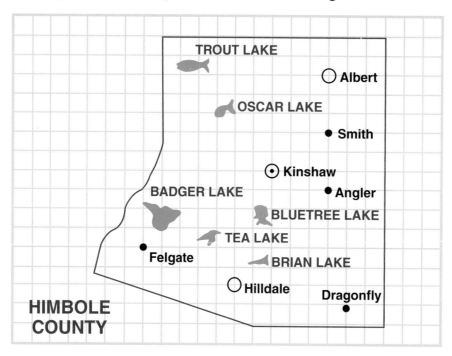

The symbol ● means that the city has between 500 and 1000 people.
The symbol ○ means that the city has between 1000 and 2000 people.
The symbol ⊙ means that the city has between 2000 and 5000 people.

Write **Part D** in the left margin of your paper. Then number it from 1 to 9.
Look at the map and answer the following questions.

1. How many people live in Kinshaw?
2. Which has a greater population, Albert or Kinshaw?
3. About how far is it from Bluetree Lake to Badger Lake?
4. How many lakes are there in Himbole County?
5. Is it farther from Bluetree Lake to Badger Lake or from Bluetree Lake to Brian Lake?
6. How many cities in Himbole County have between 500 and 1000 people?
7. How many cities have between 1000 and 2000 people?
8. How many cities have between 2000 and 5000 people?
9. How many cities have more than 1000 people?

A

What are the three things you do to find a contradiction in a passage?

• Read the following passage.

> Mary invited Fran to dinner Thursday night. She served scampi, which are large shrimp. A week later, Fran was still thinking about that dinner.
> "Remember that shrimp we ate last Wednesday?" she asked Mary. "What was the name of that again?"
> "Scampi," said Mary.
> "That was really fine food," sighed Fran.

Assume that what the writer says first is true. Which statement does the writer make that is later contradicted?
Which statement is the contradiction?
Make up an if-then statement that explains the contradiction.

• Read the following passage.

> Tom and Bob went out for a pizza. Tom had olives and pepperoni on his half and Bob had cheese and mushrooms on his. They ate the whole giant pizza.
> "Do you feel like going bowling now?" Bob asked.
> "No," replied Tom, "all those mushrooms made me sick." So Bob drove his friend home.

Assume that what the writer says first is true. Which statement does the writer make that is later contradicted?
Which statement is the contradiction?
Make up an if-then statement that explains the contradiction.

B Here's a fact:

> **During the summer, the temperature on the peak of Mount Hood is different from the temperature on nearby peaks.**

What kind of reference material would you use to support this fact?
Read the passage below and find out why the temperature on the peak of Mount Hood is different from the temperature on nearby peaks.

> Mount Hood is a volcano that has not been active for centuries. It is in the Cascade mountain range, near the city of Portland, Oregon. During the winter, great amounts of snow fall on Mount Hood and on the rest of the Cascades. In the spring, melting starts at the base of the mountains and works toward the peaks. By the middle of July, most of the snow on the peaks near Mount Hood has completely melted. However, Mount Hood, which is higher than the surrounding peaks, is still topped with a glacier of packed snow. This glacier has not melted for many years.

C Write **Part C** in the left margin of your paper. You have two minutes to copy the paragraph below.

> **There are several rules for using the words "has" and "have." If you name one thing, use the verb "has." If you name more than one thing, use the verb "have." If you use the word "you" or "I," use the verb "have."**

★

Write **Part D** in the left margin of your paper. Then number it 1 and 2.

Here's a fact:

> **You cannot do as many things with ocean water as you can with fresh water.**

Read the passage that follows and find the answer to this question:
> **Why can't you do things with ocean water that you can do with fresh water?**

   Because ocean water contains salts, it has a lower freezing temperature than fresh water. Fresh water freezes at zero degrees Celsius. For ocean water to freeze, however, the temperature must be below zero degrees Celsius.

   Ocean water contains the kind of salt that is found in salt shakers. It also contains other types of salts. Ocean water cannot be used to water most crops because the salt in the water kills the crops. Corn, wheat, tomatoes, and other garden plants would soon die if they were watered with ocean water. Ocean water doesn't kill all crops, however. Certain kinds of barley will continue to grow with ocean water. The ocean water slows growth to about one-third the normal growth rate.

---

1. Why can't you do things with ocean water that you can do with fresh water?
2. What kind of reference material would you use to support the fact?

A Here's a fact:

Jumbo jets have more than ten wheels.

What kind of reference material would you use to support this fact?
Look at the picture below and figure out how many wheels the jumbo jet has.

B What are the three things you do to find a contradiction in a passage?

• Read the following passage.

> In 1945, the United Nations was founded in San Francisco. Forty-six nations sent delegates to discuss the purpose and laws of the United Nations. They decided it would be a regulatory agency to protect nations from war. Today, the United Nations tries to distribute food, power, and wealth among nations. It tries to settle problems between countries so that those countries don't go to war with each other. Although the United Nations was founded in Ohio, the United Nations building is in New York. Many people come to visit the United Nations each year.

Assume that what the writer says first is true. Which statement does the writer make that is later contradicted?
Which statement is the contradiction?
Make up an if-then statement that explains the contradiction.

• Read the following passage.

> Mary went skating with her little brother. He had never been on ice skates before, but he was doing very well. A friend of Mary's skated over and asked him, "Where did you learn to skate like that?"
> Bill responded, "I've practiced with a skateboard. It's got the same kind of wheels as these skates have."
> "That's a smart way to learn," the friend said. "You should try out for the hockey team."

Assume that what the writer says first is true. Which statement does the writer make that is later contradicted?
Which statement is the contradiction?
Make up an if-then statement that explains the contradiction.

C Write **Part C** in the left margin of your paper. You have two minutes to copy the paragraph below.

> **Every time Richard has the opportunity to work, he refuses. He thinks we should trade skills for products instead of using currency. For instance, if you can sing, you could trade songs for dinner.**

LESSON 39

Write **Part D** in the left margin of your paper. Then number it 1 and 2.
Here's a fact:

> **The ears of an African elephant are different from the ears of an Indian elephant.**

1. Look at the picture below and tell how the elephants' ears are different.
2. What kind of reference material would you use to support the fact?

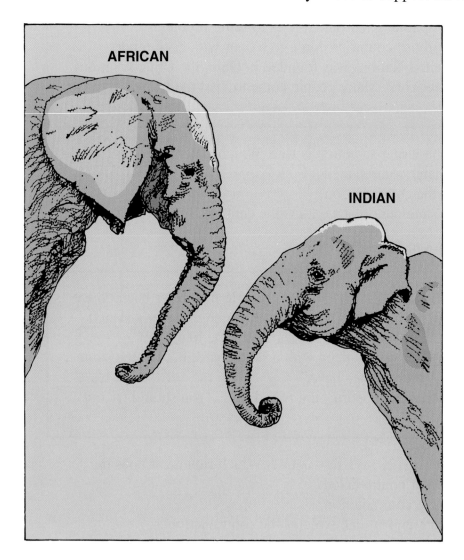

AFRICAN

INDIAN

A Here's a fact:

Chicago is on a large lake.

What kind of reference material would you use to support this fact?
Look at the map below and find the name of the lake.

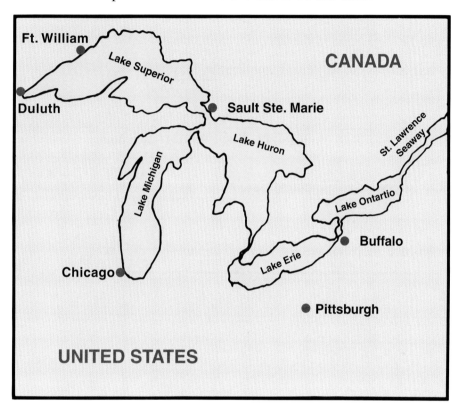

B Write **Part B** in the left margin of your paper. You have two minutes to copy the paragraph below.

A few weeks ago, my boyfriend sent me a letter that said, "Bug off, baby." I didn't know what he meant, so I marked the ambiguous phrase and sent the letter back to him.

VOCABULARY TEST. Write **Part C** in the left margin of your paper. Then number it from 1 to 4. Write the model sentence that means the same thing as each sentence below.
You have five minutes.

1. His directions were <u>unclear</u> and <u>repetitive</u>.
2. By <u>pausing</u>, she lost her <u>chance</u>.
3. The <u>rule limited</u> their parking.
4. They <u>changed</u> their Swiss <u>money</u> into Canadian <u>money</u>.

★

Write **Part D** in the left margin of your paper. Then number it 1 and 2.
Here's a fact:

Argentina is bordered by five countries.

1. Look at the map below and write the names of the countries.
2. What kind of reference material would you use to support the fact?

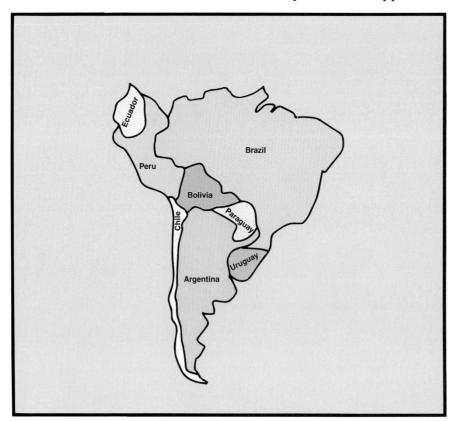

Write **Part E** in the left margin of your paper. Then number it from 1 to 5. Read the story and answer the questions.

A robot is a machine that looks and does some things like a human. You may have seen science fiction movies that show robots working for humans or even entire communities of robots living like humans.

Not every expert agrees on the origin of the word **robot.** All agree that it came from a Czechoslovakian word, and that it was first used by Karel Čapek in a play about mechanical creatures that overpowered their human creators. One encyclopedia says that Čapek based the word **robot** on the Czechoslovakian word **robotit,** which means **to drudge** (to do hard, unpleasant work). Another encyclopedia claims that Čapek got the name from the Czechoslovakian word that means **forced labor.** That word is **robota.** Still another encyclopedia says that the name came from the Czechoslovakian word **robota,** meaning **work.**

1. What is a robot?
2. Who first used the word **robot?**
3. Where was the word **robot** first used?
4. What language has the word **robota?**
5. Write one meaning for the Czechoslovakian word **robota.**

Read the passage below.

> The mudskipper lives in hot, tropical areas along the edge of muddy swamps. It has gills like most other fish. In addition, it has a special breathing system that makes it possible to get oxygen from the air. The mudskipper escapes its enemies by flipping out of the water, and then skipping across the muddy shore.

- Here is a conclusion based on the passage:

  Mudskippers escape from their enemies by hiding under rocks in the ocean.

The passage contains no evidence to support this conclusion. In fact, one sentence in the passage contradicts this conclusion.
Which sentence is that?

- Here is another conclusion:

  Mudskippers are fond of icy, arctic waters.

The passage contains no evidence to support this conclusion. In fact, one sentence contradicts this conclusion. Which sentence?

- Here is another conclusion:

  Mudskippers have a breathing system different from that of other fish.

Does the passage contain evidence to support this conclusion or evidence to contradict this conclusion?
Which sentence contains the evidence?

B Assume that the picture below is accurate. Examine the picture carefully, and then read the statements below it. Some of the statements contradict what is shown in the picture. For each contradictory statement, tell what the picture shows.

- Statement 1: **There is a crowd in the middle of the street watching the fight.**

Does that statement contradict what the picture shows?

- Statement 2: **One police officer is blowing a whistle.**

Does that statement contradict what the picture shows?

- Statement 3: **One police officer is on a horse, directing traffic.**

Does that statement contradict what the picture shows?

Write **Part B** in the left margin of your paper. Then number it from 1 to 6. Read the statements on the next page. Some of the statements contradict what the picture shows.

- Write **contradictory** or **not contradictory** for each statement.
- If a statement contradicts the picture, write what the picture shows.

1. There is a crowd in the middle of the street watching the fight.
2. One police officer is blowing a whistle.
3. One police officer is on a horse, directing traffic.
4. There are two police officers near the fight.
5. The traffic light is broken because of the fight.
6. Two dogs are fighting in the street.

Write **Part C** in the left margin of your paper. You have two minutes to copy the paragraph below.

> **Many science-fiction movies have been made about robots. In some movies, robots come to earth from another planet to find out how earth people live. In other movies, robots try to take over our planet.**

Write **Part D** in the left margin of your paper. Then number it 1 and 2. Here's a fact:

> **Thomas Edison is responsible for inventing some things that we use a lot.**

Read the passage below and find three things that Edison invented.

Thomas Edison was born in 1847. He went to school for only three months in his whole life, but he was very clever and he worked very hard. When he was only twelve years old, he started publishing his own newspaper. He worked as a telegraph operator for a while and then invented many devices to make telegraphs work better. When Edison was thirty years old, he announced his invention of the phonograph, which played sound off a tinfoil cylinder. Two years later, he introduced the electric lightbulb, his most successful invention. In 1889, he invented the kinetoscope, a machine that is something like a movie projector. Many years later, Edison used his phonograph and kinetoscope to produce the first talking pictures. He died in 1931, after making over one thousand inventions.

1. Write three things that Edison invented.
2. What kind of reference material would you use to support the fact?

Each square on the map below is five kilometers long and five kilometers wide.

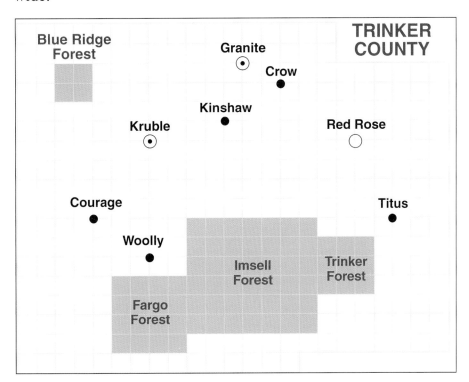

Areas that are shaded like this ▨ **are state parks.**
The symbol ● means that the city has between 1000 and 2000 people.
The symbol ○ means that the city has between 2000 and 5000 people.
The symbol ☉ means that the city has between 5000 and 10,000 people.

Write **Part E** in the left margin of your paper. Then number it from 1 to 7. Look at the map and answer the following questions.

1. How many forests are in Trinker County?
2. How many people live in Granite?
3. Which has a greater population, Kinshaw or Granite?
4. How many cities in Trinker County have between 5000 and 10,000 people?
5. How many cities have more than 2000 people?
6. Which forest is bigger, Fargo Forest or Imsell Forest?
7. Is it farther from Courage to Titus or from Courage to Kinshaw?

A Each square on the map below is one kilometer long and one kilometer wide. Assume that the map is accurate. Examine the map carefully, and then read the statements below it. Some of the statements contradict what is shown on the map. For each contradictory statement, tell what the map shows.

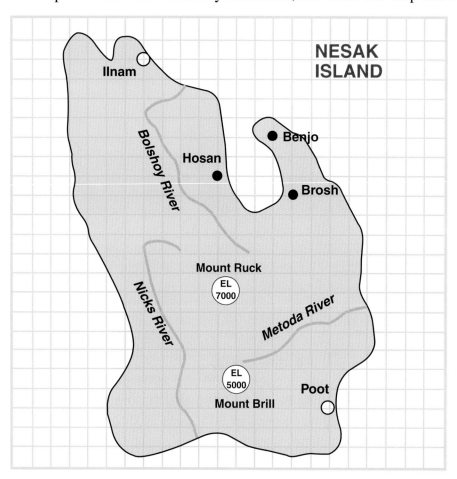

The symbol ● means that the town has between 50 and 300 people.

The symbol ○ means that the town has between 300 and 500 people.

The symbol (EL 5000) means that the mountain is 5000 meters high.

- Statement 1: **On Nesak Island, there are three towns with more than 300 people.**

Does that statement contradict what the map shows?

- Statement 2: **Nesak Island has five rivers.**

Does that statement contradict what the map shows?

- Statement 3: **All the towns in Nesak Island are within one kilometer of the shore.**

Does that statement contradict what the map shows?

Write **Part A** in the left margin of your paper. Then number it from 1 to 6. Read the statements below. Some of the statements contradict what the map shows.

- Write **contradictory** or **not contradictory** for each statement.
- If a statement contradicts the map, write what the map shows.

1. On Nesak Island, there are three towns with more than 300 people.
2. Nesak Island has five rivers.
3. All the towns on Nesak Island are within one kilometer of the shore.
4. It is farther from Benjo to Poot than it is from Benjo to Brosh.
5. On Nesak Island, there are no mountains over 3000 meters high.
6. Brosh is a town with 50 to 300 people.

Here's a new rule:

> **Just because two things happen around the same time doesn't mean that one thing causes the other thing.**

Read the rule over to yourself and get ready to say it.

The argument below is faulty because it breaks the rule.
Read the argument.

> **I went to Chicago, and it rained in Chicago. I went to Cleveland, and it rained in Cleveland. So I think I'll go to New York City and make it rain there.**

What does the writer want us to conclude?
Why does the writer think that going to a city causes rain?
Say the rule the argument breaks.

Here's how you could prove that going to a city could not cause rain. Send the person to lots of cities. If it doesn't rain **every time** the person goes to one of those cities, going to the city does not cause rain.

Read the passage below.

> The earliest advertisements were not conveyed through newspapers or radios. Thousands of years ago, peddlers wandered through city streets and advertised by shouting or singing about what they had to sell. This practice is still common in some parts of the world.

● Here is a conclusion based on the passage:

Some people continue to advertise by shouting in the streets.

Does the passage contain evidence to support this conclusion or evidence to contradict this conclusion?
Which sentence contains the evidence?

● Here is another conclusion:

There was no such thing as advertising before the invention of television.

Does the passage contain evidence to support this conclusion or evidence to contradict this conclusion?
Which sentence contains the evidence?

 Write **Part D** in the left margin of your paper. You have two minutes to copy the paragraph below.

> **Over time, the value of American currency changes around the world. For example, a number of years ago one American dollar converted to four French francs. In 1998, however, the American dollar converted to almost six and a half francs.**

Write **Part E** in the left margin of your paper. Then number it 1 and 2. Here's a fact:

Triceratops was a dinosaur that had horns.

Look at the picture below and answer the questions.

TRICERATOPS

1. How many horns did triceratops have?
2. What kind of reference material would you use to support the fact?

LESSON 43

A

Name three types of information that you can find in an encyclopedia.
Name three types of information that you can find in an atlas.
Name three types of information that you can find in a dictionary.

B

The argument below is faulty because it breaks this rule:

> **Just because two things happen around the same time doesn't mean that one thing causes the other thing.**

Read the rule over to yourself and get ready to say it.

Here's the argument:

> **If I slam the door when I get into my car, I don't run out of gas. That trick has kept my car from running out of gas for a week now.**

What does the writer want us to conclude?
Why does the writer think that slamming his car door keeps him from running out of gas?
Say the rule the argument breaks.

Here's how you could prove that slamming the car door could not keep the car from running out of gas. Make the person slam the car door **every time** that person gets into the car. If the car runs out of gas, slamming the car door does not keep the car from running out of gas.

C

Read the passage below.

> When a lumber company strips all the trees off a hillside and then promises that a new forest will grow there, it is making a promise it may not be able to keep. With no trees to stop erosion, a heavy rainfall can wash all the good soil off a hillside, making it impossible to grow anything. The result may be a barren, useless piece of land.

• Here's a conclusion:

The trees on a hillside serve no useful purpose.

Does the passage contain evidence to support this conclusion or evidence to contradict this conclusion?
The evidence in the passage contradicts the conclusion. So we can say that the evidence **refutes** the conclusion. Which sentence in the passage refutes the conclusion?

• Here's another conclusion:

More young trees may survive on flat land.

Does the passage contain evidence to support this conclusion or evidence to refute this conclusion?
Which sentence contains the evidence?

 Each square on the map below is five kilometers long and five kilometers wide. Assume that the map is accurate. Examine the map carefully, and then read the statements that follow it. Some of the statements contradict what is shown on the map. For each contradictory statement, tell what the map shows.

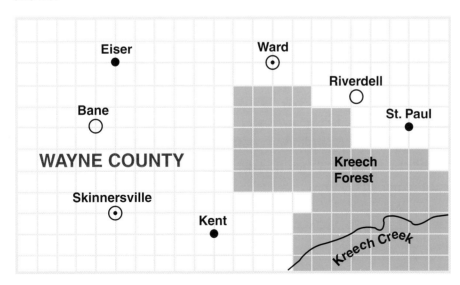

Areas that are shaded like this ▮ are state parks.
The symbol ● means that the city has between 1000 and 5000 people.
The symbol ○ means that the city has between 5000 and 10,000 people.
The symbol ⊙ means that the city has between 10,000 and 50,000 people.

- Statement 1: **The shortest distance from Bane to Kreech Forest is twenty kilometers.**

Does that statement contradict what the map shows?

- Statement 2: **Riverdell is closer to Kreech Forest than Ward is.**

Does that statement contradict what the map shows?

- Statement 3: **The population of Bane is greater than the population of Skinnersville.**

Does that statement contradict what the map shows?

Write **Part D** in the left margin of your paper. Then number it from 1 to 5. Read the statements below. Some of the statements contradict what the map shows.

- Write **contradictory** or **not contradictory** for each statement.
- If a statement contradicts the map, write what the map shows.

1. The shortest distance from Bane to Kreech Forest is twenty kilometers.
2. Riverdell is closer to Kreech Forest than Ward is.
3. The population of Bane is greater than the population of Skinnersville.
4. There are five cities in Wayne County with more than 5000 people.
5. Part of Kreech Creek lies inside Kreech Forest.

Write **Part E** in the left margin of your paper. You have two minutes to copy the paragraph below.

> Zebras and horses are related, but they look different from each other. Horses may be almost any color. Zebras, though, always have black and white stripes. The stripes blend with shadows, to help zebras hide from other creatures.

★ F Write **Part F** in the left margin of your paper. Then number it from 1 to 4. Read the story and answer the questions.

By now, you've probably figured out the types of mistakes that Mr. Nelson makes when he tries to say certain things. He exchanges the first sound of one word for the first sound of another word. Sometimes he says things that don't make any sense. Other times, however, his mistakes are funny. For example, once he was walking in the woods with Irene, his granddaughter. She had brought along some snacks, including a small bag of peanuts. As she walked along the shore of a pond with Mr. Nelson, she snacked on her peanuts.

Mr. Nelson was pointing things out to her—the trees, the little bugs swimming in the pond. Suddenly, however, he noticed that Irene had crumpled up her empty peanut bag and had tossed it into the pond.

"Shame on you," Mr. Nelson said. "You shouldn't be a bitter lug."

1. What did Mr. Nelson mean when he said, "You shouldn't be a bitter lug"?
2. What did Irene do that made Mr. Nelson say that?
3. If Mr. Nelson exchanges the first sound of one word for the first sound of another word, how would he say, "Fix that car"?
4. How would Mr. Nelson say, "Hot dog"?

Here's an argument:

> **While Thelma was on vacation in Mexico, her house burned down. Thelma says she'll never go on vacation again.**

What does the writer want us to conclude?
Why does Thelma think that going on vacation caused her house to burn down?
Say the rule the argument breaks.

Here's how you could prove that going on vacation could not cause her house to burn down. Send Thelma on lots of vacations. If her house doesn't burn down **every time** she's on vacation, then going on vacation doesn't cause her house to burn down.

Some items in the list below are human. The word **who** is used to refer to those items.
Other items in the list are not human. The word **which** is used to refer to those items.
Tell whether you would use the word **who** or **which** for each item.

1. A table
2. A person
3. People
4. A situation
5. A dog
6. A dogcatcher

Read the passage below.

> The rhinoceros has very poor eyesight, but it lives with another animal that has excellent eyesight—the tickbird. A tickbird spends almost its entire life on a rhinoceros, eating parasites such as ticks and lice that attach themselves to the rhino. When possible danger approaches, the tickbird hisses. This tells the nearsighted rhino that danger is near.

• Here's a conclusion:

 A tickbird is a good guard.

Does the passage contain evidence to support this conclusion or evidence to refute this conclusion?
Which sentence in this passage contains the evidence?

• Here's another conclusion:

 Rhinos have no parasites.

Does the passage contain evidence to support this conclusion or evidence to refute this conclusion?
Which sentence contains the evidence?

D Name three types of information that you can find in an atlas.
Name three types of information that you can find in an encyclopedia.
Name three types of information that you can find in a dictionary.

E Write **Part E** in the left margin of your paper. You have two minutes to copy the paragraph below.

> **Here's a rule that is sometimes broken in arguments: Just because two things happen around the same time doesn't mean that one thing causes the other thing. You will use the rule to attack faulty arguments.**

★ **F** Write **Part F** in the left margin of your paper. Then number it from 1 to 6. Read the story and answer the questions.

> Branding cattle is a tricky business. The idea is to burn the animal's hide so that no hair will grow on the part that is burned. At the same time, however, the branding iron should not be permitted to burn the animal seriously. If done correctly, branding frightens the young animal far more than it actually hurts it.
>
> In the early West there were no fences. There was grazing land, and frequently the cattle from different ranches grazed on the same range. Every spring, after the new calves were born, cowhands found the calves with cows wearing the brand of their ranch. The cowhands then branded the young calves. For the rest of its life, the animal had a brand — perhaps a circle with a bar through it or a horseshoe with a dot over it.
>
> A man named Sanuel A. Maverick didn't bother to brand his cattle. Neighboring ranchers began to refer to these unbranded animals as **mavericks**. Later, the name came to mean any outcast or person who wasn't part of the group.

1. How long does a brand last?
2. During what time of year is branding done?
3. Why did cattle from different ranches get mixed together?
4. How did a cowhand tell which ranch an unbranded calf belonged to?
5. Why was Samuel A. Maverick different from other ranchers?
6. What does **maverick** mean today?

Write **Part G** in the left margin of your paper. Then number it from 1 to 5. Assume that the picture below is accurate. Examine the picture carefully, and then read the statements below it. Some of the statements contradict what the picture shows.

- Write **contradictory** or **not contradictory** for each statement.
- If a statement contradicts the picture, write what the picture shows.

1. There is a family in the tent.
2. One member of the family is at the picnic table.
3. One bear sees the chicken that is cooking.
4. The bears have tipped over the garbage can.
5. A camper truck is parked near the tent.

Some items in the list below are human. The word **who** is used to refer to those items.

Other items in the list are not human. The word **which** is used to refer to those items.

Tell whether you would use the word **who** or **which** for each item in the list below.

1. Matches
2. Paint
3. A cow
4. A cowboy
5. A bird's nest
6. A bird

Here's an argument:

> **The last two times Joe tapped home plate, he hit a home run. He should always remember to tap home plate when he goes up to bat.**

What does the writer want us to conclude?
Why does the writer think that tapping home plate will cause Joe to hit a home run?
Say the rule the argument breaks.

Here's how you could prove that tapping home plate doesn't cause Joe to hit a home run. Make Joe tap home plate every time he goes up to bat. If he doesn't hit a home run **every time** he taps home plate, then tapping home plate doesn't cause him to hit a home run.

When we draw a conclusion from a rule, we start with the rule. Then we add some other evidence. Here's a rule:

> **The more you exercise, the healthier you are.**

Here's some additional evidence:

> **Sharon exercises more now than she did a year ago.**

What's the conclusion?

Sometimes, we can't draw a conclusion from a rule. This happens when the additional evidence is irrelevant. Here's a rule:

> **The more you exercise, the healthier you are.**

Here's the additional evidence:

> **Olivia takes a lot of vitamins.**

What's the conclusion? There is none. We can't draw a conclusion because the additional evidence is irrelevant to the rule.

Here's another rule:

> **The more you drive, the more you pollute the air.**

Tell if each piece of evidence below is **relevant** to the rule or **irrelevant** to the rule. Remember, if it is irrelevant, you can't draw a conclusion. Here are the pieces of evidence:

1. **This year's cars are more expensive than last year's.**
   Is this evidence relevant or irrelevant?
   So what's the conclusion?
2. **Carla uses the family car twice as much as Amanda does.**
   Is this evidence relevant or irrelevant?
   So what's the conclusion?
3. **Frank is bald.**
   Is this evidence relevant or irrelevant?
   So what's the conclusion?
4. **Henry Ford built cars on an assembly line.**
   Is this evidence relevant or irrelevant?
   So what's the conclusion?
5. **Now that Frieda has a bike, she doesn't drive as much as she used to.**
   Is this evidence relevant or irrelevant?
   So what's the conclusion?
6. **Many English words have roots that are thousands of years old.**
   Is this evidence relevant or irrelevant?
   So what's the conclusion?

Write **Part D** in the left margin of your paper. You have two minutes to copy the paragraph below.

> **Here are the rules for using "who" and "which." If the thing you're referring to is human, use the word "who." If the thing you're referring to is not human, use the word "which."**

VOCABULARY TEST. Write **Part E** in the left margin of your paper. Then number it from 1 to 4. Write the model sentence that means the same thing as each sentence below. You have five minutes.

1. They changed their Swiss money into Canadian money.
2. The rule limited their parking.
3. By pausing, she lost her chance.
4. His directions were unclear and repetitive.

★

Write **Part F** in the left margin of your paper. Then number it from 1 to 4. Each square on the map below is five miles long and five miles wide. Assume that the map is accurate.
Examine the map carefully, and then read the statements below it.
Some of the statements contradict what the map shows.

● Write **contradictory** or **not contradictory** for each statement.
● If a statement contradicts the map, write what the map shows.

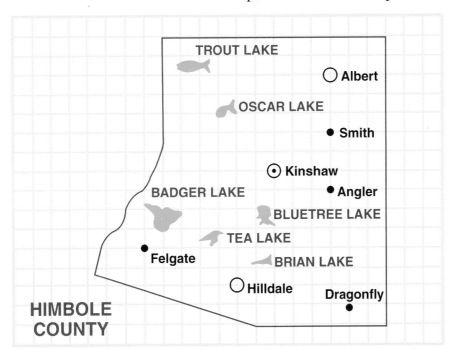

The symbol ● means that the city has between 500 and 1000 people.
The symbol ○ means that the city has between 1000 and 2000 people.
The symbol ⊙ means that the city has between 2000 and 5000 people.

1. Two cities in Himbole County have between 1000 and 2000 people.
2. Tea Lake is the biggest lake in Himbole County.
3. It is farther from Albert to Angler than it is from Smith to Kinshaw.
4. Four cities in Himbole County have more than 1000 people.

Write **Part G** in the left margin of your paper. Then number it from 1 to 5. Read the story and answer the questions.

> The Arabian horse is considered by many horse experts to be the most intelligent and sensitive of all horses. It is a white horse with just a few spots on its belly. When Arabians are young, they are not white, but spotted, and as they grow older most of the spots disappear.
>
> The Arabian horse was bred by the Arabs. The Arabs didn't wear armor in battle, so they didn't need big, heavy animals. The speed and lightness of the Arabian horse meant that it could perform well in battle. These horses became so important that many Arabs considered them to be members of the family and would sometimes let their horses sleep in their tents. At times, the horse stayed outside the tent and served as a watchdog, warning its master if an unwanted visitor came near the camp at night.
>
> Today, horse breeders frequently breed Arabian stallions with other kinds of horses. This breeding increases the intelligence of the line.

1. How does an Arabian horse's appearance change as it grows older?
2. Why didn't the Arabian people need big, heavy horses?
3. Why could Arabian horses perform well in battle?
4. Why do today's horse breeders breed Arabian stallions with other kinds of horses?
5. Where did Arabs sometimes permit their horses to sleep?

Here's a rule:

All soccer players have strong legs.

Tell if each piece of evidence below is **relevant** to the rule or **irrelevant** to the rule. Remember, if it is irrelevant, you can't draw a conclusion.
Here are the pieces of evidence:

1. **Lisa's favorite sport is skindiving.**
   Is this evidence relevant or irrelevant?
   So what's the conclusion?
2. **Carlos plays soccer.**
   Is this evidence relevant or irrelevant?
   So what's the conclusion?
3. **Margo goes skiing every weekend.**
   Is this evidence relevant or irrelevant?
   So what's the conclusion?
4. **Nanda has played in six soccer tournaments.**
   Is this evidence relevant or irrelevant?
   So what's the conclusion?

Here's a new rule:

Just because you know about a part doesn't mean you know about the whole thing.

Read the rule over to yourself and get ready to say it.
The argument below is faulty because it breaks this rule. Here's the argument:

The picture on the cover of that book is stupid. I'm sure it's a stupid book.

The argument concludes something about the whole book. What is that conclusion?
The conclusion is based on information about part of the book.
Which part is that?
Say the rule the argument breaks.
To find out whether the whole book is stupid, you would have to read the whole book.

What word do we use to refer to things that are human?
What word do we use to refer to things that are **not** human?
Tell whether you would use the word **who** or **which** to refer to each thing in the list below.

1. An animal
2. An animal trainer
3. A truck
4. A truck wheel
5. A truck driver
6. A gas station attendant
7. A gas station

Some words refer to a **whole** thing. A class, an army, and a committee are whole things. These wholes are not human; however, they are made up of humans. An **army** is not human. A **soldier** is human. The **discussion group** is not human. The **members** of the discussion group are human.

Remember, wholes are not human even though they are made up of humans.

Tell whether you would use the word **who** or **which** to refer to each item in the list below. If the item refers to a human, use **who.**
If the item refers to something that is not human, use **which.** Use **which** to refer to any whole that is made up of humans.

1. The team
2. The players
3. The committee
4. The members of the committee
5. The class
6. The students
7. The student
8. The army
9. The soldiers
10. The play
11. The actors

Write **Part D** in the left margin of your paper. You have two minutes to copy the paragraph below.

> **The Arabian horse was bred by the Arabs. The Arabs didn't wear armor; therefore, they didn't need big, heavy animals. The speed and lightness of the Arabian horse meant that it could perform well in battle.**

★

Write **Part E** in the left margin of your paper. Then number it from 1 to 6. Examine the picture carefully, and then read the statements below it. Some of the statements contradict what the picture shows.

• Write **contradictory** or **not contradictory** for each statement.
• If a statement contradicts the picture, write what the picture shows.

1. The artist is looking at a painting of her cat.
2. The artist is eating bread and drinking from a cup.
3. A basket of fruit is sitting on the table.
4. A black cat is standing under the picture.
5. The artist has three paintbrushes in her back pocket.
6. One of the table drawers is open.

A What word do we use to refer to things that are not human?
What word do we use to refer to things that are human?

Some words refer to a whole. A **class,** an **army** and a **committee** are wholes. These wholes are not human; however, they are made up of humans. A **class** is not human. A **student** is human.

Tell whether you would use the word **who** or **which** to refer to each item in the list below. If the item refers to a human, use **who.** If the item refers to something that is not human, use **which.** Use **which** to refer to any whole that is made up of humans.

1. The loggers
2. The logging crew
3. The secretarial pool
4. The secretaries
5. The queen
6. The royal family
7. The gang
8. The union members

B Here's some information that you will need.

> Some publications provide information about products and how well they perform. Photography magazines test cameras and lenses. Automotive magazines test cars. Consumer magazines such as *Consumer Reports* test different products and rate them so the consumer knows which product is the best value.

Name some other kinds of publications you could use to get information about products.

C Here's a rule:

Just because you know about a part doesn't mean you know about the whole thing.

Read the rule over to yourself and get ready to say it.

The argument below is faulty because it breaks this rule.
Here's the argument:

That tree has a dead limb. We might as well cut the tree down because I'm sure the whole tree is dead.

The argument concludes something about the whole tree.
What is that conclusion?
The conclusion is based on information about part of the tree.
Which part is that?
Say the rule the argument breaks.
Here's how you could prove the whole tree is not dead.
Find some new growth on other parts of the tree.

Here's a rule:

All planets orbit the sun.

Tell if each piece of evidence below is **relevant** to the rule or **irrelevant** to the rule. Remember, if it is irrelevant, you can't draw a conclusion.

Here are the pieces of evidence:

1. **Jupiter is a planet.**
   Is this evidence relevant or irrelevant?
   So what's the conclusion?
2. **Halley's Comet can be seen from Earth about every seventy years.**
   Is this evidence relevant or irrelevant?
   So what's the conclusion?
3. **Red giants are stars.**
   Is this evidence relevant or irrelevant?
   So what's the conclusion?
4. **Venus is a planet.**
   Is this evidence relevant or irrelevant?
   So what's the conclusion?

Write **Part E** in the left margin of your paper. You have two minutes to copy the paragraph below.

> **Here's a rule that is sometimes broken in faulty arguments: Just because you know about a part doesn't mean you know about the whole thing. To understand this rule, you need to understand parts and wholes.**

A

Here's an argument:

> **These transmissions contain our patented Dyno ball bearings. Dyno ball bearings are the toughest ball bearings used in any automobile. So these transmissions have to be tough.**

The argument concludes something about the whole transmission.
What is that conclusion?
The conclusion is based on information about part of the transmission. Which part is that?
Say the rule the argument breaks.
Here's how you could find out whether these transmissions are tough. Test the whole transmission.

B

In each sentence below, the word **which** refers to something. That thing is mentioned immediately before the word **which.**

- **She had a coat, which was yellow and red.**

What is mentioned immediately before **which?** Coat.
So what does **which** refer to? Coat.

- **Five dogs sat under a maple tree, which had spreading branches.**

What is mentioned immediately before **which?**
So what does **which** refer to?

- **That stapler, which had been on my desk, was found in the kitchen.**

What does **which** refer to?
How do you know?
The word **who** works like the word **which.** The word **who** refers to somebody. That person is mentioned immediately before the word **who.**

- **The girl, who lived next door, had six brothers.**

What does **who** refer to?
How do you know?

C

Here's an argument:

> **Teresa should always bounce the basketball before she shoots for a basket. The last few times she's done that, she's made the basket.**

What does the writer want us to conclude?
Why does the writer think that bouncing the basketball will make Teresa shoot a basket?

Say the rule the argument breaks.
How would you prove that bouncing the basketball does not cause Teresa to make a basket?

 Write **Part D** in the left margin of your paper. You have two minutes to copy the paragraph below.

> **In the Old West, cowhands had a word for cows that were not branded. They called these cows "mavericks." In time, the word "maverick" came to mean anyone who is an outsider, someone who isn't part of the group.**

★ Write **Part E** in the left margin of your paper. Then number it from 1 to 4. Read the story and answer the questions.

> It was cold. The wind was blowing like crazy, and the temperature had dropped below zero. Mr. Nelson's car wouldn't start, and he had to go to the store. Mr. Nelson wrapped himself up in his heavy winter coat and scarf. Off he trudged, bundled up like a bear.
>
> On the way to the store, he met a lad whose ears were bright red. The boy had a hat with ear flaps, but he wasn't wearing it. Instead, he had stuffed the hat in his pocket.
>
> Mr. Nelson tried to tell the boy how to keep his ears warm, but Mr. Nelson got his words mixed up. Instead of saying keep, he said heap, and instead of saying hat, he said cat. Here's what Mr. Nelson told the boy: "Your ears will be a lot warmer if you heap your cat on your head."
>
> "Oh yeah?" said the boy. "And why don't you put a rooster on your nose?"

1. What did Mr. Nelson mean to say?
2. How would Mr. Nelson say, "She won't keep her hat on"?
3. Could this story have taken place in January?
4. How do you know?

A

Here's an argument:

> **Boris belongs to the Raccoon Lodge. He's a real creep, so I'd stay away from all the Raccoons.**

The argument concludes something about all Raccoons. What is that conclusion?

The conclusion is based on information about part of the Raccoons. Which part is that?

Say the rule the argument breaks.

Here's how you could find out whether all the Raccoons are creeps. Get the names of all the other Raccoons. Talk to them.

B

The words **who** and **which** refer to what is mentioned immediately before them in a sentence.

1. **That man, who lives on the corner, washes his car every day.**
   What does the word **who** refer to?
   How do you know?
2. **She eats lots of oranges, which are high in vitamin C.**
   What does the word **which** refer to?
   How do you know?
3. **He bought a painting by Picasso, who was born in Spain.**
   What does the word **who** refer to?
   How do you know?
4. **Her dog, which just had puppies, is a collie.**
   What does the word **which** refer to?
   How do you know?

C

Here's an argument:

> **Beavers have very strong teeth, and beavers chew on wood. If you want strong teeth, chew on wood.**

What does the writer want us to conclude?

Why does the writer think that chewing on wood causes strong teeth?

Say the rule the argument breaks.

How would you prove that chewing on wood could not cause strong teeth?

Write **Part D** in the left margin of your paper. You have two minutes to copy the paragraph below.

> **Sometimes a person is considered a part and sometimes a person is considered a whole thing. If you're talking about a man and his hand, or a man and his intelligence, then the man is a whole thing.**

★

Write **Part E** in the left margin of your paper. Then number it from 1 to 6. Read the story and answer the questions.

> Braille is the system of reading and writing that blind people use. Each letter of the Braille alphabet is made with a pattern of bumps. The letter **b,** for example, is made with two bumps, one right below the other. The letter **c** consists of two bumps placed side by side. The letter **h** consists of three bumps, one above the other two. Blind people read by running their fingers across pages covered with patterns of bumps.
>
> The Braille system is named after the man who developed it, Louis Braille. Louis became blind as a child, and in 1829, when he was only twenty years old, he published his code. The code has symbols for all twenty-six letters as well as symbols to indicate capital letters, quotation marks, and other punctuation.
>
> Although Braille has helped blind people read, it is a very slow method of reading. A speed reader of Braille might be able to read 150 words per minute—about the rate at which people talk. Most Braille readers do not read more than a hundred words per minute.

1. What is Braille?
2. Where did the Braille alphabet get its name?
3. Who uses the Braille alphabet?
4. How is Braille read?
5. How is the letter **c** represented in the Braille alphabet?
6. How would a Braille reader know when a word starts with a capital letter?

LESSON 50

Write **Part A** in the left margin of your paper. You have two minutes to copy the paragraph below.

> Braille is the system of reading and writing used by blind people. Each letter of the Braille alphabet is made with a pattern of bumps. Blind people read by running their fingers across these patterns of bumps.

VOCABULARY TEST. Write **Part B** in the left margin of your paper. Then number it from 1 to 4. Write the model sentence that means the same thing as each sentence below.
You have five minutes.

1. The rule limited their parking.
2. They changed their Swiss money into Canadian money.
3. His directions were unclear and repetitive.
4. By pausing, she lost her chance.

INFORMATION TEST. Write **Part C** in the left margin of your paper. Then number it from 1 to 16. Answer each item. You have thirteen minutes.

1. What are two other names for a donkey?
2. What did **clewe** mean in Middle English?
3. What is a robot?
4. Why do today's breeders breed Arabian stallions with other kinds of horses?
5. How is Braille read?
6. What is a boar?
7. What do you do when you haze someone?
8. What do you do when you tantalize someone?
9. What does the Greek word **paragraphos** mean?
10. Why could Arabian horses perform well in battle?
11. What is a nook?
12. What is a clue?
13. Name two descendants of equus.
14. What is a maverick?
15. What is Braille?
16. Why did some types of equus become large and strong while others became slender and quick?

Write **Part D** in the left margin of your paper. Then number it from 1 to 5. Each square on the map below is five miles long and five miles wide. Assume that the map is accurate.

Examine the map carefully, and then read the statements below it. Some of the statements contradict what the map shows.

- Write **contradictory** or **not contradictory** for each statement.
- If a statement contradicts the map, write what the map shows.

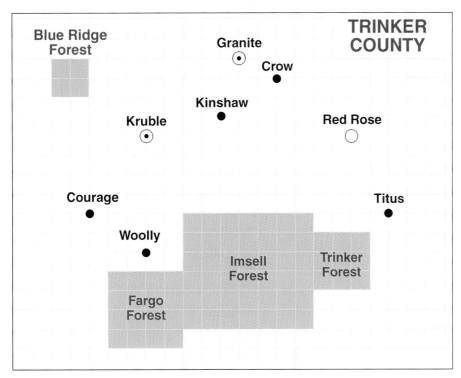

Areas that are shaded like this [ ] are state parks.

The symbol ● means that the city has between 1000 and 2000 people.

The symbol ○ means that the city has between 2000 and 5000 people.

The symbol ◉ means that the city has between 5000 and 10,000 people.

1. Two cities in Trinker County have more than 5000 people.
2. It is farther from Woolly to Kruble than it is from Woolly to Courage.
3. Red Rose is the largest city in Trinker County.
4. Trinker Forest is the smallest forest in Trinker County.
5. Five cities in Trinker County have between 1000 and 2000 people.

Write **Part E** in the left margin of your paper. Then number it from 1 to 6. Read the story and answer the questions.

The Pony Express began in 1860. The route that it followed extended from St. Joseph, Missouri, to Sacramento, California, and covered a distance of about 2000 miles. Before the Pony Express, most mail was delivered by stagecoach. The people who started the Pony Express wanted to prove that the mail could be delivered faster by the Pony Express.

It took about twenty days to get from St. Joseph to Sacramento traveling by stagecoach. Today, a jet would make that trip in about four hours! One reason the trip took so long was that the stagecoaches were pulled by horses. Horses do not have great endurance. After they run hard for a few miles, they must slow down.

The Pony Express solved the problem of tired horses by building relay stations about 12 miles apart along the route. Pony Express riders rode at top speed from station to station. When the rider reached the station, a fresh horse would be waiting—saddled, fed, watered, and ready to go. The rider would jump from his tired horse, throw the mailbags onto the fresh horse, grab a drink of water, say a few words to the stationmaster, and take off on the fresh horse. The change of horses took no more than two and a half minutes.

The riders were young men, usually between fourteen and seventeen years of age, and they were very tough. They rode day and night, and in any kind of weather.

After the first few trips, mail leaving St. Joseph on the Pony Express arrived in Sacramento eight days after it had been sent.

1. How many days did it take to deliver mail from St. Joseph to Sacramento before the Pony Express?
2. How long did the same delivery take with the Pony Express?
3. By how many days did the Pony Express reduce the time it took to deliver mail from St. Joseph to Sacramento?
4. Why was the Pony Express so much faster than the stagecoach?
5. How long would the same trip take by jet?
6. How old were the Pony Express riders?

The words **who** and **which** refer to what is mentioned immediately before them in a sentence.

1. **He planted lots of squash, which grows well in this area.**
   What does the word **which** refer to?
   How do you know?
2. **Her spouse, who works downtown, drives a sports car.**
   What does the word **who** refer to?
   How do you know?
3. **She rooms with Libby Levine, who is my sister.**
   What does the word **who** refer to?
   How do you know?
4. **The impala, which is an antelope, is native to Africa.**
   What does the word **which** refer to?
   How do you know?

In the passage below, there are four underlined words. These words can be replaced with words from the model sentences you have learned. Read each sentence. Then figure out which model-sentence word can replace each underlined word. Then say the sentence with the model-sentence word or words.

> She <u>paused</u> before reading the sign in front of the counter. Crossing the border meant she would be <u>limited</u> in certain ways. She could not bring her Swiss <u>money</u> into Russia. When she had a <u>chance</u> to speak to the guard stationed at the counter, she asked if she could keep a special Swiss coin that had been in her family for years.

Write **Part C** in the left margin of your paper. You have two minutes to copy the paragraph below.

> **Sometimes a person is considered a part and sometimes a person is considered a whole thing. If you're talking about a girl and her family or a girl and her class, then the girl is a part.**

★ **D** Write **Part D** in the left margin of your paper. Then number it from 1 to 5. Read the story and answer the questions.

> Mr. Nelson liked movies. He particularly liked mysteries—detectives, spies, and things like that. He had waited a long time to see a special movie. When it finally came to one of the local theaters, Mr. Nelson went. Unfortunately, his old car stalled on the way to the theater, and he got there late. Nearly all the seats were filled. Mr. Nelson wandered up and down the aisle trying to find an empty seat, but the theater was dark and Mr. Nelson couldn't see a thing.
>
> Finally, he found an usher in the lobby and said, "It's very dark in there. Would you kindly sew me to a sheet?" The usher threw Mr. Nelson out of the theater.

   1. What did Mr. Nelson mean to say?
   2. How would Mr. Nelson say, "You have shown me to a dirty seat"?
   3. Did the usher understand what Mr. Nelson was trying to say?
   4. How do you know?
   5. Why did Mr. Nelson get to the theater late?

E Write **Part E** in the left margin of your paper. In the passage below, there are nine underlined words. These words can be replaced with words from the model sentences you have learned. Rewrite the passage using the model-sentence words. Remember to start every sentence with a capital letter and to punctuate each sentence correctly.

> She <u>paused</u> before reading the sign in front of the counter. Crossing the border meant she would be <u>limited</u> in certain ways. She could not bring her Swiss <u>money</u> into Russia. When she had a <u>chance</u> to speak to the guard standing at the counter, she asked if she could keep a special Swiss coin that had been in her family for years. The guard's response was <u>unclear</u>. When she repeated the question, he recited some <u>repetitive</u> phrases about the <u>rules</u> of the country. She thanked him and went to the desk where <u>money</u> could be <u>changed</u> into Russian rubles.

Write **Part F** in the left margin of your paper. Then number it from 1 to 6. Assume that the passage below is true. Read the passage carefully and then read the statements below it. Some of the statements contradict facts in the passage.

- Write **contradictory** or **not contradictory** for each statement.
- If a statement contradicts a fact, write the fact that it contradicts.

In 1960, the United States government sent military advisers to Vietnam to help the South Vietnamese in their fight against the North Vietnamese. By 1965, thousands of American soldiers were fighting in Vietnam, and thousands were dying.

In the late 1960s, people in the United States began to protest the war. Young men burned their draft cards. Some were sent to jail; others fled to Canada. Students staged marches. At Kent State University in Ohio, four students were killed by the Ohio National Guard during a protest held on campus.

There were soldiers who came back from Vietnam and joined the protesters. They believed that the United States should not be fighting in Vietnam. Some people began to lose faith in the government.

---

1. The United States government sent advisers to help the Vietnamese people fight Japan.
2. Although many American citizens protested the war, none of the protesters were harmed.
3. Some American soldiers believed that the United States shouldn't be involved in Vietnam.
4. The war made all American citizens more loyal to their government.
5. Many American soldiers died in Vietnam.
6. Some people were jailed because they protested the war.

A In the passage below, there are five underlined words. These words can be replaced with words from the model sentences you have learned. Read each sentence, and figure out which model-sentence word can replace each underlined word. Then say the sentence with the model-sentence word or words.

The editor took out her blue pencil and began to cross out the <u>repetitive</u> passages in the article. When she came to a particularly <u>unclear</u> sentence, she <u>paused</u> and looked up at the author, a cub reporter. The article had to do with new <u>rules</u> about interest rates on foreign <u>money</u>.

B Here's an argument:

> **More than half of the cameras sold in the United States are imported from other countries. We can conclude that the majority of all products sold in the United States are made outside the United States.**

The argument concludes something about the majority of products sold in the United States. What is that conclusion?

The conclusion is based on information about one kind of product sold in the United States. Which is that?

Say the rule the argument breaks.

How could you prove that the majority of products sold in the United States are made inside that country?

C Write **Part C** in the left margin of your paper. You have two minutes to copy the paragraph below.

> **One day, Sally tantalized my dog by holding a bone just out of reach. Rufus got so excited that he knocked her down. He grabbed the bone and almost bit off her hand! Sally doesn't tease Rufus anymore.**

★ **D** Write **Part D** in the left margin of your paper. In the passage that follows, there are eight underlined words. These words can be replaced with words from the model sentences you have learned. Rewrite the passage using the model-sentence words. Remember to start every sentence with a capital letter and to punctuate each sentence correctly.

The editor took out her blue pencil and began to cross out the repetitive passages in the article. When she came to a particularly unclear sentence, she paused and looked up at the author, a cub reporter. The article had to do with new rules about interest rates on foreign money. The sentence that the reporter had written was a mess, but the editor changed it into a clear sentence by crossing out a few words. She said to the reporter, "When you get a chance, I want you to copy this article with the changes I've made. Try to get a feel for the way I've changed some of your unclear sentences."

Write **Part E** in the left margin of your paper. Then number it from 1 to 5. Read the story and answer the questions.

> One way to force a business to change its practices is to boycott that business. A boycott takes place when people stop buying from the business or selling to the business. If the boycott is successful, the business then has a choice: it can either change its practices or go out of business.
>
> Consumers can use the boycott against manufacturers who are not acting in a way that preserves the environment. For example, some manufacturers dump sewage into rivers. This sewage kills fish and other forms of life. It makes the river something like a sewer. If people boycotted these companies by not buying the goods they manufacture, the companies would probably become more interested in the environment.
>
> The word **boycott** came from the name of Captain Charles Boycott, an English land agent in the 1880s. This land agent tried to collect full rent from the farmers who were working the land of Boycott's employer. The crops had not done well, though, and there was no money. So, when Boycott refused to reduce the rent, the farmers refused to do business with him. They didn't gather in their crops, and they didn't pay their rent.

1. What happens when a boycott takes place?
2. From whom did the word **boycott** come?
3. Who was Charles Boycott?
4. When a successful boycott takes place, what choices does a business have?
5. What would people do to boycott oranges that are grown in Florida?

Here's an argument:

> **Senator Flopp was convicted as a criminal both before and after he was in the Senate. There can be no question about the character of the people in the Senate.**

The argument concludes something about all the people in the Senate. What is that conclusion?

The conclusion is based on information about part of the people in the Senate. Which part is that?

Say the rule the argument breaks.

How could you prove that all the people in the Senate are not criminals?

What are the three things you do to find a contradiction in a passage?

Read the passage below.

> Jane joined a volleyball team. All the girls on the team were much better players, but they helped Jane at practice. Jane had to buy green shorts and a white T-shirt for a uniform.
>
> Wednesday night she played her first game. After the game, a team member patted her shoulder. "Your serve looked good tonight," she said. "Just remember to follow through with your racket and you'll continue to do well." When Jane went home, she felt happy. She was learning to play the game.

You assume that what the writer says first is true. Which statement does the writer make that is later contradicted?

Which statement is the contradiction?

Make up an if-then statement that explains the contradiction.

Write **Part C** in the left margin of your paper. You have two minutes to copy the paragraph below.

> **The Pony Express greatly reduced the time required to deliver mail to the West Coast by stationing fresh horses along the route. The Pony Express delivered the mail until the completion of the coast-to-coast telegraph system.**

★ **D** Write **Part D** in the left margin of your paper. Then number it from 1 to 4. Read the story and answer the questions.

Mr. Nelson made one of the strangest statements he has ever said at the hardware store last spring. Mr. Nelson had performed his annual spring housecleaning. He had swept, scrubbed, waxed, and painted. One thing he painted was an old stand for a lamp. This lamp stand had been in Mr. Nelson's family for over fifty years, but Mr. Nelson didn't have a lamp for it.

Mr. Nelson went to the hardware store to purchase a lamp that would fit on his lamp stand. Unfortunately, when Nelson tried to say **lamp** he sometimes said **stamp,** and when he tried to say **stand,** he usually said **land.**

Imagine how the young woman who worked in the hardware store must have felt when Mr. Nelson walked up to the counter, smiled, and said: "Hello. The land I have is freshly painted, but now I need a stamp that will fit on it."

You can understand why the woman ran into the back room of the store calling, "Mr. Fisk, I think you'd better come out here."

1. What did Mr. Nelson mean to say?
2. How would Mr. Nelson say, "A lamp stand"?
3. Why did Mr. Nelson go to the hardware store?
4. How do you know that this story didn't take place in January?

A When you combine sentences with the word **but,** what do you do with the period of the first sentence?
What follows the comma?
When you combine sentences with the word **and,** what do you do with the period of the first sentence?
What follows the comma?
When you combine sentences with the word **therefore,** what do you do with the period of the first sentence?
What follows the semicolon?
What follows the word **therefore?**

B Look at this diagram:

The diagram contradicts part of these instructions:

1. Make a square.
2. Make a **T** above the square.
3. Write the word **regulation** to the right of the square.

Say the instruction that the diagram contradicts.
What does the diagram show?
How would you change the diagram so that it is consistent with the instructions?

C Write **Part C** in the left margin of your paper. You have two minutes to copy the paragraph below.

> **For many years, the United Farm Workers asked consumers to boycott iceberg lettuce and green grapes. The reason for the boycott was that the farm workers felt they weren't getting paid enough for picking lettuce and grapes.**

Here's a rule:

The bigger a fire is, the more oxygen it needs.

Tell if each piece of evidence below is relevant to the rule or irrelevant to the rule. Remember, if it is irrelevant, you can't draw a conclusion.
Here are the pieces of evidence:

1. **The fire in our fireplace is bigger than the fire on our stove.**
   Is this evidence relevant or irrelevant?
   So what's the conclusion?
2. **A candle's flame is smaller than the flames of a bonfire.**
   Is this evidence relevant or irrelevant?
   So what's the conclusion?
3. **After running five kilometers, Janice was breathing hard.**
   Is this evidence relevant or irrelevant?
   So what's the conclusion?
4. **When I put dry wood on the fire, the fire got bigger.**
   Is this evidence relevant or irrelevant?
   So what's the conclusion?

When you combine sentences with the word **however,** what do you do with the period of the first sentence?
What follows the semicolon?
What follows the word **however?**
   When you combine sentences with the word **so,** what do you do with the period of the first sentence?
What follows the comma?
   When you combine sentences with the word **therefore,** what do you do with the period of the first sentence?
What follows the semicolon?
What follows the word **therefore?**

Write **Part C** in the left margin of your paper. You have two minutes to copy the paragraph below.

> **When you draw a conclusion from a rule, you start with the rule. Then you add other evidence. If the evidence is relevant, you can draw a conclusion. When the evidence is irrelevant, you can't draw a conclusion.**

VOCABULARY TEST. Write **Part D** in the left margin of your paper. Then number it from 1 to 4. Write the model sentence that means the same thing as each sentence below. You have five minutes.

1. By <u>pausing</u>, she lost her <u>chance</u>.
2. His directions were <u>unclear</u> and <u>repetitive</u>.
3. They <u>changed</u> their Swiss <u>money</u> into Canadian <u>money</u>.
4. The <u>rule</u> <u>limited</u> their parking.

INFORMATION TEST. Write **Part E** in the left margin of your paper. Then number it from 1 to 18 and answer each item. You have sixteen minutes.

1. How many days did it take to deliver mail from St. Joseph, Missouri, to Sacramento, California, before the Pony Express?
2. How long did mail delivery from St. Joseph to Sacramento take with the Pony Express?
3. Why was the Pony Express so much faster than regular mail delivery?
4. Why did the feet of eohippus change over the centuries?
5. What happens when a boycott takes place?
6. Why did some types of equus become large and strong while others became slender and quick?
7. Why do today's breeders breed Arabian stallions with other kinds of horses?
8. What is Braille?
9. How do we know that eohippus was related to a modern horse?
10. When a successful boycott takes place, what choices does a business have?
11. Name the earliest-known close relative of the horse.
12. How did eohippus defend itself?
13. What do we call the group of animals that modern horses belong to?
14. What is a robot?
15. What is a maverick?
16. Why could Arabian horses perform well in battle?
17. How is Braille read?
18. What does the Greek word **paragraphos** mean?

Write **Part F** in the left margin of your paper. Then number it from 1 to 5. Assume that the picture below is accurate. Examine the picture carefully, and then read the statements below it. Some of the statements contradict what the picture shows.

- Write **contradictory** or **not contradictory** for each statement.
- If a statement contradicts the picture, write what the picture shows.

1. Two buttons on the man's pants are unbuttoned.
2. The man is holding his hands up to his mouth.
3. There is a bone on the man's plate.
4. All of the silverware is on the plate.
5. The man didn't finish his milk or his bread.

A Some words in the rules below are underlined.

- **All dogs can swim.** What words are underlined?

So evidence is relevant if it tells that something is a dog.

- **Most blerbs are gibbers.** What words are underlined?

So evidence is relevant if it tells that something is a blerb.

- **Trees are stationary.** What word is underlined?

So evidence is relevant if it tells that something is _____.

- **Hot air is light.** What words are underlined?

So evidence is relevant if it tells that something is _____.

- **Some planets have moons.** What words are underlined?

So evidence is relevant if it tells that something is _____.

There are no underlined words in the rules below.

- **China cups break.** What should be underlined?

So evidence is relevant if it tells that something is _____.

- **Molecules are very small particles.** What should be underlined?

So evidence is relevant if it tells that something is _____.

- **Some birds are blue.** What should be underlined?

So evidence is relevant if it tells that something is _____.

- **Every large bluper has candy stripes.** What should be underlined?

So evidence is relevant if it tells that something is _____.

B Here's a new model sentence:

Her response was replete with extraneous details.

Read the sentence to yourself. Study the sentence until you can say it without looking at it.

Here's what the model means:

Her answer was filled with irrelevant details.

Which word in the model means **answer?**

Which word in the model means **filled?**

Which word in the model means **irrelevant?**

For each item, say a sentence that means the same thing.

1. His movements were <u>filled</u> with nervous jerks.
2. The teacher's <u>irrelevant</u> <u>answers</u> confused me.

Write **Part C** in the left margin of your paper. You have two minutes to copy the paragraph below.

> **When you write, avoid extraneous details. Extraneous details clutter what you write and make your meaning ambiguous. If you choose words carefully and try to be brief, your writing will be much easier for someone else to understand.**

★

Write **Part D** in the left margin of your paper. Then number it from 1 to 6. Assume that the passage below is true. Read the passage carefully, and then read the statements below it. Some of the statements contradict facts in the passage.

- Write **contradictory** or **not contradictory** for each statement.
- If a statement contradicts a fact, write the fact that it contradicts.

> While Americans were worrying about the Vietnam War, an incident occurred in Washington, D.C., that would later shake the country. Some men were caught breaking into the national headquarters of the Democratic party, which were located in Washington, D.C. The scandal that followed became known as the Watergate scandal because the headquarters were in an office building called Watergate. Reporters from *The Washington Post* newspaper discovered that the burglars had been hired by men who worked closely with President Nixon. An investigation followed. It resulted in Nixon resigning as president of the United States. United States citizens were angry when they discovered that their president had been closely linked to criminal activities.

1. CIA agents discovered who was involved in the Watergate scandal.
2. The scandal was called Watergate because the basement of the building was flooded with water.
3. The Watergate burglars were hired by people close to President Nixon.
4. The Watergate incident took place just before World War II.
5. The Watergate scandal did not affect President Nixon's life.
6. The Watergate incident took place in Washington, D.C.

E Write **Part E** in the left margin of your paper. Then number it from 1 to 6. Read the story and answer the questions.

> Mr. Nelson says some funny things when he exchanges the first parts of words. These funny things are called **spoonerisms.** Spoonerisms are named after the Reverend William A. Spooner, who is probably the all-time master of the spoonerism. He said things such as, "It is kisstomary to cuss the bride," instead of "It is customary to kiss the bride," and "You are occupewing the wrong pie," instead of "You are occupying the wrong pew." Instead of saying "half-formed wish," he once said "half-warmed fish."
>
> Spooner was a teacher, and he became very popular. The students never knew when he would say something like "man to pleat you," instead of "plan to meet you." Although Spooner died in 1930, his name lives on.

1. How do you make a spoonerism?
2. Who are spoonerisms named after?
3. Why are spoonerisms named after him?
4. Make a spoonerism from "plugged a drain."
5. Make a spoonerism from "first base."
6. Why was Spooner a popular teacher?

A

Here's the latest model sentence you learned:

Her response was replete with extraneous details.

What sentence means the same thing?

What word means **answer?**

What word means **filled?**

What word means **irrelevant?**

What's another way of saying,

His <u>answers</u> were <u>filled</u> with <u>irrelevant</u> information?

B

Some words in the rules below are underlined.

• **All <u>mammals</u> are warm-blooded.** What words are underlined?
So evidence is relevant if it tells that something is a mammal.

• **<u>Muscles</u> don't move the bones they cover.**
What word is underlined?
So evidence is relevant if it tells that something is _____.

• **Every <u>fish</u> swims.** What words are underlined?
So evidence is relevant if it tells that something is _____.

• **All <u>gleeks</u> have flammers.** What words are underlined?
So evidence is relevant if it tells that something is _____.

No words are underlined in the rules below.

• **Some people are left-handed.** What should be underlined?

So evidence is relevant if it tells that something is _____.

• **All amphibians are born in water.** What should be underlined?
So evidence is relevant if it tells that something is _____.

• **Most rizzos are bloopers.** What should be underlined?
So evidence is relevant if it tells that something is _____.

• **Birds have feathers.** What should be underlined?
So evidence is relevant if it tells that something is _____.

Write **Part C** in the left margin of your paper. You have two minutes to copy the paragraph below.

> **Some words, like "class" or "army," refer to wholes. The wholes are not human; however, they are made up of humans. Because the wholes are not human, use the word "which" when you refer to them.**

★

Write **Part D** in the left margin of your paper. Then number it from 1 to 5. Read the story and answer the questions.

> Houston, Texas, was founded in 1836 and was named after Sam Houston, a leader who helped Texas become a state. Two things stimulated Houston's growth. The first was a railroad that connected Houston with cities to the north and east. The second was a canal connecting Houston with the Gulf of Mexico, making it possible for ships to reach the city.
>
> Today, Houston is the largest city in the South. It is the largest inland seaport in the United States. It is a center for shipping cotton and cattle to all parts of the world, and it is one of the fastest-growing cities in the United States.

1. In what state is Houston?
2. In what year was Houston founded?
3. Is Houston a seaport?
4. What important products are shipped from Houston?
5. What two things stimulated Houston's growth?

Here's the latest model sentence you learned:

Her response was replete with extraneous details.

What sentence means the same thing?

What word means **answer?**

What word means **filled?**

What word means **irrelevant?**

What's another way of saying,

Jo's answer was filled with irrelevant comments?

Write **Part B** in the left margin of your paper. You have two minutes to copy the paragraph below.

Today, Houston, Texas, is the largest city in the southern part of the United States. Although Houston is inland, it is a large seaport, which is a center for shipping products to all parts of the world.

★ **C** Write **Part C** in the left margin of your paper. Then number it from 1 to 5. Read the story and answer the questions.

> One American president you've probably never heard much about is Millard Fillmore, the thirteenth president of the United States. The reason Fillmore is not famous is that he didn't do very much while he was president. He was moderate in his views, which means that he didn't take a strong stand on anything.
>
> Fillmore was born in 1800. He left school when he was young, worked and studied in law offices, and became a lawyer when he was twenty-three years old. In 1848, he was elected vice-president when Zachary Taylor was elected president. When Taylor died two years later, Fillmore became president. During the short time of his presidency, he tried to keep the trouble between the North and the South from getting out of hand. His moderate approach delayed the conflict between the North and the South, but it didn't solve the real problems. In 1861, eight years after Fillmore left the office of the presidency, the Civil War broke out between the North and the South.

1. When did Fillmore become vice-president?
2. When did Fillmore become president?
3. Who was president immediately before Fillmore?
4. In what year did Fillmore's term as president end?
5. What do we mean when we say that Fillmore was moderate in his views?

You learned a model sentence that means:

Her answer was filled with irrelevant details.

Say that model sentence.

What word in the model sentence means **answer?**

What word in the model sentence means **filled?**

What word in the model sentence means **irrelevant?**

Write **Part B** in the left margin of your paper. You have two minutes to copy the paragraph below.

> **We tried a new Greek restaurant last night. They served us a delicious meal: black olives, Greek salad, spinach pie, and barbecued lamb. A regulation is posted which restricts the occupancy to thirty people, so reservations are a good idea.**

Write **Part C** in the left margin of your paper. Then number it from 1 to 5. Each square on the map below is ten miles long and ten miles wide. Assume that the map is accurate. Examine the map carefully and then read the statements below it. Some of the statements contradict what the map shows.

- Write **contradictory** or **not contradictory** for each statement.
- If a statement contradicts the map, write what the map shows.

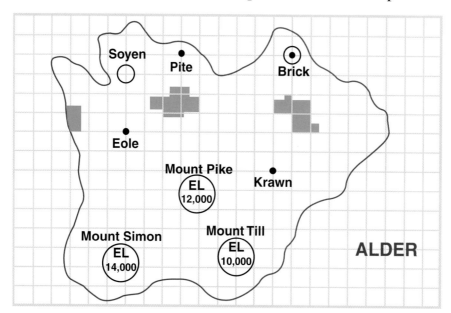

Areas that are shaded like this ▮ are state parks.
The symbol ● means that the city has between 10,000 and 50,000 people.
The symbol ◯ means that the city has between 50,000 and 100,000 people.
The symbol ⊙ means that the city has between 100,000 and 1,000,000 people.

The symbol (EL 15000) means that the mountain is 15,000 feet high.

1. Krawn is more than 100 miles from Brick.
2. There are three state parks in the state of Alder.
3. There are four cities in Alder with a population between 10,000 and 50,000 people.
4. Mount Simon is taller than Mount Till.
5. Soyen has between 50,000 and 100,000 people.

Write **Part A** in the left margin of your paper. You have two minutes to copy the paragraph below.

In 1996, the people in the United States elected a new president. Abraham Lincoln and Franklin Roosevelt are famous presidents. Other presidents, like William Henry Harrison, are mentioned briefly in history books, because they were in office a short time.

VOCABULARY TEST. Write **Part B** in the left margin of your paper. Then number it from 1 to 5. Write the model sentence that means the same thing as each sentence below. You have six minutes.

1. They changed their Swiss money into Canadian money.
2. Her answer was filled with irrelevant details.
3. The rule limited their parking.
4. His directions were unclear and repetitive.
5. By pausing, she lost her chance.

INFORMATION TEST. Write **Part C** in the left margin of your paper. Then number it from 1 to 18 and answer each item. You have sixteen minutes.

1. How do you make a spoonerism?
2. Who was president of the United States immediately before Millard Fillmore?
3. When a successful boycott takes place, what choices does a business have?
4. What is a robot?
5. Why do today's horse breeders breed Arabian stallions with other kinds of horses?
6. How is Braille read?
7. Why was the Pony Express so much faster than regular mail delivery?
8. What two things stimulated Houston's growth?
9. What are two other names for a donkey?
10. What do you do when you haze someone?
11. Why could Arabian horses perform well in battle?
12. How many days did it take to deliver mail from St. Joseph, Missouri, to Sacramento, California, before the Pony Express?
13. What happens when a boycott takes place?
14. What do we mean when we say that Millard Fillmore was moderate in his views?

15. Name two descendants of equus.
16. What is a maverick?
17. What is Braille?
18. How long did mail delivery from St. Joseph to Sacramento take with the Pony Express?

★ Write **Part D** in the left margin of your paper. Rewrite the passage below in three or four sentences. Combine consistent sentences with **and** or **therefore.** Combine inconsistent sentences with **but** or **however.**

> Herman's car is over twenty-five years old. He has trouble finding parts for it. He works on his car every weekend. His car never seems to run. Herman does his own repair work. His repairs cost less than if he took his car to a mechanic's shop. Herman has been saving money for over two years. He still doesn't have enough to make a down payment on a new car.

If evidence is relevant to a rule, it must tell about certain words in the rule.
Here's a rule:

> **All green plants produce oxygen.**

What words should be underlined?
So relevant evidence must tell that something is _____.
Here's some relevant evidence:
A caladium is a green plant.
This evidence tells that something is a green plant.
Here's some irrelevant evidence:
Lilies produce oxygen.
This evidence is irrelevant because it doesn't tell that something is a green plant.
Here's another rule:

> **All fruits contain some vitamin C.**

What words should be underlined?
So relevant evidence must tell that something is _____.

Figure out which evidence below is relevant to the rule.

- **A banana contains some vitamin C.**
Is that evidence relevant to the rule?

- **Oranges and lemons are fruits.**
Is that evidence relevant to the rule?

- **A grape is a fruit.**
Is that evidence relevant to the rule?

- **Cantaloupes contain lots of vitamin C.**
Is that evidence relevant to the rule?

If evidence is irrelevant, you can't draw a conclusion.
Here's the rule again:
All fruits contain some vitamin C.
Here's some irrelevant evidence: **A banana contains some vitamin C.**
What's the conclusion? There is none.
Here's some more evidence: **Oranges and lemons are fruits.**
What's the conclusion?
Here's some more evidence: **A grape is a fruit.**
What's the conclusion?
Here's some more evidence: **Cantaloupes contain lots of vitamin C.**
What's the conclusion?

B Paragraphs sometimes have a main-idea sentence. It's the sentence that tells what the paragraph is about.

Here's the main-idea sentence for a paragraph:

| The collision occurred at 2 A.M. |

Read the sentence to yourself and get ready to say it.

Tell if each sentence below provides more information about the main idea.

- **Two cars collided at the intersection of Fourth and Grand.**

Does that sentence provide more information about the main idea?

- **The river was beautiful in the moonlight.**

Does that sentence provide more information about the main idea?

- **One car, a red sports car, was driven by Emil Brock.**

Does that sentence provide more information about the main idea?

- **The second vehicle was a 1971 compact car.**

Does that sentence provide more information about the main idea?

- **A couple was singing and playing a banjo on the bank of the river.**

Does that sentence provide more information about the main idea?

- **Driftwood was scattered along the riverbank.**

Does that sentence provide more information about the main idea?

- **Both cars suffered extensive damage.**

Does that sentence provide more information about the main idea?

- **Brock's car skidded fifty meters before striking the compact car.**

Does that sentence provide more information about the main idea?

- **Although the river looked clear, it was polluted.**

Does that sentence provide more information about the main idea?

You have learned that just because you know about a part of something doesn't mean you know about the whole thing. Some arguments break important rules that are similar to this one. Here are those rules:

> - **Just because you know about a part doesn't mean you know about another part.**
> - **Just because you know about a whole thing doesn't mean you know about every part.**

Here are some arguments that involve parts and wholes. See if you can figure out which rule each argument breaks.

- That company is very well known and respected. How can the treasurer be a crook?
- I saw the kitchen in their house, and it was fabulous. I'll bet they have the best-looking living room on the block.
- You can tell that Linda comes from a poor family. She only makes $150 a week.
- She must get good grades in all her classes. She got an A in algebra last semester.
- I'm sure he sings very well, because he whistles beautifully.

Write **Part D** in the left margin of your paper. You have two minutes to copy the paragraph below.

> **Bob was walking by the river one night when he heard screams. Without hesitating, he jumped in and swam to a girl who was thrashing in the water. "Swimming here is restricted to daylight," Bob gasped, after he pulled her to shore.**

Paragraphs sometimes have a main-idea sentence. It's the sentence that tells what the paragraph is about.

Here's the main-idea sentence for a paragraph:

> **Oil spills in the ocean cause lots of damage.**

Read the sentence to yourself and get ready to say it.

Tell if each sentence below provides more information about the main idea.

• **An ocean liner can cross the Atlantic in several days.**

Does that sentence provide more information about the main idea?

• **When birds get oil on their feathers, they starve, drown, or die of pneumonia.**

Does that sentence provide more information about the main idea?

• **Oil in the water kills thousands of fish.**

Does that sentence provide more information about the main idea?

• **Ocean water is salty.**

Does that sentence provide more information about the main idea?

• **Some oil tankers hold over one million liters of oil.**

Does that sentence provide more information about the main idea?

• **When fish are killed by oil spills, fishers have no way to make a living.**

Does that sentence provide more information about the main idea?

 Here's a new model sentence:

> **They devised an appropriate strategy.**

Read the sentence to yourself. Study the sentence until you can say it without looking at it.

Here's what the model means:

> **They made up a fitting plan.**

Which word in the model means **made up?**

Which word in the model means **fitting?**

Which word in the model means **plan?**

For each item, say a sentence that means the same thing.

1. The committee <u>made up</u> a <u>fitting</u> schedule.
2. The <u>plan</u> was <u>made up</u> by the director.

Here's a rule:

All plectognaths are tropical fish.

What words should be underlined?
So relevant evidence must tell that something is _____.
Figure out which evidence below is relevant to the rule.

● **A triggerfish is a plectognath.**
Is that evidence relevant to the rule?

● **A swordtail is a tropical fish.**
Is that evidence relevant to the rule?

● **Puffers are plectognaths.**
Is that evidence relevant to the rule?

● **A guppy is a tropical fish.**
Is that evidence relevant to the rule?

If evidence is irrelevant, you can't draw a conclusion.
Here's the rule again:
All plectognaths are tropical fish.
Here's some irrelevant evidence: **A swordtail is a tropical fish.**
What's the conclusion? There is none.
Here's some more evidence: **A triggerfish is a plectognath.**
What's the conclusion?
Here's some more evidence: **Puffers are plectognaths.**
What's the conclusion?
Here's some more evidence: **A guppy is a tropical fish.**
What's the conclusion?

You have learned that just because you know about a part of something doesn't mean you know about the whole thing. Some arguments break important rules that are similar to this one. Here are those rules:

> • **Just because you know about a part doesn't mean you know about another part.**
> • **Just because you know about a whole thing doesn't mean you know about every part.**

Here are some arguments that involve parts and wholes. See if you can figure out which rule each argument breaks.

- Joe was a good student. I'm looking forward to teaching his sister.
- I took a lesson on how to change a flat tire. Therefore, I feel quite confident about taking care of my own car.
- An ad said that this refrigerator is made of the highest-quality steel, but I can't imagine a refrigerator with a steel light bulb in it.

Write **Part E** in the left margin of your paper. You have two minutes to copy the paragraph below.

> **Here's a rule that is sometimes broken in faulty arguments: Just because you know about a whole thing doesn't mean you know about every part. Don't get this rule confused with the other rules about parts and wholes.**

A

Here's the latest model sentence you learned:

They devised an appropriate strategy.

What sentence means the same thing?

What word means **made up?**

What word means **fitting?**

What word means **plan?**

What's another way of saying,

The plan the president made up was not fitting?

B

You can change a sentence into a part of a sentence by using **who** or **which.**
Here's a sentence with some words underlined:

The car was on the street.

Here's how to change the sentence: **which** was on the street.
Here's a different sentence: **Those workmen had a big job.**
Here's how to change the sentence: **who** had a big job.

Change each sentence by saying **who** or **which** for the underlined part.
1. The team was playing baseball.
2. Five dogs sat in the yard.
3. My siblings were tired.
4. The arrows narrowly missed him.
5. The dancer was six feet tall.
6. The club will meet on Friday.

C

Here's a rule:

Insecticides are designed to kill insects.

What word should be underlined?
So relevant evidence must tell that something is _____.
Figure out which evidence below is relevant to the rule.

• **Locusts are insects.**
Is that evidence relevant to the rule?

• **Chlordane and DDT are insecticides.**
Is that evidence relevant to the rule?

• **A grasshopper is an insect.**
Is that evidence relevant to the rule?

• **Fire ants are insects.**
Is that evidence relevant to the rule?

If evidence is irrelevant, you can't draw a conclusion.

Here's the rule again:

Insecticides are designed to kill insects.

Here's some irrelevant evidence: **Locusts are insects.**

What's the conclusion? There is none.

Here's some more evidence: **Chlordane and DDT are insecticides.**

What's the conclusion?

Here's some more evidence: **A grasshopper is an insect.**

What's the conclusion?

Here's some more evidence: **Fire ants are insects.**

What's the conclusion?

 Write **Part D** in the left margin of your paper. You have two minutes to copy the paragraph below.

> **Paragraphs sometimes have a main-idea sentence. The main-idea sentence is the sentence that tells what the paragraph is about. The rest of the sentences in the paragraph usually provide more details about the main-idea sentence.**

★ Write **Part E** in the left margin of your paper. Rewrite the passage below in four or five sentences. Combine consistent sentences with **so** or **therefore.** Combine inconsistent sentences with **but** or **however.**

> Tokyo, Japan, has many earthquakes. Very few buildings there are destroyed by quakes. Buildings made of paper and wood do not usually break when an earthquake hits. Many people in Tokyo live in houses of paper and wood. Most of the buildings in Tokyo were destroyed by an earthquake in 1923. One hotel survived. It had a special foundation designed not to crack during earthquakes.

Here's the latest model sentence you learned:
They devised an appropriate strategy.
What sentence means the same thing?
What word means **made up?**
What word means **fitting?**
What word means **plan?**
What's another way of saying,
The coach made up a fitting plan for winning?

Write **Part B** in the left margin of your paper. You have two minutes to copy the paragraph below.

Here's a rule that is sometimes broken in faulty arguments: Just because you know about a part doesn't mean you know about another part. Don't get this rule confused with the other rules about parts and wholes.

Paragraphs sometimes have a main-idea sentence. It's the sentence that tells what the paragraph is about.
Here's the main-idea sentence for a paragraph:

> **Chess is a game that is played in many countries.**

Read the sentence to yourself and get ready to say it.

Tell if each sentence below provides more information about the main idea.

- **Chess champions have come from Turkey, Italy, Spain, and India.**

Does that sentence provide more information about the main idea?

- **Backgammon is a game that was played in ancient Greece and Rome.**

Does that sentence provide more information about the main idea?

- **The game of chess has been spread by traders and travelers for over 1400 years.**

Does that sentence provide more information about the main idea?

- **Worldwide chess matches are held every few years.**

Does that sentence provide more information about the main idea?

 You learned a model sentence that means:
    They made up a fitting plan.
Say that model sentence.
What word in the model sentence means **made up?**
What word in the model sentence means **fitting?**
What word in the model sentence means **plan?**

Here's how to combine sentences using **who** or **which.**

> 1. Find what's common to both sentences.
> 2. Change the second sentence by using **who** or **which.**
> 3. Put a comma before **who** or **which.**

Here's a pair of sentences. The underlined words are common to both sentences.
She complained about the band. The band was very loud.
What's common to both sentences?
Change the second sentence by using **who** or **which.**
Say the combined sentence.
What punctuation do you need before **which?**

Here's another pair of sentences.

She went out with Nita's brother. Nita's brother is very tall.

What's common to both sentences?

Change the second sentence by using **who** or **which.**

Say the combined sentence.

What punctuation do you need before **who?**

Here's another pair of sentences.

They had fifty sheep. Those fifty sheep were skinny.

What's common to both sentences?

Change the second sentence by using **who** or **which.**

Say the combined sentence.

What punctuation do you need before **which?**

Write **Part D** in the left margin of your paper. You have two minutes to copy the paragraph below.

> **Over the past forty years, people have become increasingly interested in a subject called ecology. The word "ecology" comes from an old Greek word that means "house." The house that is referred to by the word "ecology" is our earth.**

VOCABULARY TEST. Write **Part E** in the left margin of your paper. Then number it from 1 to 6. Write the model sentence that means the same thing as each sentence below. You have seven minutes.

1. By pausing, she lost her chance.
2. His directions were unclear and repetitive.
3. They changed their Swiss money into Canadian money.
4. The rule limited their parking.
5. Her answer was filled with irrelevant details.
6. They made up a fitting plan.

A

Here's how to combine sentences using **who** or **which**.

> 1. Find what's common to both sentences.
> 2. Change the second sentence by using **who** or **which**.
> 3. Put a comma before **who** or **which**.

Here's a pair of sentences. The underlined words are common to both sentences.

She loves to eat mangoes. Mangoes are a sweet tropical fruit.

What's common to both sentences?

Change the second sentence by using **who** or **which**.

Say the combined sentence.

What punctuation do you need before **which?**

Here's another pair of sentences.

The lawyer questioned the witness. The witness was very nervous.

What's common to both sentences?

Change the second sentence by using **who** or **which**.

Say the combined sentence.

What punctuation do you need before **who?**

Here's another pair of sentences.

Milk contains lots of vitamin D. Vitamin D is necessary for normal bone growth.

What's common to both sentences?

Change the second sentence by using **who** or **which**.

Say the combined sentence.

What punctuation do you need before **which?**

B

Here are two main ideas.

Main idea for paragraph 1:

> **Frank was getting ready to go fishing.**

Main idea for paragraph 2:

> **Frank had an accident and nearly drowned.**

Each of the following sentences belongs to either paragraph 1 or paragraph 2. Read each sentence. Then tell which paragraph the sentence belongs to.

• **His pole fell in the water and he jumped in after it.**

Which paragraph does that sentence belong to?

- **He got his boots and gear ready the night before.**

Which paragraph does that sentence belong to?

- **He told his mother he would bring some trout home for dinner.**

Which paragraph does that sentence belong to?

- **His clothes became heavy with water and dragged him to the bottom of the stream.**

Which paragraph does that sentence belong to?

- **Holding his breath, he took off his boots and struggled out of his clothes.**

Which paragraph does that sentence belong to?

- **He went to bed early so that he could get an early start the next morning.**

Which paragraph does that sentence belong to?

- **He bought some new hooks and lures.**

Which paragraph does that sentence belong to?

- **He swam to the surface and gasped for air.**

Which paragraph does that sentence belong to?

- **The stream carried him under some low-hanging branches, which he grabbed onto.**

Which paragraph does that sentence belong to?

- **He dragged himself out of the water and lay panting on the bank of the stream.**

Which paragraph does that sentence belong to?

- **He had marked the places where he wanted to fish on some maps.**

Which paragraph does that sentence belong to?

 Write **Part C** in the left margin of your paper. You have two minutes to copy the paragraph below.

> **A hundred years ago, people were not concerned about ecology. Wild animals seemed to be as plentiful as weeds; therefore, people believed that there was no end to different types of wildlife. Nobody worried about killing these animals.**

★ **D** Write **Part D** in the left margin of your paper. Then number it from 1 to 5. Assume that the picture below is accurate. Examine the picture carefully, and then read the statements below it. Some of the statements contradict what the picture shows.

- Write **contradictory** or **not contradictory** for each statement.
- If a statement contradicts the picture, write what the picture shows.

1. The woman is standing on a stool to get a basket of fruit.
2. There are two boxes on the top shelf of the open cabinet.
3. The cat is sitting on the floor and looking at the woman.
4. The fork and the food dish are on the floor.
5. A banana is lying beside the fruit basket.

Here are two main ideas.
Main idea for paragraph 1:

> **He studied piano for ten years.**

Main idea for paragraph 2:

> **On his nineteenth birthday, he gave a concert with the local orchestra.**

Each sentence below belongs to either paragraph 1 or paragraph 2. Read each sentence. Then tell which paragraph the sentence belongs to.

- **He bought a tuxedo for the performance.**

Which paragraph does that sentence belong to?

- **He went to a music camp for several summers.**

Which paragraph does that sentence belong to?

- **He used to mow lawns to pay for extra lessons.**

Which paragraph does that sentence belong to?

- **He amazed the audience with his ability.**

Which paragraph does that sentence belong to?

- **Over the years, he had half a dozen different teachers.**

Which paragraph does that sentence belong to?

- **When he was younger, his friends teased him about how much time he spent practicing.**

Which paragraph does that sentence belong to?

- **At the end of the last piece, the audience stood up and cheered.**

Which paragraph does that sentence belong to?

- **He used to travel hundreds of miles to hear great pianists.**

Which paragraph does that sentence belong to?

- **He played two encores.**

Which paragraph does that sentence belong to?

- **Local writers reviewed the performance in the newspapers.**

Which paragraph does that sentence belong to?

- **After the performance, members of the orchestra congratulated him.**

Which paragraph does that sentence belong to?

B The argument below is faulty because it breaks this rule:

> **Just because words are the same**
> **doesn't mean they have the same meaning.**

Read the rule over to yourself and get ready to say it.

Here's an argument:

> **Emma must be color-blind. She told me she was blue,**
> **but she looks the same color she always does.**

What does the writer want us to conclude?

What evidence does the writer use to support this conclusion?

To show that the argument is faulty, you point out that the evidence has two meanings.

What meaning of **blue** does the writer use?

What's the other meaning?

If the evidence has two meanings, the writer's conclusion is not the only conclusion that is possible. Another conclusion is that Emma was feeling sad, not that she was the color blue.

C Write **Part C** in the left margin of your paper. You have two minutes to copy the paragraph below.

> **Here's how to combine sentences using the word "who" or the word "which." Find what's common to both sentences. Change the second sentence by using "who" or "which." Put a comma before the word "who" or "which."**

The argument below is faulty because it breaks this rule:

**Just because words are the same
doesn't mean they have the same meaning.**

Read the rule over to yourself and get ready to say it.
Here's an argument:

> **Lou must be an artist because I know he draws a lot of flies.**

What does the writer want us to conclude?
What evidence does the writer use to support this conclusion?
To show that the argument is faulty, you point out that the evidence has two meanings. What meaning of **draw** does the writer use?
What's the other meaning?
If the evidence has two meanings, the writer's conclusion is not the only conclusion that is possible. Another conclusion is that Lou attracts flies to him, not that he makes pictures of them.

B Look at the graph below.

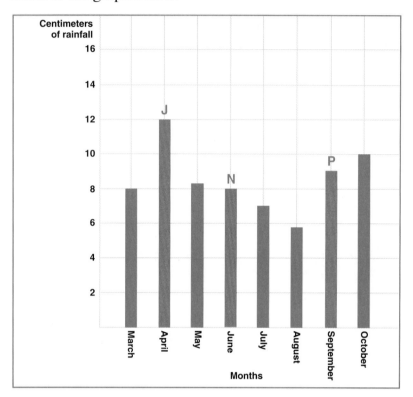

What do the up-and-down numbers on the graph show?
What do the words across the bottom show?

- Find the letter **N.**

N shows how many centimeters of rainfall occurred in a certain month. To find the month for **N,** go this way: ↓

What month is **N** above?
To find the number of centimeters of rainfall for **N,** go this way: ⟵ . How many centimeters is **N** next to?
So **N** shows 8 centimeters of rainfall for the month of June.

- Find the letter **J.**

J shows the number of centimeters of rainfall for a different month. To find the month for **J,** which way do you go?
What month is **J** above?
To find the number of centimeters of rainfall for **J,** which way do you go?
How many centimeters is **J** next to?
So **J** shows 12 centimeters of rainfall for the month of April.

- Find the letter **P.**

P shows the centimeters of rainfall for one month. What month?
How many centimeters?

Remember the three things you do to combine sentences with **who** or **which**.

1. Find what's common to both sentences.
2. Change the second sentence by using **who** or **which**.
3. Put a comma before **who** or **which**.

Here's a pair of sentences.
The woman lost her wallet. The wallet was brown.
What's common to both sentences?
Change the second sentence by using **who** or **which**.
Say the combined sentence.
What punctuation do you need?

Here's another pair of sentences.
He stared at Jenny. Jenny was beautiful.
What's common to both sentences?
Change the second sentence by using **who** or **which**.
Say the combined sentence.
What punctuation do you need?

Write **Part D** in the left margin of your paper. You have two minutes to copy the paragraph below.

> **Animal species are endangered when only a few of the species are alive. When the number of babies born each year becomes smaller than the number of animals that die each year, the population of the species becomes very small.**

A Look at the graph below.

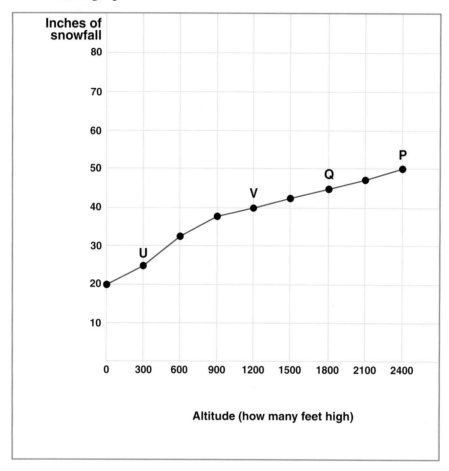

What do the up-and-down numbers on the graph show?
What do the numbers across the bottom show?

- Find the letter **V.**

V shows how many inches of snowfall occurred at a certain altitude. To find the altitude for **V**, go this way: ↓
What altitude is **V** above?
To find the number of inches of snowfall for **V**, go this way: ←. How many inches is **V** next to?
So **V** shows that 40 inches of snowfall occurred at 1200 feet.

- Find the letter **U.**

U shows the number of inches of snowfall at a different altitude. What altitude? How many inches?

Write **Part A** in the left margin of your paper. Then number it from 1 to 4. Answer the questions about what is shown on the graph.

● The letter **Q** shows the inches of snowfall at a certain altitude.

1. What altitude?
2. How many inches?

● The letter **P** shows the inches of snowfall at a certain altitude.

3. What altitude?
4. How many inches?

For some rules, relevant evidence tells what something **is not** or **does not do.**
    Cats are mammals.
Evidence is relevant if it tells that something is a cat.
Evidence is also relevant if it tells that something is not a mammal.

Here's a deduction with evidence that tells that something is not a mammal:

> **Cats are mammals.**
> **A marabou is not a mammal.**
> **Therefore, a marabou is not a cat.**

Read each rule below and say the answers to the items.

● **Monkeys have fingers.**
Evidence is relevant if it tells that something is _____.
Evidence is relevant if it tells that something does not _____.
Make up a deduction using evidence that something does not have fingers.

● **Fires need oxygen.**
Evidence is relevant if it tells that something is _____.
Evidence is relevant if it tells that something does not _____.
Make up a deduction using evidence that something does not need oxygen.

Here's an argument:

> **I heard that Eskimos survive on blubber, but I could never figure out how crying a lot would help them survive.**

What does the writer want us to conclude?
What do you point out to show that the argument is faulty?
What part of the evidence has more than one meaning?
Make up a conclusion that is based on the other meaning of that evidence.

Write **Part D** in the left margin of your paper. You have two minutes to copy the paragraph below.

> **Here's a rule that is sometimes broken in faulty arguments: Just because words are the same doesn't mean they have the same meaning. See if you can make up some funny arguments that break this rule.**

Write **Part A** in the left margin of your paper. You have two minutes to copy the paragraph below.

> **I can't tell when my friend is teasing. Sometimes she gets the most ambiguous expressions on her face, and it's hard to tell whether she is serious. Yesterday she told me that it would be appropriate to wear jeans to the prom.**

VOCABULARY TEST. Write **Part B** in the left margin of your paper. Then number it from 1 to 6. Write the model sentence that means the same thing as each sentence below. You have seven minutes.

1. His directions were unclear and repetitive.
2. The rule limited their parking.
3. They made up a fitting plan.
4. By pausing, she lost her chance.
5. Her answer was filled with irrelevant details.
6. They changed their Swiss money into Canadian money.

INFORMATION TEST. Write **Part C** in the left margin of your paper. Then number it from 1 to 18 and answer each item. You have fourteen minutes.

1. The word **ecology** comes from a Greek word meaning what?
2. Why weren't people concerned with ecology a hundred years ago?
3. What is a basic goal of all living things?
4. What do we mean when we say that an animal is herbivorous?
5. What would happen to carnivorous animals if there were no herbivorous animals?
6. What did **clewe** mean in Middle English?
7. When you study ecology, what do you study?
8. What is an endangered species?
9. What is the only type of living thing that produces its own food?
10. What would happen to herbivorous animals if there were no plants?
11. What do you do when you haze someone?
12. What does it mean when we say that a type of animal is extinct?
13. How many species of animals are currently endangered?
14. For plants to manufacture food, what three ingredients must be present?
15. What do we mean when we say that an animal is carnivorous?

16. What do you do when you tantalize someone?

17. Why did some types of equus become large and strong while others became slender and quick?

18. What is a clue?

 ★ Write **Part D** in the left margin of your paper. Then number it from 1 to 6. Look at the graph below. Then answer the questions about what is shown on the graph.

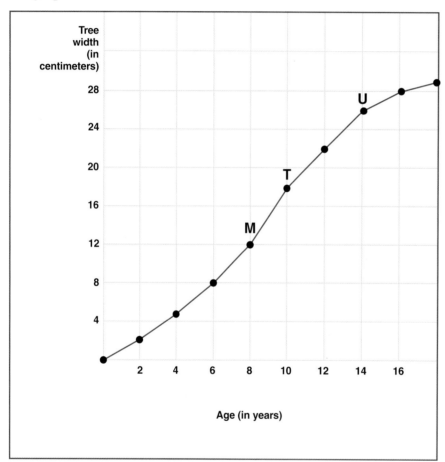

• The letter **U** shows the number of centimeters for a certain age.

1. What age?

2. How many centimeters?

• The letter **M** shows the number of centimeters for a certain age.

3. What age?

4. How many centimeters?

- The letter **T** shows the number of centimeters for a certain age.

5. What age?
6. How many centimeters?

Here are some words that will be in some editing activities. Test yourself to make sure that you know what the words mean.

catastrophe—A catastrophe is a terrible event that results in death and destruction. Earthquakes, fires, and floods are catastrophes. Here is a sentence that uses the word **catastrophe:**
 The plane crash was the worst catastrophe in the history of northern Indiana.

inquiries—Inquiries are questions. Here is a sentence that uses the word **inquiries:**
 The lawyer's inquiries made the witness nervous.

overpopulated—When a place is overpopulated, too many things are living there. An overpopulated city is a city that has too many people in it. Here is a sentence that uses the word **overpopulated:**
 The area became overpopulated with rabbits because all the coyotes were killed.

temporary—Situations that are temporary do not last forever. They change. Here is a sentence that uses the word **temporary:**
 She had a temporary job as a waitress.

wildlife—Wildlife is made up of wild plants and wild animals. Here's a sentence that uses the word **wildlife:**
 The hikers saw lots of wildlife as they went down into the canyon.

A

Read each rule below and say the answers to the items.

- **Dinosaurs are extinct.**

Evidence is relevant if it tells that something is _____.
Evidence is relevant if it tells that something does not _____.
Make up a deduction using evidence that something is not extinct.

- **Green plants produce oxygen.**

Evidence is relevant if it tells that something is _____.
Evidence is relevant if it tells that something does not _____.
Make up a deduction using evidence that something does not produce oxygen.

B

Here's an argument:

> **When Jim came to the party dressed like Zorro, Mrs. Thompson said that he had poor taste. If he can't taste anything, I guess I won't invite him for dinner anymore. It would be a waste of good food.**

What does the writer want us to conclude?
What do you point out to show that the argument is faulty?
Make up a conclusion that is based on the other meaning of that evidence.
What rule does the argument break?

C

Write **Part C** in the left margin of your paper. You have two minutes to copy the paragraph below.

> **Green plants manufacture their own food; therefore, they don't have to hunt for food. For green plants to produce food, they need sunlight, water, and carbon dioxide, which are converted into green vegetation. The conversion process used by plants is called photosynthesis.**

Write **Part D** in the left margin of your paper. Then number it from 1 to 6. Look at the graph below. Then answer the questions about what is shown on the graph.

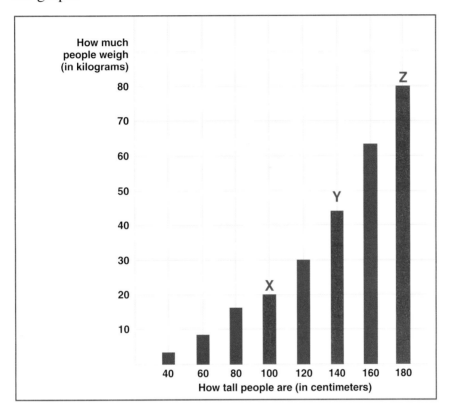

• The letter **X** shows the weight for people who are a certain height.

1. What height?
2. What weight?

• The letter **Y** shows the weight for people who are a certain height.

3. What height?
4. What weight?

• The letter **Z** shows the weight for people who are a certain height.

5. What height?
6. What weight?

A Read each rule below and say the answers to the items.

- **Herbivorous animals eat plants.**

Evidence is relevant if it tells that something is _____.
Evidence is relevant if it tells that something does not _____.
Make up a deduction using evidence that something does not eat plants.

- **Chisels are used to shape stone.**

Evidence is relevant if it tells that something is _____.
Evidence is relevant if it tells that something does not _____.
Make up a deduction using evidence that something is not used to shape stone.

B Write **Part B** in the left margin of your paper. You have two minutes to copy the paragraph below.

> A catastrophe is a terrible event that results in death and destruction. Earthquakes, tornadoes, and hurricanes are catastrophes. Here is a sentence that uses the word "catastrophe": The big fire was the worst catastrophe in the history of the city.

The main idea of a passage is the most important idea. When you remember the main idea, the other ideas that the author expresses in a selection are easier to remember.

The main idea is not necessarily one of the sentences in the passage. The main idea tells about everything that is covered in the passage. What does the main idea tell about?

● Here's the main idea of a passage:

> **Some older trees are very large.**

Read the main idea to yourself and get ready to say it.

Read each passage below. Then tell whether the main idea describes passage 1, passage 2, or passage 3.

Passage 1. Trees keep on growing as long as they live. Trees in some areas of the country have a "rest" period during part of the year. They do not grow during the winter months. At temperatures below the freezing point, sap inside the tree cannot flow. If sap doesn't flow, the growing parts of the trees receive no water or food from the roots. Only when warm weather returns does the sap begin to flow, and trees start growing again.

Passage 2. Trees keep on growing as long as they live. There are trees in California that are nearly 5000 years old. They are the oldest living things on earth. Since trees keep growing for as long as they live, some trees that live for hundreds of years become very large. In fact, the largest living thing on Earth is a tree—a sequoia in California that is about eighty-two meters tall and twenty-four meters around!

Passage 3. Trees keep on growing as long as they live. Each year until their death, trees add a layer of new wood during the growing season and then "rest" during the cold months. These layers form the rings that you see when you cut through a tree trunk. Because one layer is added every year, you can figure out how old a tree is by counting its rings.

The main idea is: **Some older trees are very large.** Does that main idea best fit passage 1, passage 2, or passage 3?

• Here's the main idea of another passage:

> **Camels are noisy animals.**

Read the main idea to yourself and get ready to say it.

Read each passage below. Then tell whether the main idea describes passage 4, passage 5, or passage 6.

Passage 4. Camels are useful animals, but they have some very peculiar traits. Camels groan and grumble, just as some people do. If you put a load on a camel's back, the camel will moan. If you take the load off, the camel may make the same sound! Some people who work with camels think that camels enjoy grumbling.

Passage 5. Camels are useful animals, but they have some very peculiar traits. A camel might start to run as soon as its rider dismounts. Such behavior could leave a person stranded in the desert, far from water. Sometimes a camel simply won't do what its rider wants it to do. It ignores the rider's commands and goes where it pleases. Sometimes it kneels quickly, throwing the astonished rider to the ground.

Passage 6. Camels are useful animals, and they live in places besides sandy deserts. Some camels live where winters are very cold and there is much snow. These camels have long hair and their feet are well designed both for moving over sand and for traveling over snow and ice. Not many people know that camels are so well fitted to live in colder regions.

The main idea is: **Camels are noisy animals.** Does that main idea best fit passage 4, passage 5, or passage 6?

 Write **Part B** in the left margin of your paper. You have two minutes to copy the paragraph below.

> **Animals must hunt for food. Carnivorous animals eat other animals, and herbivorous animals eat plants. If there were no plants, herbivorous animals would have nothing to eat. If there were no herbivorous animals, carnivorous animals would become extinct.**

The main idea of a passage is the most important idea. When you remember the main idea, the other ideas that the author expresses in a selection are easier to remember.

The main idea is not necessarily one of the sentences in the passage. The main idea tells about everything that is covered in the passage. What does the main idea tell about?

• Here's the main idea of a passage:

> **What to do when you feel an earthquake.**

Read the main idea to yourself and get ready to say it.

Read each passage below. Then tell whether the main idea describes passage 1, passage 2, or passage 3.

Passage 1. An earthquake results when pressure causes the earth's crust to buckle and crack. Earthquakes haven't been known to damage a ship at sea; however, earthquakes can be felt aboard ship. One person who was on a ship during an earthquake said that it felt as if the ship had struck a reef. Another said it felt as if the ship had lost a blade of its propeller.

Passage 2. An earthquake results when pressure causes the earth's crust to buckle and crack. People of ancient times had a different explanation for earthquakes. They believed that Earth was balanced on the head of a huge animal. Sooner or later the animal that held up the world would shake or scratch itself. According to the belief, this would start an earthquake in some parts of the world.

Passage 3. An earthquake results when pressure causes the earth's crust to buckle and crack. If you should feel the ground or floor start to shake beneath your feet, and if you see walls starting to move, you may be caught in an earthquake. If you are inside a building, get under anything that will protect you from a falling ceiling. If you are outside, get away from buildings as fast as you can. Open places are the safest.

The main idea is: **What to do when you feel an earthquake.** Does that main idea best fit passage 1, passage 2, or passage 3?

Write **Part B** in the left margin of your paper. You have two minutes to copy the paragraph below.

> **When a place is overpopulated, too many things are living there. An overpopulated city is a city that has too many people. Here is a sentence that uses "overpopulated": The area became overpopulated with field mice because all the hawks were killed.**

★

Write **Part C** in the left margin of your paper. Rewrite the passage below in three sentences. Combine consistent sentences with **and** or **so.** Combine inconsistent sentences with **but** or **however.** Combine some sentences with **who** or **which.**

> Douglas fir trees are named after David Douglas. David Douglas was the first person to study these trees. More than half of the trees in the northwestern part of the United States are Douglas firs. Douglas fir lumber is the principal lumber for construction there. Christmas decorations are often made with Douglas fir cones. The cones are often over three inches long.

Write **Part D** in the left margin of your paper. Then number it from 1 to 4. Look at the graph below. Then answer the questions about what is shown on the graph.

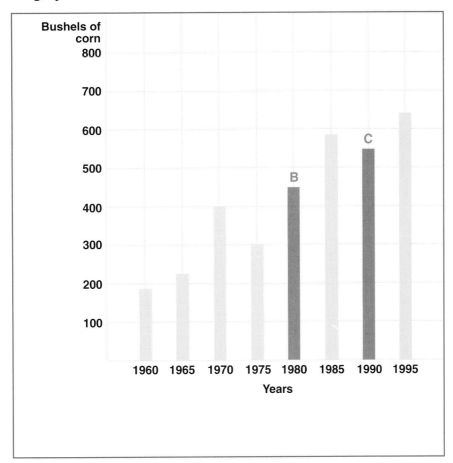

- The letter **B** shows bushels of corn for one year.

1. What year?
2. How many bushels?

- The letter **C** shows bushels of corn for one year.

3. What year?
4. How many bushels?

Write **Part E** in the left margin of your paper.
  Here's the main idea of a passage:

> **Gloves used to be symbols of bad things to come.**

Read each passage below. Then tell whether the main idea describes
passage 1, passage 2, or passage 3.

Passage 1. Many everyday objects, such as gloves, have interesting
or unusual histories. Trick gloves were popular among wealthy people
during the 1600s. Sometimes people put powder into gloves that they
sent to a friend. The powder made the friend's hands and wrists itch.
Sometimes the fingers of gloves were sewn together so that the person
couldn't get his or her hand into the glove.

Passage 2. Many everyday objects, such as gloves, have interesting
or unusual histories. For example, people used to be superstitious about
gloves. They thought that if a person lost a glove, that person would
suffer a great disappointment.

Passage 3. Many everyday objects, such as gloves, have interesting
or unusual histories. Years ago, wedding guests were often given white
gloves, which later reminded guests of the happy wedding. The white
gloves were received not only by those who attended the wedding, but
also by all friends of the bride and groom. To cut down on the cost of
supplying so many gloves, some families gave paper gloves.

  The main idea is: **Gloves used to be symbols of bad things to come.**
Does that main idea best fit passage 1, passage 2, or passage 3?

For the rules below, some of the relevant evidence tells what something is not or what something does not do.

Rule 1. **All reptiles are cold-blooded.**
Evidence A. **Marmosets are not cold-blooded.**
Evidence B. **A rodent is not cold-blooded.**
Evidence C. **A Gila monster is a reptile.**

Rule 2. **Stars are burning things.**
Evidence D. **Venus is not a burning thing.**
Evidence E. **The sun is a star.**
Evidence F. **Peru is not a burning thing.**

The main idea of a paragraph is the most important idea. When you remember the main idea, the other ideas that the author expresses in a selection are easier to remember.

Here's the main idea of a passage:

Businesses use music to sell more products.

Read the main idea to yourself and get ready to say it.

Read each passage that follows. Then tell whether the main idea describes passage 1, passage 2, or passage 3.

Passage 1. Music influences the way people behave. Some businesses have recently taken advantage of this fact, but the idea is not new. The legend of the Pied Piper has been around for hundreds of years. According to this legend, the piper played his flute and lured children to follow him. Aristotle, who lived before Christ, wrote a great deal about music and how it influenced people. He thought that "wild" music caused people to do bad things.

Passage 2. Music influences the way people behave. When you have some friends over, try this experiment. First play some soft, slow music. The conversation will probably become quiet and calm. Then play some rock 'n' roll. Most likely, the conversation will become more lively, and people will start moving around.

> **Passage 3.** Music influences the way people behave. Some businesses have recently taken advantage of this fact. For example, some stores pipe in "pleasant" music. The idea is that the music will make you feel better. If you feel good, you will want to stay in the store, and if you stay in the store, you'll probably end up spending more money.

The main idea is: **Businesses use music to sell more products.**
Does that main idea best fit passage 1, passage 2, or passage 3?

 Write **Part C** in the left margin of your paper. You have two minutes to copy the paragraph below.

> **The main idea of a passage is the most important idea. When you remember the main idea, the other ideas that the author expresses in a selection are easier to remember. The main idea is not necessarily one of the sentences in the passage. The main idea tells about everything that is covered in the passage.**

 VOCABULARY TEST. Write **Part D** in the left margin of your paper. Then number it from 1 to 6. Write the model sentence that means the same thing as each sentence below. You have seven minutes.

1. The <u>rule</u> <u>limited</u> their parking.
2. By <u>pausing</u>, she lost her <u>chance</u>.
3. His directions were <u>unclear</u> and <u>repetitive</u>.
4. They <u>made up</u> a <u>fitting</u> <u>plan</u>.
5. They <u>changed</u> their Swiss <u>money</u> into Canadian <u>money</u>.
6. Her <u>answer</u> was <u>filled</u> with <u>irrelevant</u> details.

★ Write **Part E** in the left margin of your paper.
Here's the main idea of a passage:

| **Wind can make unpredictable changes.** |

Read each passage on the next page. Then tell whether the main idea describes passage 1, passage 2, or passage 3.

Passage 1. The study of wind can be fascinating. In medieval times, people used several formulas for getting rid of wind. All the bells in town were rung when a storm was approaching, and people clanked metal dishes and yelled in hopes of scaring the wind away. Sometimes people even shot huge cannons into the wind. Some primitive tribes went to war against the wind, throwing rocks, shells, and spears into the storm in hopes of conquering it.

Passage 2. The study of wind can be fascinating. The chinook is a warm wind that can change the temperature during the winter by more than eight degrees Fahrenheit in just a few minutes. The weather bureau in Montana has a record of a chinook that, early one morning, raised the temperature sixty degrees in three minutes. For a few hours before sunrise, it was like a spring day. Then, just as suddenly, the temperature dropped down to twenty degrees, and it was winter again.

Passage 3. The study of wind can be fascinating. Many superstitions have been created about wind. For centuries, people believed that wind came from caves. For this reason, sailors were afraid to take their boats out of sight of land. They figured that the wind would not blow on the open ocean where there were no caves.

The main idea is: **Wind can make unpredictable changes.** Does that main idea best fit passage 1, passage 2, or passage 3?

 Write **Part F** in the left margin of your paper. Rewrite the passage below in four sentences. Combine consistent sentences with **and** or **therefore.** Combine inconsistent sentences with **but** or **however.** Combine some sentences with **who** or **which.**

> Americans who watch television in Britain are often surprised. There is almost no advertising on British television stations. British television stations are sponsored by the government. The British people find advertising very distasteful. They pay for their television stations with their taxes. The few ads on British television are different from American ads. American ads are offensive to many Britishers.

For the rules below, some of the relevant evidence tells what something is not or what something does not do.

Rule 1. **Astringent substances draw things together.**
Evidence A. **Alum is an astringent substance.**
Evidence B. **Water does not draw things together.**
Evidence C. **Paper does not draw things together.**

Rule 2. **Consumers buy things.**
Evidence D. **John does not buy things.**
Evidence E. **Most Canadians are consumers.**
Evidence F. **Parrots do not buy things.**

Write **Part B** in the left margin of your paper. You have two minutes to copy the paragraph below.

> **Herbivorous animals are well designed for grazing. Their teeth are flat, which is helpful for grinding grass, leaves, and seeds. The eyes of herbivorous animals are positioned so that they can eat and watch out for enemies at the same time.**

Write **Part C** in the left margin of your paper.
     Here's the main idea of a passage:

> **The color of a sunset is not the same as the color of a sunrise.**

Read each of the following passages. Then tell whether the main idea describes passage 1, passage 2, or passage 3.

> **Passage 1.** The color of the sky changes because light passes through particles in the air. The basic rule is this: The more particles the light passes through, the greater the change in color of the light. At sunset and sunrise, the light from the sun is close to the horizon; therefore, it must pass through many particles to reach you. That's why the sky appears to be colored.

Passage 2. There is no atmosphere on the moon, which means that there are no particles in the air for the light to pass through. The sky is therefore black. There can be no sunset on the moon, because the light does not pass through particles. The sky is never colored—it's always black.

Passage 3. During the daytime, the color of the sky on earth is usually blue. However, the color of the sky is different at sunrise from what it is at sunset. The reason is that the earth rotates from west to east. When the earth is moving away from the light of the sun, the light tends to turn red. When the earth is moving toward the light, the light turns blue. Since the earth is turning toward the east, it turns toward the light in the morning and away from the light in the evening. Therefore, at most sunrises, the sky has a bluish color, and at most sunsets, the sky has a reddish color.

The main idea is: **The color of a sunset is not the same as the color of a sunrise.** Does that main idea best fit passage 1, passage 2, or passage 3?

A Here's a sentence:

> **Before she got home, she stopped at the store <u>and then went to her house.</u>**

Explain why the underlined part is redundant. Do this by completing the sentence below.

If you know that she got home, you already know that _____.

● Here's another sentence:

> **Production at the factory was raised <u>when production was increased.</u>**

Explain why the underlined part is redundant. Do this by completing the sentence below.

If you know that production at the factory was raised, you already know that

_____.

● Here's another sentence:

> **This catastrophe is the worst <u>disaster</u> I've ever seen.**

Explain why the underlined part is redundant. Do this by completing the sentence below.

If you know that what happened is a catastrophe, you already know that

_____.

B Here's an argument for where to locate a new business:

> Hilldale is the best location for new business in Hinker County. Here's why Hilldale is the best choice:

● Hilldale is located at the intersection of Route 5 and Route 30.
● Hilldale is only sixteen kilometers from Benjamin.
● Hilldale is the largest town in Hinker County.
● Hilldale is only fourteen kilometers from Muckster.

When you consider all these reasons, you see that there could not be a more convenient location for a new business.

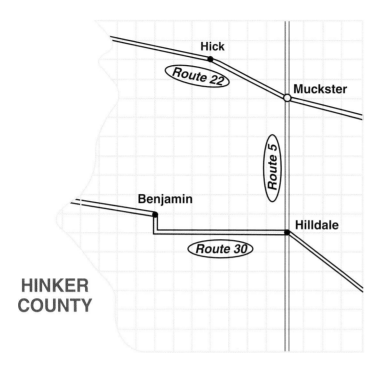

HINKER COUNTY

Each square on the map is two kilometers long and two kilometers wide.
The symbol ● means that the city has between 1000 and 5000 people.
The symbol ○ means that the city has between 5000 and 10,000 people.
The symbol ⟨Route 5⟩ means that the road is named Route 5.

Part of the argument is contradicted by the map above. Look at the map and figure out which part.
What does the map show?

When you combine sentences with the word **and,** what do you do with the period of the first sentence?
What word follows the comma?

When you combine sentences with the word **however,** what do you do with the period of the first sentence?
What follows the semicolon?
What follows the word **however?**

When you combine sentences with the word **but,** what do you do with the period of the first sentence?
What word follows the comma?

D Write **Part D** in the left margin of your paper. You have two minutes to copy the paragraph below.

> **Wildlife is made up of wild plants and wild animals. In the last one hundred years, many forms of wildlife have become extinct. Today there are several clubs that have been organized to help protect wildlife that is currently endangered.**

★ **E** Write **Part E** in the left margin of your paper.

Here's the main idea of a passage:

Changes in weather can affect military battles.

Read each passage below. Then tell whether the main idea describes passage 1, passage 2, or passage 3.

Passage 1. A few drops of rain at the right time could change the history of the world. In fact, the threat of rain once played an important role in the outcome of a battle. One morning in 1815, Napoleon had planned to attack the British at daybreak, but when daybreak came, the sky was full of clouds. He didn't want to fight in the rain, so he waited. By noon, the sky still hadn't cleared, but Napoleon gave the command to attack. By waiting for the weather, Napoleon had given the British enough time to receive badly needed reinforcements. Napoleon suffered a terrible defeat at this famous battle—the Battle of Waterloo.

Passage 2. A few drops of rain at the right time could change the history of the world. And Dr. Irving Langmuir wanted to figure out how to produce these drops of rain. Dr. Langmuir had been looking for a long time for a way to make clouds rain on demand. One day, he left the door to his freezer open. When he realized what he had done, he put a chunk of dry ice into the freezer to cool the freezer down. Later, when he stuck his head in the freezer to retrieve the dry ice, he exhaled, causing hundreds of tiny snowflakes to appear right in front of his face. Dr. Langmuir's discovery led to successful experiments in producing rain from real clouds.

Passage 3. Plutarch, an ancient Greek, noticed that many large military battles were accompanied by rain. He suggested that military battles affect the weather. He said that maybe the gods made it rain because they were angry about all the killing. Other people thought that all of the blood, sweat, and tears shed during a battle were absorbed by the clouds and then rained back down on the battlefield. Still others suggested that it was actually the noise of the battle that caused the rain.

The main idea is: **Changes in weather can affect military battles.** Does that main idea best fit passage 1, passage 2, or passage 3?

The argument below is faulty because it breaks this rule:

Just because the writer presents some choices doesn't mean there aren't other choices.

Read the rule over to yourself and get ready to say it.

Here's an argument:

> **You should go to college. If you don't, you'll either have to join the army or get a job pumping gas.**

What does the writer want us to conclude?

What choices does the writer use as evidence for this conclusion?

Say the rule that the argument breaks.

Here's how to show that the argument is faulty. Name a choice that the writer doesn't mention.

Here's a sentence:

These temporary problems will go away in time.

Explain why the underlined part in the sentence is redundant. Do this by completing the sentence below:

If you know that these problems are temporary, you already know that

_____.

• Here's another sentence:

Anybody can see the point I'm trying to make because it is very obvious.

Explain why the underlined part is redundant. Do this by completing the sentence below:

If you know that anybody can see the point I'm trying to make, you already know that _____.

• Here's another sentence:

"I will not take part in this," he said, refusing to get involved.

Explain why the underlined part is redundant. Do this by completing the sentence below:

If you know that he will not take part, you already know that

_____.

C

Here are three main ideas:

> Main idea A. **Native Americans stampeded a herd.**
> Main idea B. **Native Americans used poison.**
> Main idea C. **Native Americans waited for game.**

Each main idea fits one of the passages below. After reading all the passages, figure out which main idea goes with each passage.

Passage 1. Native Americans had many ways of obtaining food. One method of hunting buffaloes was particularly clever. Native Americans would get behind a buffalo herd and make a lot of noise. The buffaloes charged forward, running from the noise. The Native Americans then moved the herd in the direction of a cliff. The stampeding buffaloes were unable to stop at the edge of the cliff and plunged to their deaths on the rocks below.

Passage 2. Native Americans had many ways of obtaining food. One Indian method of hunting large game is known as still-hunting. An Indian sat by a pool in a deep forest and waited for animals to come to him. With his bow and arrow ready, he remained perfectly still for hours. Sooner or later, a deer would come within range. Then the Indian would shoot an arrow, killing the deer.

Passage 3. Native Americans had many ways of obtaining food. Some of them picked pokeberries or jack-in-the-pulpits, which are both poisonous plants. Then the people mashed up these plants and dropped them into ponds or slow-moving streams. The poisonous plants killed the fish, which floated to the top. The Native Americans picked the dead fish from the surface of the water and ate them. The poison in the fish didn't bother the people.

- Main idea A is: **Native Americans stampeded a herd.** Which passage does main idea A best fit?

- Main idea B is: **Native Americans used poison.** Which passage does main idea B best fit?

- Main idea C is: **Native Americans waited for game.** Which passage does main idea C best fit?

Write **Part D** in the left margin of your paper. You have two minutes to copy the paragraph below.

> Some sentences have redundant parts. To figure out if a part is redundant, you need to know what the part means. If you listen closely to ads on radio and television, you'll probably hear a lot of redundant parts.

★

Write **Part E** in the left margin of your paper. Then number it 1 and 2.

Here is a conclusion:

The old man enjoys watching dogs fighting in his garden.

The evidence is below. Some evidence is contradicted by the picture.

- The old man stopped working on the garden to watch the fight.
- Two other people tried to stop the fight while the old man watched.
- The old man laughed at the two people trying to break up the fight.
- The old man did not use his shovel or his hose to break up the fight.

If you see all these things, you can conclude that the old man likes to watch dogs fighting in his garden.

1. Which evidence is contradicted by the picture?
2. What does the picture show?

LESSON 79

A Here are three main ideas:

> Main idea A. **Johnny can't read because there's something wrong with his health.**
> Main idea B. **Johnny can't read because of social problems.**
> Main idea C. **Johnny can't read because he was improperly taught.**

Each main idea fits one of the passages below. After reading all the passages, figure out which main idea goes with each passage.

Passage 1. It's obvious that Johnny has reading problems. There may be something wrong with his eyes or with his diet. Sometimes children have difficulty seeing the chalkboard because they need glasses. If they can't see the chalkboard, they can't follow the lesson and they don't learn. Or Johnny may be in the habit of skipping breakfast. Children need food for energy during the day. If they don't eat properly, they become tired and don't feel like learning anything.

Passage 2. It's obvious that Johnny has reading problems. Look at his social background. He just moved here from Chicago and is having trouble making friends. If he is lonely or unhappy, he may be unable to concentrate on what the teacher is saying. His older sister has a record of bad grades. I would suggest placing him in a low-performers' group and encouraging him in the use of color crayons. He may have a hidden talent for art.

Passage 3. It's obvious that Johnny has reading problems. However, the main reason is that he was not taught very well. Whoever taught him the alphabet never made sure that Johnny knew the difference between **b** and **d**. Whoever taught him to read never made sure that he read each word properly. But with a lot of work on his part and a lot of work on my part, Johnny will be reading pretty well before the year is over.

- Main idea A is: **Johnny can't read because there's something wrong with his health.** Which passage does main idea A best fit?

- Main idea B is: **Johnny can't read because of social problems.** Which passage does main idea B best fit?

- Main idea C is: **Johnny can't read because he was improperly taught.** Which passage does main idea C best fit?

The argument below is faulty because it breaks this rule:

**Just because the writer presents some choices
doesn't mean there aren't other choices.**

Read the rule over to yourself and get ready to say it.

Here's an argument:

> **The coal miners are on strike and the country needs coal. There are only two possible solutions—send in the army to take over the mines or sit by while we freeze to death. Personally, I don't want to freeze to death.**

What does the writer want us to conclude?

What choices does the writer use as evidence for this conclusion?

Say the rule that the argument breaks.

Here's how to show that the argument is faulty. Name a choice that the writer doesn't mention.

Write **Part C** in the left margin of your paper. You have two minutes to copy the paragraph below.

> **Here's a rule that is sometimes broken in faulty arguments: Just because the writer presents some choices doesn't mean there aren't other choices. Be careful that you don't break this rule when you write arguments or when you argue with somebody.**

Write **Part D** in the left margin of your paper. Then number it 1 and 2.

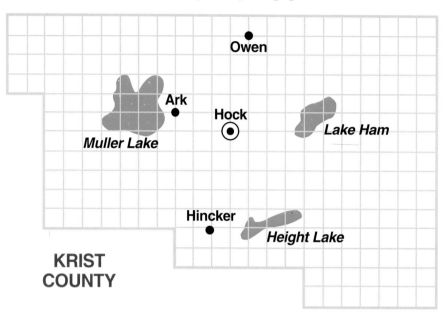

The symbol ● means that the city has between 10,000 and 50,000 people.
The symbol ⊙ means that the city has more than 50,000 people.

Although the report doesn't tell exactly where the accident took place, we know that it took place in Krist County. From other information, we can conclude that it took place in Hock. The evidence is below. Some evidence is contradicted by the map.

- The accident took place between two lakes, Lake Ham and Muller Lake.
- The accident took place in the largest city in Krist County.
- The accident took place in the city that is closest to Muller Lake.
- The accident took place near the middle of the county.

1. Which evidence is contradicted by the map?
2. What does the map show?

Write **Part E** in the left margin of your paper. Then number it from 1 to 3. Here are three main ideas:

Main idea A. **Many Irish came to America.**
Main idea B. **The Irish and English battled on Easter.**
Main idea C. **The Republic of Ireland was formed on Easter.**

Each main idea fits one of the passages below. After reading all the passages, figure out which main idea goes with each passage.

Passage 1. Part of Ireland has been ruled by England for hundreds of years. During those centuries, the Irish have often tried to establish their independence. Many Irish people finally left Ireland. They didn't want to pay heavy taxes to English landlords, and the potato famines of the 1840s caused the starvation of hundreds of Irish people. During that time, many Irish sailed from Ireland to America, where they were treated very poorly. NINA was a word often found in job listings. NINA meant "No Irish Need Apply."

Passage 2. Part of Ireland has been ruled by England for hundreds of years. On Easter morning in 1949, Ireland broke its last ties to England and became the Republic of Ireland. Since then, five-sixths of Ireland has been a free country. One-sixth of Ireland is called Northern Ireland and is still part of England. Many bitter, bloody battles for freedom have been fought in Northern Ireland.

Passage 3. Part of Ireland has been ruled by England for hundreds of years. During those centuries, the Irish have often tried to establish their independence. On Easter morning in 1916, two men named Collins and Pearse led a rebellion against the English. The rebellion failed because it was badly organized. Some leaders were sentenced to death by the English. Other rebels were put in jail. The rebellion was called the Easter Rebellion. Although it failed, the rebellion excited most Irish people and increased their anger toward England.

1. Main idea A is: **Many Irish came to America.** Which passage does main idea A best fit?
2. Main idea B is: **The Irish and English battled on Easter.** Which passage does main idea B best fit?
3. Main idea C is: **The Republic of Ireland was formed on Easter.** Which passage does main idea C best fit?

F Write **Part F** in the left margin of your paper. Then number it from 1 to 4. Look at the graph below. Then answer the questions about what is shown on the graph.

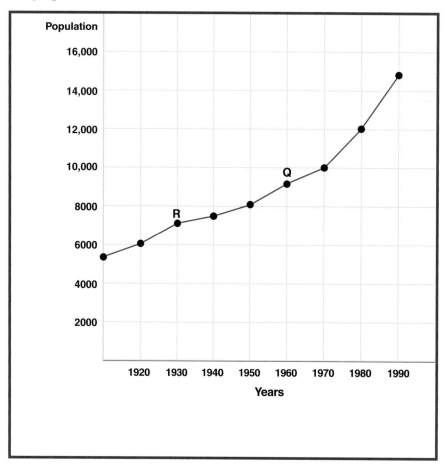

• The letter **Q** shows the population for one year.

1. What year?
2. How many people?

• The letter **R** shows the population for one year.

3. What year?
4. How many people?

Write **Part A** in the left margin of your paper. You have two minutes to copy the paragraph below.

> A carnivorous animal is well designed to hunt other animals. Its teeth are pointed and sharp; therefore, the animal can tear its food into chunks. The eyes of a carnivorous animal look straight ahead so it can see what it is hunting.

VOCABULARY TEST. Write **Part B** in the left margin of your paper. Then number it from 1 to 6. Write the model sentence that means the same thing as each sentence below. You have seven minutes.

1. Her answer was filled with irrelevant details.
2. They made up a fitting plan.
3. By pausing, she lost her chance.
4. They changed their Swiss money into Canadian money.
5. His directions were unclear and repetitive.
6. The rule limited their parking.

★

Write **Part C** in the left margin of your paper. Then number it 1 and 2.

Here is a conclusion:

A cat knocked over the plant while it was trying to grab a muffin.

The evidence is below. Some evidence is contradicted by the picture.

- The man wasn't looking, but the boy clearly saw a cat sitting on the counter.
- There were twelve muffins near the window.
- The plant fell over right below the window.
- The cat had come in through the open window.

We can conclude that the cat wanted to eat a muffin and that it knocked over the plant while trying to get one.

1. Which evidence is contradicted by the picture?
2. What does the picture show?

 Here are some words that will be in some editing activities. Test yourself to make sure that you know what the words mean.

affirmed—When you affirm something, you agree with it. Here's a sentence that uses the word **affirmed:**

The committee voted and affirmed the new regulations.

audibly—When you say something audibly, you say it loud enough for people to hear you. Here's a sentence that uses the word **audibly:**

She speaks quite audibly, even in a large room.

imitation—Something that is fake is an imitation. Imitation mayonnaise looks like real mayonnaise. Here's a sentence that uses the word **imitation:**

Her coat is made of imitation fur but it was still very expensive.

remote—A remote area is an area that is far from towns or cities. Very few people live in remote areas. Here's a sentence that uses the word **remote:**

She settled in a remote part of Alberta because she liked peace and quiet.

Here are three main ideas:

> Main idea A. **The United States fought communism.**
> Main idea B. **Americans were afraid of communism.**
> Main idea C. **Senator Joseph McCarthy was investigated by the Senate.**

Each main idea fits one of the passages below. After reading all the passages, figure out which main idea goes with each passage.

Passage 1. In the 1950s, the United States and the former Soviet Union were involved in a "cold war." That means that although the two countries were not actually using guns, the countries were close to being in a shooting war. At the same time, the United States was involved in a shooting war in Korea, where American soldiers were fighting Chinese communists and North Koreans. In 1950, a man named Joseph McCarthy, a United States Senator, became famous when he accused more than fifty employees of the State Department of being communists.

Passage 2. In the 1950s, the United States and the former Soviet Union were involved in a "cold war." Communism produced much anxiety in the United States. If someone accused a person of being communist, others believed that the person was a communist. Many people lost their jobs because Senator Joseph McCarthy said they were communists. Some people even committed suicide. From 1950 to 1954, Senator McCarthy was one of the most powerful people in the United States.

Passage 3. In the 1950s, the United States and the former Soviet Union were involved in a "cold war." That means that although the two countries were not actually using guns, the countries were close to using guns. In 1950, Joseph McCarthy started his own war, accusing many people of being communists. But, by 1954, many Americans were tired of hearing Joe McCarthy accuse people of being communists. In April 1954, McCarthy and his group were investigated by a Senate subcommittee. When asked to prove some of his accusations, McCarthy could provide no real evidence. The Senate criticized McCarthy for not behaving as a senator should behave.

- Main idea A is: **The United States fought communism.** Which passage does main idea A best fit?

- Main idea B is: **Americans were afraid of communism.** Which passage does main idea B best fit?

- Main idea C is: **Senator Joseph McCarthy was investigated by the Senate.** Which passage does main idea C best fit?

Here's an argument:

> **We can send food to the rest of the world or we can keep all the food here and have enough for the people in our country. I don't think we should send food to others while our people starve.**

What does the writer want us to conclude?
What choices does the writer use as evidence for this conclusion?
Say the rule that the argument breaks.
To show that the argument is faulty, what do you do?
Name one.

Write **Part C** in the left margin of your paper. You have two minutes to copy the paragraph below.

> **The world's saltiest body of water is the Dead Sea. The water of the Dead Sea is about seven times as salty as the water in the Atlantic or Pacific Ocean. The reason that the Dead Sea is so salty is that it is shrinking.**

★ Write **Part D** in the left margin of your paper. Then number it from 1 to 3.
Here are three main ideas:

> **Main idea A.** People worship the moon.
> **Main idea B.** The moon makes people and animals behave strangely.
> **Main idea C.** We keep learning more about what the moon is like.

Each main idea fits one of the passages that follow. After reading all the passages, figure out which main idea goes with each passage.

Passage 1. Ever since humans first looked up at the night sky, they have believed that the moon has magical powers. Some people still believe that the best time to plant seeds is at the time of the new moon (when the moon is invisible). Another belief is that the full moon causes strong feelings, such as love or hate. People who lived thousands of years ago wanted to explain the powers of the moon, so they created a moon goddess. People prayed to this goddess. They promised to do favors for the goddess if the goddess would give them a good farming season.

Passage 2. Ever since humans first looked up at the night sky, they have believed that the moon has magical powers. Today, scientists think that there is a certain amount of truth in the old beliefs. Scientists have observed that some animals are more excited during the full moon than they are when the moon is not full. Also, some people have more trouble sleeping during the full moon. In some big cities, more police are assigned to night duty during the time of the full moon. Why? Because there is some evidence that more crimes are committed on those nights.

Passage 3. Ever since humans first looked up at the night sky, they have believed that the moon has magical powers. Today, we know a great deal about what the moon is. We know because we've observed the moon through giant telescopes. We also know because people have actually walked on the moon. In 1969, Neil Armstrong was the first person to do this. Others have followed. Our moon is not the only moon in our solar system. Scientists have predicted that someday astronauts will visit these moons and the planets they circle.

1. Main idea A is: **People worship the moon.** Which passage does main idea A best fit?
2. Main idea B is: **The moon makes people behave strangely.** Which passage does main idea B best fit?
3. Main idea C is: **We keep learning more about what the moon is like.** Which passage does main idea C best fit?

LESSON 82

Here's an argument:

> **"But, Dad, you have to let me stay out past ten o'clock. If you don't, everyone will think I'm a baby or that there's something wrong with me."**

What does the writer want us to conclude?
What choices does the writer use as evidence for this conclusion?
Say the rule that the argument breaks.
To show that the argument is faulty, what do you do?
Name one.

Write **Part B** in the left margin of your paper. You have two minutes to copy the paragraph below.

> **In the 1950s, the United States and the former Soviet Union were involved in a cold war. That means that although the two countries were not actually using guns, the countries were close to being in a shooting war. Many Americans were afraid of communism.**

★

Write **Part C** in the left margin of your paper. Then number it from 1 to 3.
   Here are three main ideas:

> Main idea A. **A famous man painted the Mona Lisa.**
> Main idea B. **The Mona Lisa was stolen.**
> Main idea C. **The Mona Lisa has a remarkable smile.**

   Each main idea fits one of the passages that follows. After reading all the passages, figure out which main idea goes with each passage.

> **Passage 1.** The Mona Lisa is one of the most famous paintings in the world. It is a picture of an Italian woman, and it was painted around 1500 by Leonardo da Vinci. One thing that makes the painting so famous is the Mona Lisa's mysterious smile. Many people have theories to explain what is strange about her smile. Some people say that it shows that she's in love, and others say it shows that she is insane.

Passage 2. The Mona Lisa is one of the most famous paintings in the world. For three hundred years, it hung in the Louvre, now a famous museum in Paris. But, in 1911, the museum reported that the Mona Lisa was missing. No one had a clue as to what had happened to it. For two years, detectives were unable to find a single clue. Finally, in 1913, the painting was found in Italy. An Italian worker had stolen it. He said that the Mona Lisa should remain in Italy because it was painted in Italy. In 1914, the Mona Lisa was returned to the Louvre in Paris.

Passage 3. The Mona Lisa is one of the most famous paintings in the world. The man who painted it, Leonardo da Vinci, was one of the most remarkable people who ever lived. He was born in 1452, and he died in 1519. During da Vinci's lifetime, he studied many things. He was an inventor, a musician, and a scientist. He studied the human body and drew plans for airplanes and submarines.

1. Main idea A is: **A famous man painted the Mona Lisa.** Which passage does main idea A best fit?
2. Main idea B is: **The Mona Lisa was stolen.** Which passage does main idea B best fit?
3. Main idea C is: **The Mona Lisa has a remarkable smile.** Which passage does main idea C best fit?

A Write **Part A** in the left margin of your paper. You have two minutes to copy the paragraph below.

> **The Mona Lisa is one of the most famous paintings in the world. The man who painted it, Leonardo da Vinci, was one of the most remarkable people who ever lived. He was born in 1452, and he died in 1519.**

★ Write **Part B** in the left margin of your paper. Then number it from 1 to 3. Here are three main ideas:

> Main idea A. **Plans were devised to build the coast-to-coast railroad.**
> Main idea B. **The coast-to-coast railroad was finished.**
> Main idea C. **The railroad companies encountered problems.**

Each main idea fits one of the passages that follow. After reading all the passages, figure out which main idea goes with each passage.

> **Passage 1.** People in the United States dreamed of building a railroad that would connect the east coast to the west coast. This railroad would enable trains to carry freight, mail, and passengers across the country faster and more safely. But there were some big obstacles in the way of building that railroad—laying tracks over the Rocky Mountains and tunneling through California's High Sierra Mountains. President Lincoln signed the Pacific Railroad Act in 1862. This act provided government money for building the railroad.

> **Passage 2.** People in the United States dreamed of building a railroad that would connect the east coast to the west coast. In 1862, two major railway companies began this great task. The Union Pacific Railroad began in the Midwest and laid track westward toward California. At the same time, the Central Pacific began laying track from California eastward. Both railroad companies encountered great problems. Native Americans often attacked work crews on the Union Pacific. The problems of the Central Pacific were different. The railroad passed through high mountains in California. To make a path for the railroad, tunnels had to be built and cliffs had to be dynamited. Hundreds of workers lost their lives from rock slides and accidental explosions.

Passage 3. People in the United States dreamed of building a railroad that would connect the east coast to the west coast. On May 10, 1869, this dream came true. The railroad crews of the Central Pacific and Union Pacific railroads met at Promontory Point, Utah. The long railroad track, begun on opposite sides of the United States, was finally joined. The final spike to be driven into the track was made of pure gold. When that spike was driven in, a great cheer went up. The building of the coast-to-coast railroad had been completed in seven years. The trip between Nebraska and California had taken weeks by stagecoach. Now that same trip could be made in four days.

1. Main idea A is: **Plans were devised to build the coast-to-coast railroad.** Which passage does main idea A best fit?
2. Main idea B is: **The coast-to-coast railroad was finished.** Which passage does main idea B best fit?
3. Main idea C is: **The railroad companies encountered problems.** Which passage does main idea C best fit?

LESSON 84

A When you combine sentences with the word **who** or **which,** what punctuation do you need before **who** or **which?**

When you combine sentences with the word **therefore,** what do you do with the period of the first sentence?

What follows the semicolon?

What follows the word **therefore?**

When you combine sentences with the word **but,** what do you do with the period of the first sentence?

What word follows the comma?

B Write **Part B** in the left margin of your paper. You have two minutes to copy the paragraph below.

> **People in the United States dreamed of building a railroad that would connect the east coast to the west coast. Trains would then be able to carry freight, mail, and passengers across the country faster and more safely than any other kind of transportation.**

★

C Write **Part C** in the left margin of your paper. Then number it from 1 to 3.

Here are three main ideas:

> Main idea A. **Oil spills affect people who ship oil.**
> Main idea B. **Oil spills affect the sea.**
> Main idea C. **Oil spills affect the people who make their living from the sea.**

Each main idea fits one of the passages that follows. After reading all the passages, figure out which main idea goes with each passage.

> **Passage 1.** "Twenty-six million tons of oil were dumped into the sea off the coast of France. Hundreds of birds are dead or dying. We won't be able to save even half of them. The water is poisoned. Fish and plants are dead. The fine white sand on the beaches has turned black. It will be many years before the oil is gone from the water. It will be at least fifty years before sea life returns to normal here."

Passage 2. "Twenty-six million tons of oil were dumped into the sea off the coast of France. My family has fished these waters for two hundred years. I fish for a living like my father and his father before him. Like them, I have to support a family on what I can fish from the sea. But now, I can't fish. That's my fishing boat out there in that black water. See the dead fish floating around it? It will take fifty years before anybody will be able to fish in that sea."

Passage 3. "Twenty-six million tons of oil were dumped into the sea off the coast of France. But it was an accident. Apparently, the ship ran onto some rocks while the captain was talking with someone. The rocks tore holes in the ship, and the oil spilled into the sea. Our company realizes how terrible this is, but we think it could have happened to anybody. Our company will suffer a great deal. Think of the money we lost. Instead of trying to put restrictions on oil companies and oil freighters, we should all work together and stop crying about this unfortunate event."

1. Main idea A is: **Oil spills affect people who ship oil.** Which passage does main idea A best fit?
2. Main idea B is: **Oil spills affect the sea.** Which passage does main idea B best fit?
3. Main idea C is: **Oil spills affect people who make their living from the sea.** Which passage does main idea C best fit?

A Here's a new model sentence:

> **A strange phenomenon caused the anxiety that she exhibited.**

Read the sentence to yourself. Study the sentence until you can say it without looking at it.

Here's what the model means:

> **A strange event caused the fear that she showed.**

Which word in the model means **event?**

Which word in the model means **fear?**

Which word in the model means **showed?**

For each item, say a sentence that means the same thing.

1. A strange <u>event</u> caused the behavior that they <u>showed</u>.
2. The horror movie caused an outcome of <u>fear</u>.

B Write **Part B** in the left margin of your paper. You have two minutes to copy the paragraph below.

> **Carnivorous animals that kill are called predators. Wolves, lions, tigers, and sharks are fierce predators. Frogs and robins are also predators. Frogs eat flies and robins eat worms. The eagle is a predator with good eyesight and very strong claws.**

C **VOCABULARY TEST.** Write **Part C** in the left margin of your paper. Then number it from 1 to 6. Write the model sentence that means the same thing as each sentence below. You have seven minutes.

1. They <u>changed</u> their Swiss <u>money</u> into Canadian <u>money</u>.
2. The <u>rule</u> <u>limited</u> their parking.
3. His directions were <u>unclear</u> and <u>repetitive</u>.
4. By <u>pausing</u>, she lost her <u>chance</u>.
5. They <u>made up</u> a <u>fitting</u> <u>plan</u>.
6. Her <u>answer</u> was <u>filled</u> with <u>irrelevant</u> details.

★ **D**

Write **Part D** in the left margin of your paper. Then number it 1 and 2.
Here's a fact:

> **The Canadian province of Alberta has four national parks.**

1. In what kind of reference book would you look to find evidence to support this fact?
2. Look at the map below. Then write the names of the national parks.

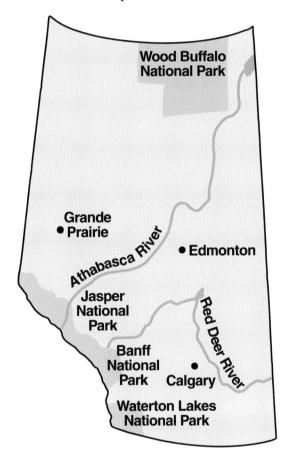

Here's the latest model sentence you learned:

> **A strange phenomenon caused the anxiety that she exhibited.**

What sentence means the same thing?
What word means **event?**
What word means **fear?**
What word means **showed?**
What's another way of saying,

A strange event caused the fear that she showed?

Write **Part B** in the left margin of your paper. You have two minutes to copy the paragraph below.

> **Parasites are carnivorous animals that do not kill. They attach themselves to another animal and suck nourishment from their host, but they do not kill the host. The host does the work of hunting for food while the parasite feasts on the host.**

Write **Part C** in the left margin of your paper. Then number it from 1 to 5. Assume that the picture below is accurate. Examine the picture carefully, and then read the statements below it. Some of the statements contradict what the picture shows.

- Write **contradictory** or **not contradictory** for each statement.
- If a statement contradicts the picture, write what the picture shows.

1. A boy is sitting at a desk looking at a television set.
2. Two books are on the shelf of the television stand.
3. The boy has a cookie in one hand and a pencil in the other hand.
4. There are two books on the desk but only one is open.
5. A glass and a plate of cupcakes are on the desk.

A Read the passage and look at the graph. Then answer the questions. Answers to some of the questions are found in the passage. Answers to other questions are found in the graph. Some answers are found in both the passage and the graph.

> Rising prices can make the dollar less valuable, which means the dollar buys less. In 1890, a dollar could buy three gallons of milk. That same dollar in 1930 bought less than two gallons of milk. In 1890, a pound of round steak cost $.12. In 1930, a pound of round steak cost $.43.
>
> When the cost of living goes up, the buying power of the dollar goes down. An increase in the cost of living is called inflation. For many years, economists have been trying to explain what causes inflation. They hope that understanding inflation will point the way to controlling it. As the graph shows, inflation is still with us, and it doesn't seem to show any signs of letting up.

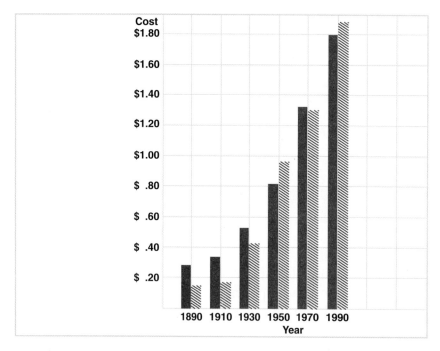

This kind of bar ▮ shows how much one gallon of milk cost.

This kind of bar ▨ shows how much one pound of round steak cost.

Write **Part A** in the left margin of your paper. Then number it from 1 to 14. Write the answers to the questions. Some of the questions ask where you found the answer. Use this key:

- Write **G** if the answer is in the graph.
- Write **P** if the answer is in the passage.
- Write **GP** if the answer is in both the graph and the passage.

1. In 1910, which cost more—a gallon of milk or a pound of round steak?
2. Where did you find the answer to question 1?
3. What is inflation?
4. Where did you find the answer to question 3?
5. How much did a pound of round steak cost in 1890?
6. Where did you find the answer to question 5?
7. In 1990, which cost more—a gallon of milk or a pound of round steak?
8. Where did you find the answer to question 7?
9. What happens to the buying power of the dollar when the cost of living increases?
10. Where did you find the answer to question 9?
11. Why do economists want to understand what causes inflation?
12. Where did you find the answer to question 11?
13. How much did a pound of round steak cost in 1990?
14. Where did you find the answer to question 13?

Here's the latest model sentence you learned:

> **A strange phenomenon caused the anxiety that she exhibited.**

What sentence means the same thing?
What word means **event?**
What word means **fear?**
What word means **showed?**
What's another way of saying,
    A strange event caused the fear that she showed?

Write **Part C** in the left margin of your paper. You have two minutes to copy the paragraph below.

> **Scavengers are carnivorous animals that do not kill. Instead of killing animals, scavengers wait for animals to die or to be killed by predators. After the predators have eaten what they want, the scavengers eat the remains of the animals.**

D Write **Part D** in the left margin of your paper. Then number it from 1 to 3. Here are three main ideas:

> Main idea A. **What to do if you get frostbite.**
> Main idea B. **Why we were stranded on the mountain.**
> Main idea C. **You can recognize frostbite.**

Each main idea fits one of the passages below. After reading all the passages, figure out which main idea goes with each passage.

> **Passage 1.** Frostbite results from extreme cold. Frostbite most often affects the ears, nose, hands, and feet. At first, a frostbitten body part feels cold and stings. Then it becomes numb, losing all feeling. The frostbitten part may sometimes appear gray or yellow in color, and it will feel extremely cold when you touch it.

> **Passage 2.** Frostbite results from extreme cold. Frostbite most often affects the ears, nose, hands, and feet. Some people mistakenly believe that you should rub the frostbitten body part with snow or ice. This is not only wrong, it is dangerous. If a doctor cannot be reached, the frostbitten part should be warmed slowly in lukewarm water or against a warm part of someone's body, such as between the thighs or under the arm.

> **Passage 3.** It was getting dark, and there was no sign that the snow would let up. The cold northern wind was getting harsher. It was impossible to start a fire in this weather, so we sat huddled together in our tent. This was the third night we had spent here, halfway up Mount McKinley. We were unable to go higher or lower on the mountain because of the foul weather.

1. Main idea A is: **What to do if you get frostbite.** Which passage does main idea A best fit?
2. Main idea B is: **Why we were stranded on the mountain.** Which passage does main idea B best fit?
3. Main idea C is: **You can recognize frostbite.** Which passage does main idea C best fit?

A

You learned a model sentence that means:

A strange event caused the fear that she showed.

Say that model sentence.
What word in the model sentence means **event?**
What word in the model sentence means **fear?**
What word in the model sentence means **showed?**

B

Read the passage and look at the map on the following page. Then answer the questions. Answers to some of the questions are found in the passage. Answers to other questions are found on the map. Some answers are found both in the passage and on the map.

> For part of the eighteenth and nineteenth centuries, Alaska was owned by Russia. In 1867, the United States bought Alaska for $7,200,000, which was less than two cents an acre. Alaska did not become a state until January 3, 1959, when it became the forty-ninth state to join the United States.
>
> Alaska is closer to the North Pole than any other state in the United States. The town in Alaska that is closest to the North Pole is Barrow, which is 300 kilometers north of the Arctic Circle. This means that for over half the year, it is daytime in Barrow. The sun comes up in the month of April, and it doesn't go down again until September. From April through September, the sun never sets. If you went outside at midnight, you would see the sun.
>
> Alaska has the largest area of any state in the United States. With over 1.5 million square kilometers, it has more than twice the area of Texas. However, Alaska has the smallest population of any state. In Alaska, there is only about one person for every square kilometer. In the state of New York, there are over 140 people for every square kilometer.
>
> Anchorage is Alaska's largest city. It has a population of 305 thousand people. Anchorage is located on Alaska's southern coast, on Cook Inlet. About 300 kilometers north of Anchorage is Alaska's tallest mountain, Mount McKinley. Mount McKinley has an altitude of 6194 meters, which makes it the tallest mountain in North America.
>
> Alaska is a growing state with many natural resources. It has an abundance of oil and natural gas. These resources are becoming more and more important to the United States.

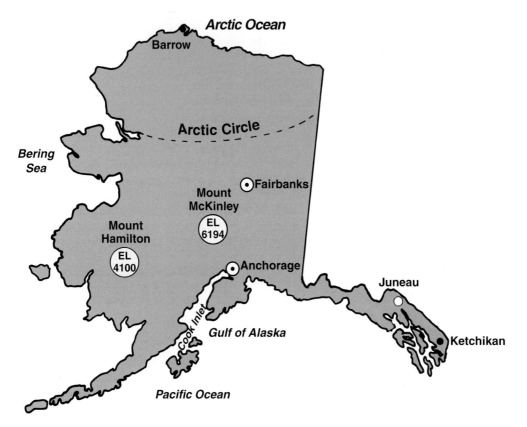

The symbol ● means that the city has under 10,000 people.

The symbol ○ means that the city has between 10,000 and 50,000 people.

The symbol ◉ means that the city has over 50,000 people.

The symbol (EL 4176) means that the mountain is 4176 meters high.

Write **Part B** in the left margin of your paper. Then number it from 1 to 14. Write the answers to the questions. Some of the questions ask where you found the answer. Use this key:

- Write **M** if the answer is on the map.
- Write **P** if the answer is in the passage.
- Write **MP** if the answer is both on the map and in the passage.

1. What is the population of Fairbanks?
2. Where did you find the answer to question 1?
3. When did Alaska become a state?
4. Where did you find the answer to question 3?
5. What town in Alaska is north of the Arctic Circle?
6. Where did you find the answer to question 5?
7. Who owned Alaska before the United States?
8. Where did you find the answer to question 7?
9. How tall is Mount McKinley?
10. Where did you find the answer to question 9?
11. What are two important resources in Alaska?
12. Where did you find the answer to question 11?
13. What ocean is north of Barrow?
14. Where did you find the answer to question 13?

Write **Part C** in the left margin of your paper. You have two minutes to copy the paragraph below.

> **Frostbite results from extreme cold. Frostbite most often affects the ears, nose, hands, and feet. At first, a frostbitten body part feels cold and stings. Then it becomes numb, losing all feeling. The frostbitten part may appear gray or yellow in color.**

★ **D**   Write **Part D** in the left margin of your paper. Then number it from 1 to 3. Here are three main ideas:

> Main idea A. **Nesting places for bluebirds are disappearing.**
> Main idea B. **Bluebirds are forced out of their nesting places.**
> Main idea C. **People build nesting places for bluebirds.**

Each main idea fits one of the passages below. After reading all the passages, figure out which main idea goes with each passage.

Passage 1. Bluebirds are disappearing from North America. One reason is the increased population of sparrows and starlings, which are not native to North America. Sparrows and starlings like to nest in the same places that bluebirds like. Bluebirds are mild-mannered, peaceful animals, so the frisky sparrows find it easy to drive the bluebirds away and move into the stolen homes.

Passage 2. Bluebirds are disappearing from North America. They have always preferred to nest in old fence posts and rotting trees near farms and on the outskirts of towns. As our cities grow larger, most rotten trees are cut down, and metal fence posts have largely replaced the old wooden kind. Consequently, it is getting harder and harder for bluebirds to find proper places to build nests and raise their young. The population of bluebirds is declining steadily.

Passage 3. Bluebirds are disappearing from North America. But as more and more people become concerned, a determined effort to save this friendly bird is growing. People all over the country are building nesting boxes for the bluebirds and mounting them on fence posts and tree trunks. The boxes are designed to keep the larger starlings out, as well as to protect the bluebirds from cold weather and predators. In areas where the boxes are plentiful, the population of bluebirds is starting to increase.

1. Main idea A is: **Nesting places for bluebirds are disappearing.** Which passage does main idea A best fit?
2. Main idea B is: **Bluebirds are forced out of their nesting places.** Which passage does main idea B best fit?
3. Main idea C is: **People build nesting places for bluebirds.** Which passage does main idea C best fit?

A

When you combine sentences with **who** or **which,** what punctuation do you need before **who** or **which?**

When you combine sentences with the word **so,** what do you do with the period of the first sentence?
What word follows the comma?

When you combine sentences with the word **however,** what do you do with the period of the first sentence?
What follows the semicolon?
What follows the word **however?**

B

Read the passages below. Then answer the questions. Answers to some of the questions are found in passage A. Answers to other questions are found in passage B. Some answers are found in both passage A and passage B.

Passage A. A coal strike started in Ike, Pennsylvania, today. Mine workers are striking over wage disputes. Wage negotiations are presently going on between the coal mining companies and the miners' union. The president of Ike Coal Company said in reaction to the strike, "This strike is poorly timed. There's a high demand for coal at this time of year, and we need to work at full capacity. The union is being unfair, undiplomatic, and is not considering the good of the nation as a whole."

The president of the Ike, Pennsylvania, mine workers' union today said, "The Ike Coal Company has been making larger and larger profits from our work. It's time we got a fair share for doing work that is hard and dangerous."

The strike is expected to go on for a long time.

Passage B. At one minute after midnight this morning, the mine workers in Ike, Pennsylvania, walked out of their jobs and began a strike that is expected to last for months. The mine workers' union has a large strike fund and can afford to strike for a long time. Negotiations between the coal companies and the union are going on right now, but no one is hopeful that there will be an early end to the strike.

Jeremy Plob, the president of the striking coal workers' union, said today, "The coal companies have been making larger and larger profits from our work."

Plob also cites foul-smelling gas in the mines as one reason for the walkout.

Write **Part B** in the left margin of your paper. Then number it from 1 to 9. Write the answers to the questions. Some of the questions ask where you found the answer. Use this key:

- Write **A** if the answer is in passage A.
- Write **B** if the answer is in passage B.
- Write **AB** if the answer is in passage A and passage B.

1. Where is the coal strike taking place?
2. Where did you find the answer to question 1?
3. Why are the coal miners striking?
4. At what time did the strike begin?
5. Where did you find the answer to question 4?
6. Why can the union afford to strike for a long time?
7. Where did you find the answer to question 6?
8. Name a coal company that is being struck.
9. Where did you find the answer to question 8?

Write **Part C** in the left margin of your paper. You have two minutes to copy the paragraph below.

> **Bluebirds are disappearing from North America. One reason for this is the increased population of sparrows and starlings, which are not native to North America. Sparrows and starlings like to nest in the same places that bluebirds like—old fence posts and rotting trees.**

★

Write **Part D** in the left margin of your paper. Then number it from 1 to 3.
Here are three main ideas:

Main idea A. **Alcoholism is a disease.**
Main idea B. **People are taught about alcoholism.**
Main idea C. **Alcoholism is tied to other social problems.**

Each main idea fits one of the passages that follows. After reading all the passages, figure out which main idea goes with each passage.

Passage 1. Alcohol abuse is one of the biggest health and social problems in the United States today. There are ten million "problem drinkers" in the United States. Seven million of these people are serious alcoholics who require counseling or medical attention. It has been known for a long time that alcohol abuse leads to serious physical damage. In the last thirty years, though, medical researchers have begun to recognize that alcoholism, like other diseases, can be cured.

Passage 2. Alcohol abuse is one of the biggest health and social problems in the United States today. There are ten million "problem drinkers" in the U.S. Seven million of these people are serious alcoholics who require counseling or medical attention. Many social problems are often associated with alcohol. It is believed that over half of this country's crimes are committed by people who have been drinking. Poverty and family conflicts are also frequently tied to alcohol abuse.

Passage 3. Alcohol abuse is one of the biggest health problems in the United States today. Public education about alcoholism is growing rapidly, as community groups use television and radio to reach the population. Community groups are trying to accomplish two things. First, they want people to recognize that alcoholics are sick, not irresponsible or lazy. Second, they want people to recognize the early signs of alcoholism, so that victims of the disease can get treatment before serious physical or mental damage is done.

1. Main idea A is: **Alcoholism is a disease.** Which passage does main idea A best fit?
2. Main idea B is: **People are taught about alcoholism.** Which passage does main idea B best fit?
3. Main idea C is: **Alcoholism is tied to other social problems.** Which passage does main idea C best fit?

LESSON 90

A

Write **Part A** in the left margin of your paper. You have two minutes to copy the paragraph below.

> **Alcohol abuse is one of the biggest health and social problems in the United States today. It is believed that over half of this country's crimes are committed by people who have been drinking. Family conflicts are also frequently tied to alcohol abuse.**

B

VOCABULARY TEST. Write **Part B** in the left margin of your paper. Then number it from 1 to 7. Write the model sentence that means the same thing as each sentence below. You have eight minutes.

1. A strange event caused the fear that she showed.
2. His directions were unclear and repetitive.
3. The rule limited their parking.
4. They made up a fitting plan.
5. By pausing, she lost her chance.
6. They changed their Swiss money into Canadian money.
7. Her answer was filled with irrelevant details.

★

C

Write **Part C** in the left margin of your paper. Rewrite the passage below in three or four sentences. Combine consistent sentences with **so** or **therefore.** Combine inconsistent sentences with **but** or **however.** Combine some sentences with **who** or **which.**

> The Federal Trade Commission supervises advertising. It is anxious to hear your complaints. There is a lot of honest, informative advertising. There is also misleading and dishonest advertising. The Federal Trade Commission would like to stop all dishonest advertising. Dishonest advertising is against the law.

Here are some words that will be in some editing activities. Test yourself to make sure that you know what the words mean.

clarity—Something that has clarity is very clear. A diamond with great clarity is a very clear diamond. Here's a sentence that uses the word **clarity:**
The clarity of his argument answered many questions.

cautious—When you are cautious, you are very careful. Here's a sentence that uses the word **cautious:**
She was a very cautious driver, especially in heavy traffic.

sorrow—Sorrow is sadness. When you are filled with sorrow, you are very sad. Here's a sentence that uses the word **sorrow:**
He showed great sorrow when his dog died.

A Read the passage and look at the graph below. Then answer the questions on the next page. Answers to some of the questions are found in the passage. Answers to other questions are found in the graph. Some answers are found in both the passage and the graph.

Ten thousand Americans in California died of scurvy in the year 1849 because they were cut off from a steady source of fresh fruits and vegetables. In the United States today, such an event would be unlikely. Modern machinery and new farming methods have made the land more productive than ever before. In addition, our transportation system makes fresh food available to nearly everyone.

For all the problems that technology has solved, it has also created some problems. Specialized machines are now doing a large part of the hard physical work once done by humans. Automobiles have almost eliminated walking for some people. People's appetites, however, have not decreased as much as their exercise has.

For the first time in history, millions of people are eating far more food than their bodies can use. In western Europe and in North America, excess weight is now recognized as a serious risk to the health of millions of people. Research shows that being as little as 10 percent overweight seriously increases the risk of early death.

The graph shows how an increase in weight is related to early deaths in men. For men who are overweight by 10 percent, the number of early deaths is 13 percent over normal. At 20 percent overweight, the number of early deaths in men is 25 percent over normal. As the graph indicates, the percentage of early deaths increases as the amount that men are overweight increases.

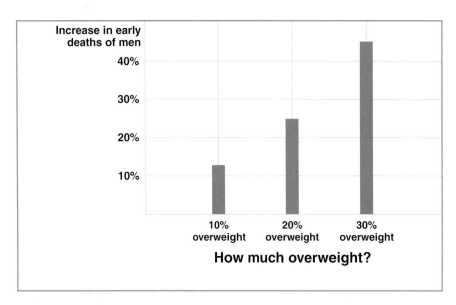

Write **Part A** in the left margin of your paper. Then number it from 1 to 12. Write the answers to the questions. Some of the questions ask where you found the answer. Use this key:

- Write **G** if the answer is in the graph.
- Write **P** if the answer is in the passage.
- Write **GP** if the answer is in both the passage and the graph.

1. Tell one good effect of progress.
2. Where did you find the answer to question 1?
3. Is being extremely overweight more serious than being just a little overweight?
4. Where did you find the answer to question 3?
5. What's a good way to prevent scurvy?
6. Where did you find the answer to question 5?
7. As you become more overweight, what happens to your chances of dying?
8. Where did you find the answer to question 7?
9. For men who are 30 percent overweight, what is the expected increase in early deaths?
10. Where did you find the answer to question 9?
11. For men who are 20 percent overweight, what is the expected increase in early deaths?
12. Where did you find the answer to question 11?

Write **Part B** in the left margin of your paper. Read the passage below.

B

You will probably have many job interviews during your life. Knowing how to be interviewed is very important. You will do well on a job interview if you remember certain things. Here are a few pointers to keep in mind when you're being interviewed. First, make sure that your clothes are neat and well pressed. They don't have to be expensive or high-fashion clothes—just clean and ironed. If you look as if you care about yourself, the employer will think you will care about your job. The second thing to remember is to be on time for the interview. If you arrive late, your chances of getting hired are probably pretty small. A third point is to find out as much about the job as you can during the interview. Ask what kind of work you will be doing and what you will be paid. Ask about benefits, such as insurance and vacations. The last thing to remember is to be relaxed during an interview. Many people are so nervous when they are interviewed that the employer thinks they can't do the job. So if you smile, relax, and ask questions, your chances of getting hired are very good.

The main idea of the passage you just read is: **What to do on a job interview.**

The author gives four tips on what you should do on a job interview. The first tip is: **Make sure your clothes are clean and neat.** What are the other three tips?

Copy the main idea and the four points on your paper just as they appear in the outline below. Label the main idea roman numeral one. To show that the points are under the main idea, indent them and label them **A, B, C,** and **D.**

I. What to do on a job interview
    A. Make sure your clothes are neat and clean
    B. Arrive on time
    C. Find out as much about the job as you can
    D. Be relaxed

Read the passage below.

> Small details are very important when you apply for credit. An important reason that people are not given credit has to do with their handwriting. They write illegibly. The writing may be so poor that the credit manager cannot figure out where the person lives. The credit manager may not even be able to figure out who sent in the form. Sometimes the credit manager looks at the sloppy handwriting and concludes that if the person who is applying for credit does not take care in filling out the form, that person will not take care in repaying the loan.

The main idea of the passage is: **What can happen if you write illegibly on a credit application.** The author makes three points that fall under the main idea. Write the main idea and the three points in outline form. Label the points **A, B,** and **C,** and indent them under the main idea.

Write **Part C** in the left margin of your paper. You have two minutes to copy the paragraph below.

> **Some parasites attach themselves to animals. Other parasites attach themselves to plants. Dodder grows on the stalks of plants and sucks sap from them. Mistletoe is a part-time parasite that grows in the tops of trees and takes nourishment from them.**

D Write **Part D** in the left margin of your paper. Then number it 1 and 2. Here's an argument for where not to build a bicycle path.

> The proposed bicycle path should not be built in Goshen Park. Here's why.

- The bicycle path will have to be between four and five meters above the interstate highway to give trucks enough room to pass underneath.
- The interstate highway has four lanes.
- Bicyclists will have to dodge the traffic on the interstate highway.
- The proposed bicycle path will go through Goshen Park and cross the interstate highway.

It is obvious that crossing the interstate highway at Goshen Park will be very dangerous for bicyclists.

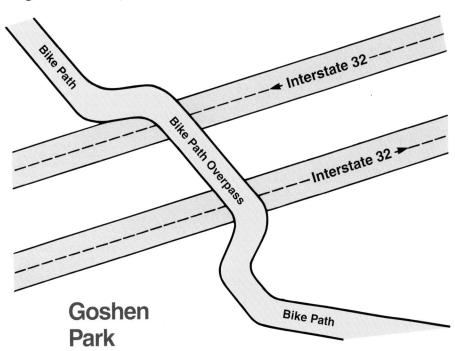

1. Part of the argument is contradicted by the map. Which part is contradicted?
2. What does the map show?

E Write **Part E** in the left margin of your paper. In the passage below, there are eight underlined words. These words can be replaced with words from the model sentences you have learned. Rewrite the passage using the model-sentence words. Remember to start every sentence with a capital letter and to punctuate each sentence correctly.

Pat was a mountain climber who had never experienced <u>fear</u>. As she neared the snowcapped mountain, she <u>paused</u>. She checked <u>her</u> route, but the map was <u>unclear</u>. Pat radioed base camp for help, but there was no <u>answer</u>. A light fog in the area <u>limited</u> visibility, but she continued to climb. Soon darkness fell and Pat had missed her last <u>chance</u> to turn back. Pat was lost, and as the night grew colder, she <u>showed fear</u> in her eyes for the first time.

Write **Part A** in the left margin of your paper. Read the passage below.

> Humans have gained power over all other animals. Humans have controlled the temperature of their environment, making it warm in winter and cool in summer. If humans are hungry, they don't have to go out and kill a deer or a rabbit—they merely go to the store and buy something to eat. How did humans become the most powerful of all? One possible reason for the power of humans is the human brain. The human brain is capable of figuring out problems that would stump any other animal. Another possible reason is that no other animal has hands with four fingers and a thumb that can touch each of the fingers. With these hands, humans made tools with which to kill other animals. Humans made fires to keep warm and shelters to protect themselves. Still another possible reason is that humans have a written language. With written language, humans transmitted ideas and accounts of the past. What one generation learned could be passed on to the next generation through written language.

This sentence expresses the main idea: **There are several possible reasons why humans have gained control over all other animals.** The author gives three points that fall under the main idea. What are those three points?

Write the main idea and the three points in outline form. Label the points **A, B,** and **C,** and indent them under the main idea.

Write **Part B** in the left margin of your paper. You have two minutes to copy the paragraph below.

> **There are several reasons why humans have gained power over other animals. The human brain is capable of figuring out problems that other animals couldn't. Humans have four fingers and a thumb that can touch each of the fingers. Humans have a written language.**

★ C   Write **Part C** in the left margin of your paper. Then number it from 1 to 14. Read the passage and look at the map on the next page. Then write the answers to the questions.

> Sri Lanka is an island. India is the country that is closest to Sri Lanka. Sri Lanka was once the British colony of Ceylon, and gained its independence in 1948. It joined the United Nations in 1955.
>
> Sri Lanka has an area of about 25,600 square miles. Since it has about 18 million people, Sri Lanka is very crowded, with more than 700 people in every square mile. The capital of Sri Lanka is Colombo. Colombo is also Sri Lanka's largest city, with almost a million people.
>
> Sri Lanka exports tea, rubber, and coconut products. These products go mostly to Britain, the United States, Japan, India, and Germany.

Some of the questions below ask where you found the answer. Use this key:

• Write **M** if the answer is on the map.
• Write **P** if the answer is in the passage.
• Write **MP** if the answer is both on the map and in the passage.

  1. What ocean surrounds Sri Lanka?
  2. Where did you find the answer to question 1?
  3. What is Sri Lanka's nearest neighbor?
  4. Where did you find the answer to question 3?
  5. What are Sri Lanka's most common exports?
  6. Where did you find the answer to question 5?
  7. On what river is Colombo located?
  8. Where did you find the answer to question 7?
  9. When did Sri Lanka join the United Nations?
10. Where did you find the answer to question 9?
11. When did Sri Lanka gain independence?
12. Where did you find the answer to question 11?
13. What is the capital of Sri Lanka?
14. Where did you find the answer to question 13?

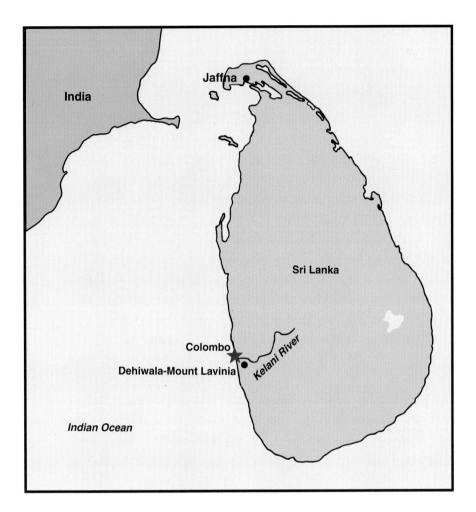

The symbol ★ means that the city is the capital of the country.

Write **Part D** in the left margin of your paper. In the passage below, the underlined words can be replaced with words from the model sentences you have learned. Rewrite the passage using the model-sentence words. Remember to start every sentence with a capital letter and to punctuate each sentence correctly.

The ranger's expression <u>showed</u> his <u>fear</u> as he <u>paused</u> to observe the progress of the raging fire. The land near the river, once <u>filled</u> with wildlife and trees, was about to be <u>changed</u> into a barren wasteland. The fire fighters were waiting anxiously for the ranger to <u>make up</u> a <u>plan</u> to <u>limit</u> the spreading fire. The situation was not the least bit <u>unclear</u>—they must act soon or lose the <u>chance</u> to contain the fire.

Write **Part E** in the left margin of your paper. Then number it from 1 to 6. Read the story and answer the questions. Some of the questions are not answered in this passage, but you should already know the answers.

Not all scavengers are full-time scavengers. Some will kill when they are quite hungry and scavenge when it is more convenient to scavenge. Turtles, crows, and coyotes are part-time scavengers, but the bear is the most famous part-time scavenger. If you leave hot dogs on the grill in bear country, you may have a guest for dinner. You may find that your guest will eat nearly everything that you eat—pancakes, eggs, candy bars, and ice cream. The bear is not fussy. But don't be confused by the bear's willingness to let somebody else do the hunting. Bears can kill. You've probably seen pictures of bears fishing from streams. They make it look easy, but if you've ever tried grabbing a large, strong salmon from a stream, you'll know just how quick and how strong bears are. They can catch small animals that are fairly quick. And if a bear gets angry, it will attack nearly any animal, particularly if the bear is a mother with young cubs.

One of the most powerful bears is the grizzly, which is now nearly extinct. The grizzly is heavier than the black or brown bear. The grizzly is so heavy that it cannot climb trees. But the grizzly bear is like other bears in one important way. If it has a choice of hunting for a meal or taking a meal away from someone else, it will probably stand up on its back legs, make a lot of noise, and act as if it is the rightful owner of the meal!

1. What do scavengers eat?
2. How are parasites and scavengers the same?
3. How are parasites and scavengers different?
4. Name two part-time scavengers.
5. What do we mean when we say that grizzly bears are almost extinct?
6. How is a grizzly bear different from other kinds of bears?

Here are some words that we use to tell how often something happens:

- **Usually** means **most of the time.**
- **Occasionally** means **once in a while.**
- **Rarely** means **almost never.**

What word means **most of the time?**
What word means **once in a while?**
What word means **almost never?**

Here's a sentence with a word that means she did it most of the time:
She usually went to the store.
Say the sentence with a word that means she did it most of the time.
Say the sentence with a word that means she did it once in a while.
Say the sentence with a word that means she almost never did it.

Write **Part A** in the left margin of your paper. Then number it from 1 to 3. For each item, write a sentence that uses the word **usually, occasionally,** or **rarely.**

1. The girl (most of the time) rode her bike to school.
2. Those hunters (almost never) shot any ducks.
3. (Once in a while) that dog comes onto our porch.

Write **Part B** in the left margin of your paper. You have two minutes to copy the paragraph below.

Not all scavengers are full-time scavengers. Some will kill when they are quite hungry and scavenge when it is more convenient to scavenge. Turtles, crows, and coyotes are part-time scavengers, but the bear is the most famous part-time scavenger.

Write **Part C** in the left margin of your paper. Read the passage below.

When you hear a piece of music, you may listen for the sound of each instrument, or you may listen to the sound of all the instruments blended together. In an orchestra, there are four major sections of sound. The first section is the woodwinds, and it contains instruments such as oboes and clarinets. The woodwind instruments are some of the earliest instruments ever devised by humans. The second section of the orchestra contains the stringed instruments, such as violins and cellos. Another section is the brass section, which contains horns such as trumpets, French horns, and tubas. The last section is one you are all familiar with. The percussion section contains such instruments as drums, chimes, and clashing cymbals. This section maintains the rhythm of a piece of music. The next time you listen to a CD or attend a concert, try to listen to each separate section of the orchestra. You will learn a lot about how the different sounds of the instruments blend together.

This sentence expresses the main idea: **There are four major types of instruments in an orchestra.** The author makes four points that fall under the main idea. Write the main idea and the four points in outline form. Label the points **A, B, C,** and **D,** and indent them under the main idea.

Write **Part D** in the left margin of your paper. Then number it from 1 to 12. Read the passages that follow. Then write the answers to the questions.

Passage A. Diamonds are now being mined from the ocean floor. Most of the diamonds from the ocean are of a higher quality than those from land. All of the undersea mining is done with huge vacuum cleaners that suck the gravel off the ocean floor. Every ton of gravel yields about one carat in diamonds. But there are some disadvantages to ocean mining. When the gravel is removed, the creatures that live there are disturbed. Then the processed gravel is dumped back into the sea, leaving huge brown clouds of silt and sand in the water. By the time the mining is done, the environment is no longer suitable for many of the ocean animals.

Passage B. Diamonds are being mined from the floor of the ocean. This practice has been questioned by some leading economists. They contend that the practice presents two serious problems. The first is the damage to the underwater environment. Vacuuming material from the bottom of the ocean disturbs the underwater life as far as eight kilometers from the mining site.

The second problem is the value of diamonds. According to the economists, the major mines in Africa could mine diamonds at ten times their present rate if they wished. They do not mine at this rate, however, because the value of diamonds would drop. A diamond valued at $1000 would not be as rare as it is now, and the price might drop to $100. The mines produce diamonds at a slow rate so that the value of diamonds stays high. But what will happen if large amounts of diamonds are mined from the ocean floor? The value of diamonds will drop and everyone will suffer, including the ocean miners. They will have to work hard to mine gems that are not very valuable.

Some of the questions below ask where you found the answer. Use this key:

- Write **A** if the answer is found in passage A.
- Write **B** if the answer is found in passage B.
- Write **AB** if the answer is found in both passage A and passage B.

  1. What kind of mining is being done on the ocean floor?
  2. Where did you find the answer to question 1?
  3. How are ocean diamonds different from land diamonds?
  4. Where did you find the answer to question 3?
  5. Why do diamond mines produce diamonds at a slow rate?
  6. Where did you find the answer to question 5?
  7. How many carats of diamonds does one ton of ocean gravel yield?
  8. Where did you find the answer to question 7?
  9. How does the vacuuming process affect sea creatures?
 10. Where did you find the answer to question 9?
 11. What will happen to the value of diamonds if large amounts of diamonds are mined from the ocean floor?
 12. Where did you find the answer to question 11?

LESSON 94

A There is a redundant part in each sentence below.

- **The ambiguity of the situation was increased by the unclearness of what was happening.**

What's the redundant part?
Why is that part redundant?

- **At a rapid pace, she moved quickly.**

What's the redundant part?
Why is that part redundant?

B Here are some words that we use to tell how often something happens:

- **Usually** means **most of the time.**
- **Occasionally** means **once in a while.**
- **Rarely** means **almost never.**

What word means **most of the time?**
What word means **once in a while?**
What word means **almost never?**

Here's a sentence with a word that means we do it almost never: **We rarely go jogging in the morning.**
Say the sentence with a word that means we do it almost never.
Say the sentence with a word that means we do it once in a while.
Say the sentence with a word that means we do it most of the time.

Write **Part B** in the left margin of your paper. Then number it from 1 to 3. For each item, write a sentence that uses the word **usually, occasionally,** or **rarely.**

1. Tilly is home (once in a while) by 4 o'clock.
2. Chad (almost never) watches television.
3. They (once in a while) play tennis after school.

C Write **Part C** in the left margin of your paper. You have two minutes to copy the paragraph below.

> **You will probably have many job interviews during your life. When you go for an interview, remember to dress neatly, arrive on time, ask questions, and be relaxed. If you remember these things, your chances of getting hired will be much better.**

★ **D** Write **Part D** in the left margin of your paper. Read the passage below.

> Probably one of the oldest meals in human history is bread and cheese. If you are interested in experimenting with cheeses, remember that there are three basic types. Hard cheeses, which include Swiss and cheddar, are very popular in the United States. Semisoft cheeses include Muenster, Gouda, and mozzarella. Mozzarella is good for cooking, since it melts easily and blends well with other flavors. It is a cheese you eat in pizza and many other Italian dishes. Soft cheeses are often eaten for dessert. Soft cheeses include Camembert and Brie. These cheeses have an edible "crust," which adds to their unique flavor. The next time you're too full for a dessert like pie or ice cream, try a wedge of Camembert—you may be pleasantly surprised.

This sentence expresses the main idea: **There are three basic types of cheese.** The author makes three points that fall under the main idea. Write the main idea and the three points in outline form. Label the points **A, B,** and **C,** and indent them under the main idea.

E Write **Part E** in the left margin of your paper. Then number it from 1 to 12. Read the passage and look at the graphs on the next page. Then write the answers to the questions.

> Like most adults, Sharon receives income every year. Her income for last year was $19,000. Not everybody receives income in the same way that Sharon does. Some people receive income from insurance policies. Sharon doesn't. Some people have Social Security income. Sharon doesn't. Sharon receives most of her income from her job. She works as a secretary and earns $15,000 per year.
>
> Sharon's income is shown in graph 1. The largest part is from her secretarial job. The smaller parts of the graph show that Sharon receives money from her stocks and from renting out her garage. Graph 2 shows what Sharon does with her income. The largest part shows that she spends the greatest amount of her money on house payments. Her other expenses are for food, new clothes, car payments, and miscellaneous items.

Graph 1. Income

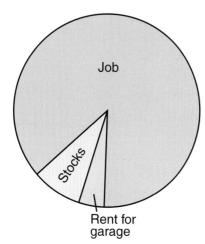

Job

Stocks

Rent for garage

Graph 2. Expenses

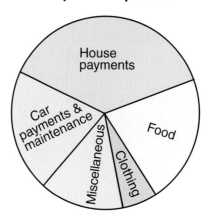

House payments

Car payments & maintenance

Miscellaneous

Clothing

Food

Some of the questions below ask where you found the answer. Use this key:

- Write **G** if the answer is in one of the graphs.
- Write **P** if the answer is in the passage.
- Write **GP** if the answer is both in a graph and in the passage.

1. What was Sharon's income last year?
2. Where did you find the answer to question 1?
3. Where does most of Sharon's income come from?
4. Where did you find the answer to question 3?
5. What are some other kinds of income besides the ones Sharon has?
6. Where did you find the answer to question 5?
7. How much does Sharon make at her job?
8. Where did you find the answer to question 7?
9. What is Sharon's largest expense?
10. Where did you find the answer to question 9?
11. Name all the things that Sharon spends her money on.
12. Where did you find the answer to question 11?

There is a redundant part in the sentence below.

- **His argument was full of inconsistent parts that did not agree with each other.**

What's the redundant part?
Why is that part redundant?

Each passage below contains a word you may not know.

> - Jesse James was a <u>notorious</u> outlaw, wanted in several states for robbery and murder. His crimes were notorious for their daring and success. As he held up more and more banks, he became more notorious. Hundreds of articles and books were written about him. He became so notorious that many other outlaws began to imitate him.

Notorious probably means:
a velvety texture   well known   pudgy   kind

How do you know that **notorious** does not mean **a velvety texture?** We know this because parts of the passage contradict the idea that **notorious** means **a velvety texture.** The passage indicates that Jesse James was a notorious outlaw, and a person is not usually described as having a velvety texture.

How do you know that **notorious** does not mean **pudgy?** Because parts of the passage contradict the idea that **notorious** means **pudgy.** The passage indicates that his crimes were notorious for their daring and success.

How do you know that **notorious** does not mean **kind?**

Find a sentence in the passage that contradicts the idea that **notorious** means **kind.**

> - She is so <u>magnanimous</u> that she would give her last dollar to a friend or her last bit of food to a hungry dog. Her magnanimous behavior wins her many friends. Sometimes I am afraid that she is too magnanimous and that people might try to take advantage of her.

Magnanimous probably means:
a form of cabbage   generous   stingy

Find a sentence in the passage that contradicts the idea that **magnanimous** means **stingy.**

- One rainy Sunday, a deep <u>malaise</u> engulfed me, making me feel sad without knowing exactly why. I was restless and dissatisfied, wanting to cry, but I had no reason to weep. I had a family, a home, a job—what caused this malaise? I was alone and lonely, and I felt that I belonged to nothing and to no one.

Malaise probably means:
        mayonnaise mixed with lemon   a feeling of cheerfulness
                    a feeling of depression
     Find a sentence in the passage that contradicts the idea that **malaise** means **a feeling of cheerfulness.**

You learned some words that tell how often something happens.
What word means **almost never?**
What word means **once in a while?**
What word means **most of the time?**
     Here's a sentence: **They <u>usually</u> went to the movies.**
Say that sentence with a word that means they went once in a while.
Say that sentence with a word that means they went most of the time.
Say that sentence with a word that means they almost never went.

Write **Part C** in the left margin of your paper. Then number it from 1 to 3. For each item, write a sentence that uses the word **usually, occasionally,** or **rarely.**

1. He (almost never) eats in a restaurant.
2. (Most of the time) she does her laundry on Saturday.
3. The Chan family (almost never) takes a vacation.

Write **Part D** in the left margin of your paper. You have two minutes to copy the paragraph below.

> **There are three basic types of cheese. The group of hard cheeses includes Swiss and cheddar. The group of semisoft cheeses includes Muenster, Gouda, and mozzarella. The last group of cheeses is the soft cheeses, including Camembert and Brie.**

VOCABULARY TEST. Write **Part E** in the left margin of your paper. Then number it from 1 to 7. Write the model sentence that means the same thing as each sentence below. You have eight minutes.

1. Her answer was filled with irrelevant details.
2. By pausing, she lost her chance.
3. The rule limited their parking.
4. A strange event caused the fear that she showed.
5. His directions were unclear and repetitive.
6. They made up a fitting plan.
7. They changed their Swiss money into Canadian money.

★

Write **Part F** in the left margin of your paper. Read the passage below.

> Because desert animals don't have many opportunities to drink water, they need desert plants. These plants provide the animals with both food and water. To protect themselves from the animals that feed on them, these plants have developed some strange defenses. One is thorns. If you've ever seen a prickly pear cactus, you know how hard it is to touch one without getting thorns in your hand. The leaves of other plants contain sour and sometimes poisonous juices. Still other plants do not have appetizing leaves—only leathery stems that tempt very few animals. These unattractive physical characteristics prevent desert animals from eating certain desert plants.

This sentence expresses the main idea: **Desert plants have ways to defend themselves.** The author makes three points that fall under the main idea. Write the main idea and the three points in outline form. Label the points **A, B,** and **C,** and indent them under the main idea.

G Write **Part G** in the left margin of your paper. Then number it 1 and 2. Here's a fact: **The fins of whales do not have the same name as the fins of fish.**

1. In what kind of reference book would you look to find evidence to support this fact?
2. Read the passage below and write the name for the fins of whales.

> When we study bones of ancient animals, we discover that the whale was once a land animal. Because whales used the sea for their food, their bodies changed over the centuries so that they were better adapted to live in the water. Their front legs became little flippers while their back legs became fins, called flukes. Today, whales do not live on land; in fact, they cannot live on land. Their skeletons could not support the weight of their bodies. If a whale is washed up on shore, it may die simply because its body is so heavy that its lungs collapse. When a whale's lungs collapse, the whale cannot breathe and it dies.

Each passage below contains a word you may not know.

> • Sherry was in an ebullient mood, joking and singing while she worked. The people around her were infected with her ebullience and started laughing and playing. Sherry grinned ebulliently, a wide-toothed grin of such joy that even the boss stopped yelling at everyone and slunk back into his office.

Ebullient probably means: sad   joyful   purple

Find a sentence in the passage that contradicts the idea that **ebullient** means **sad.**

Find a sentence in the passage that contradicts the idea that **ebullient** means **purple.**

> • My mother taught me that it was uncouth to chew with my mouth open. She claimed that it was a disgusting sight. Since then I have been angered by other people who are uncouth enough to talk while they eat. People with beautiful manners delight me; unfortunately, there seem to be many more people with uncouth habits, particularly at the dinner table.

Uncouth probably means:
understandable   a box   graceful   vulgar

Find a sentence in the passage that contradicts the idea that **uncouth** means **understandable.**

Find a sentence in the passage that contradicts the idea that **uncouth** means **a box.**

Find a sentence in the passage that contradicts the idea that **uncouth** means **graceful.**

Some statements tell what we should do or what ought to happen. These statements often contain the word **ought** or **should.** These statements tell how things ought to be, so they are called **statements of ought.** Here are some statements of ought:

• People should not go near the ocean during a bad storm.
• You should obey your parents.
• You ought to get enough sleep and exercise.

Some statements simply tell what is or what happens. These are not statements of ought. They are **statements of fact.** Statements of fact do **not** tell how things ought to be. They tell how things are. Here are some statements of fact:

- Nearly half of the people in Canada go to the doctor once a year.
- On the average, people who get enough sleep and exercise live three years longer than people who don't.
- Children who obey their parents usually don't get into as much trouble.
- In Peru, seven people were drowned in the surf because they went near the ocean during a bad storm.

Tell whether each statement below is a **statement of ought** or a **statement of fact.**

1. He went swimming.
2. He wanted to go swimming.
3. We should go swimming.
4. People ought to eat the right kinds of food.
5. We should outlaw nuclear power.
6. He exercised every day.
7. Exercising makes the body stronger.
8. You ought to exercise.
9. Smoking is dangerous to your health.
10. People shouldn't smoke.
11. Cars with bigger engines should be outlawed.
12. Cars with bigger engines burn more gas than cars with smaller engines.
13. Many people throw garbage along the highway.
14. We ought to stop people from throwing garbage along the highway.

 Write **Part C** in the left margin of your paper. You have two minutes to copy the paragraph below.

> **Desert plants provide desert animals with both food and water. To protect themselves from the animals that feed on them, many desert plants have developed some strange defenses. Some of these defenses are sharp thorns, poisonous or sour juices, and leathery stems.**

★ Write **Part D** in the left margin of your paper. Then number it from 1 to 3. Here are three main ideas:

Main idea A. **Living things protect themselves from desert sun.**
Main idea B. **Some living things can produce water from fat.**
Main idea C. **Living things can sleep through dry spells.**

Each main idea fits one of the passages below. After reading all the passages, figure out which main idea goes with each passage.

> **Passage 1.** There are many ways in which living things adapt to a desert environment. During the months when there is almost no water to be found, many animals hibernate. This means that they curl up in a safe place and sleep for a long period of time. Because they are sleeping and using very little energy, fat in the animals' bodies can last a long time. Some animals can hibernate for many weeks without becoming weak. When water becomes more plentiful, they wake up and resume an active life.

> **Passage 2.** There are many ways in which living things adapt to a desert environment. The camel is an interesting example of how desert creatures survive without much water. When a camel eats and drinks, extra food is stored in its hump in the form of fat. Later, when there is nothing to eat or drink, the fat in this hump is digested by the camel. As the fat is digested, hydrogen is released. As the camel breathes, oxygen from the air combines with the hydrogen. The combination of these two elements is H_2O—water!

> **Passage 3.** There are many ways in which living things adapt to a desert environment. Human beings have developed many different ways to cope with the heat of the harsh sun. For example, members of a certain tribe in Australia wear very little clothing. They do most of their hunting for food in the early morning hours and at dusk, when the sun is not so hot. In the daytime, they sleep in holes dug in the ground, or rest in the shade of trees. Tribes in the Sahara Desert survive in a very different fashion. To protect themselves from the blistering heat, they wrap themselves with many layers of clothing. Using clothes for insulation works well as long as you don't work too hard.

1. Which passage does main idea A best fit?
2. Which passage does main idea B best fit?
3. Which passage does main idea C best fit?

A The passage below contains a word you may not know.

> • That rich old man is so <u>penurious</u> that he saves his broken shoelaces
> and uses them for dental floss. He wouldn't loan a dime to his best
> friend. His house is falling apart, but he refuses to spend money on
> fixing it up. What good is all his money if he's too penurious to
> spend it?

Penurious probably means: generous   handkerchief   stingy

Find a sentence in the passage that contradicts the idea that **penurious**
means **generous.**

Find a sentence in the passage that contradicts the idea that **penurious**
means **handkerchief.**

B Statements of ought always tell how things ought to be. Statements of fact
simply tell what is true.

Tell whether each statement below is a **statement of ought** or a
statement of fact.

• Their goal was to climb the mountain.
  What kind of statement?
• We should climb that mountain.
  What kind of statement?
• They ought to stop at Mike's house after school.
  What kind of statement?
• They were supposed to stop at Mike's house after school.
  What kind of statement?
• They stopped at Mike's house after school.
  What kind of statement?

C Write **Part C** in the left margin of your paper. You have two minutes to copy
the paragraph below.

> **Any living thing is called an organism. Some organisms are so
> small that we cannot see them without using a strong magnifying
> glass. Different types of organisms live in different parts of our
> body and they perform different jobs for us.**

★ **D** Write **Part D** in the left margin of your paper. Then number it from 1 to 3. Here are three main ideas:

Main idea A. **Plants respond to noise around them.**
Main idea B. **Plants are different from animals.**
Main idea C. **Plants protect themselves from predators.**

Each main idea fits one of the passages below. After reading all the passages, figure out which main idea goes with each passage.

Passage 1. Plants differ greatly from animals. For instance, animals, including human beings, breathe in oxygen and exhale carbon dioxide. Plants do just the opposite—they "breathe in" carbon dioxide and "exhale" oxygen. Plants are also the only living things that can make their own food, using sunlight, water, and carbon dioxide.

Passage 2. Plants differ greatly from other living things, but there is one danger they share with almost all other forms of life—predators. Some desert plants have developed spikes and thick outer fibers to discourage animals from eating them. Many plants, such as walnut and filbert trees, drop seeds that are protected by hard outer shells. Like all other living things, plants have developed their own survival skills.

Passage 3. Plants differ greatly from animals. They don't have eyes, and they don't talk, bark, crawl, or run. They don't seem to have much in common with animals, but recently scientists have made some interesting discoveries. They have found that plants grow poorly when exposed to harsh, jarring music, and they grow well when exposed to soothing music. This indicates that plants respond to sound. Plants may not be able to see, touch, smell, or taste, but they can "hear."

1. Main idea A is: **Plants respond to noise around them.** Which passage does main idea A fit best?
2. Main idea B is: **Plants are different from animals.** Which passage does main idea B fit best?
3. Main idea C is: **Plants protect themselves from predators.** Which passage does main idea C fit best?

Written accounts about an event don't always agree. The two accounts below tell about the same event. The accounts contradict each other on an important point. When you read these accounts, look for contradictions.

Passage 1. Last night, the police were on the scene of an accident as it happened. The police car was behind a black sedan at a four-way intersection. A blue sedan failed to stop, skidded through the intersection, and sailed into the black sedan, inflicting serious damage to both vehicles. Almost before the two drivers could step from their cars, Officer Jeffrey Daniels had his ticket pad in hand. Fortunately, nobody was injured; however, Officer Daniels wasted no time in issuing two tickets to Sidney Grapp, driver of the blue vehicle. One ticket was for failing to stop at a stop sign, and the other was for driving without proper control of the vehicle. According to city officials, Officer Daniels now holds the record for issuing tickets quickly. The accident occurred at 9:34 P.M., and the tickets were issued by 9:37 P.M. This record may stand for some time.

Passage 2. Last night, a blue sedan drove past a stop sign. As the sedan crossed the intersection, the driver slammed on the brakes and the car nearly came to a stop before hitting a black sedan. The driver of the blue sedan slowly stepped from his car to assess the damage. He commented that the only damage to the black sedan was a little scratch in the side of the car and a dented hubcap. The driver of the blue sedan then looked at his own vehicle. The front bumper, the grill, and the hood were badly dented. The damages amounted to over $1000. The driver of the blue sedan was later ticketed for $100 because he had failed to stop at a stop sign.

These accounts contradict each other on one big point. What point is that?

Write **Part A** in the left margin of your paper. Then number it from 1 to 12. Answer each question. Some of the questions ask where you found an answer. Write **passage 1, passage 2,** or **passages 1 and 2** for these questions.

1. At what time did the accident take place?
2. Where did you find the answer to question 1?
3. How many dollars' worth of damage did the blue sedan suffer?
4. Where did you find the answer to question 3?
5. Which vehicle was at fault?
6. Where did you find the answer to question 5?
7. What parts of the blue sedan were damaged?
8. Where did you find the answer to question 7?
9. Who was in the car behind the black sedan?
10. Where did you find the answer to question 9?
11. How did the police officer set a record?
12. Where did you find the answer to question 11?

B Write **Part B** in the left margin of your paper. Read the passage below.

> All animals need water. A camel can drink up to 100 liters of water in a few minutes. The grasshopper mouse drinks very little, obtaining most of its water from the insects it eats. There are three basic ways in which animals can obtain water. The first and most obvious way is to drink it. A human being working in the heat of a desert must drink a lot of water—about eight liters a day! A second way of obtaining water is through food. The grasshopper mouse eats insects, which may be up to 85 percent water. Some animals can derive all the water they need from plants. A third way to obtain water is to manufacture it, as the camel does.

This sentence expresses the main idea: **Animals obtain water in different ways.** The author makes three points that fall under the main idea. What are those three points?

Write the main idea and the three points in outline form. Label the points **A, B,** and **C,** and indent them under the main idea.

 Write **Part C** in the left margin of your paper. You have two minutes to copy the paragraph below.

> **Plants don't seem to have much in common with animals, but recently scientists have made some interesting discoveries. They found that plants grow poorly when exposed to harsh, jarring music, and that they grow well when exposed to soothing music.**

Write **Part D** in the left margin of your paper. Read the passage below.

> When the Old West was being settled, there were no cars, airplanes, trains, or buses. People devised several ways to haul supplies, passengers, and mail between the east coast and the west coast. The "bull train" was one early type of transportation. It was an ordinary train of wagons pulled by oxen. Bull trains hauled freight from Missouri to California, a distance of about 2000 miles. The stagecoaches were another means of transporting freight and people. Six horses pulled a stage at a rate of about five miles an hour. Bull trains took about two months to haul freight between Missouri and California, while stagecoaches took several weeks to make the same journey. The Pony Express was another early form of transportation. A rider rode his horse at a dead run for a short distance and then exchanged his tired horse for a fresh one. In this way, it took the mail only eight days to get across the country. Perhaps the least-known means of early transportation in the United States was camels. The camels were well suited to hauling things between Texas and California. Americans were familiar with horses, mules, and oxen, but they couldn't figure out how to deal with camels, so many camels were turned loose in the desert.

This sentence expresses the main idea: **There were several means of transportation in the Old West.** The author makes four points that fall under the main idea. Write the main idea and the four points in outline form. Label the points **A, B, C,** and **D,** and indent them under the main idea.

The two accounts below contradict each other on an important point. Make sure you find that contradiction when you read the accounts.

Passage 1. Two college students were arrested yesterday for throwing soap into a fountain. The students were arrested near the fountain, which is in City Park. The fountain overflowed with bubbles, which drifted into the streets and caused traffic jams. The students were apprehended by a quick-thinking police officer.

"I spotted them right away," said Officer Blub. "They were carrying a big box of laundry detergent."

The students were released on $200 bail.

Passage 2. Traffic became snarled yesterday when hundreds of bubbles drifted into the streets. A two-car accident occurred near City Park as a direct result of the bubbles. One of the cars was carrying three dozen eggs, which smashed all over the inside of the vehicle. The driver, Mrs. Mooch of 129 Hilyard Avenue, was very upset.

"Eggs don't come cheap these days," she sobbed.

The bubbles came from a nearby fountain. Apparently, two students had dumped an unknown chemical substance into the fountain. The students were arrested. Later, they were released on $200 bail.

These accounts contradict each other on one big point. What point is that?

Write **Part A** in the left margin of your paper. Then number it from 1 to 12. Answer each question. Some of the questions ask where you found an answer. Write **passage 1, passage 2,** or **passages 1 and 2** for these questions.

1. Where was the fountain?
2. Where did you find the answer to question 1?
3. What did the bubbles do?
4. Where did you find the answer to question 3?
5. Where does Mrs. Mooch live?
6. Where did you find the answer to question 5?
7. How did the police officer know who committed the crime?
8. Where did you find the answer to question 7?
9. What happened to the students?
10. Where did you find the answer to question 9?
11. How much bail did the students have to pay?
12. Where did you find the answer to question 11?

B Write **Part B** in the left margin of your paper. You have two minutes to copy the paragraph below.

> **All animals need water to stay alive. Some animals drink the water that they need. Some animals get the water they need from food that contains lots of water. That food may be plants or animals. Some animals, like the camel, manufacture their own water.**

★ **C** Write **Part C** in the left margin of your paper. Read the passage below.

> Here are a few tips on how to grow a vegetable garden. First, you must prepare the land. This preparation involves digging it up and mixing the earth with fertilizer. The second step is to plant your seeds. Space the seeds so that the plants will have room to grow. Most seeds will take only a few days to sprout. When you see the sprouted seedlings, the third step is to "mulch" the garden. Lay down straw or hay between the seedlings. This protective mulch will stop weeds from growing around your plants. Now your garden is on its way. The last thing you must remember is to water the garden daily. If enough water is available, water your garden in the early morning and evening. Soon you'll have plenty of vegetables for the table!

This sentence expresses the main idea: **Growing a vegetable garden involves several important steps.** The author makes four points that fall under the main idea. Write the main idea and the four points in outline form. Label the points **A, B, C,** and **D,** and indent them under the main idea.

Write **Part A** in the left margin of your paper. You have two minutes to copy the paragraph below.

> **Ancient Egyptian kings believed that when they died, they would join the sun and rise and set with it forever. They had huge pyramids built over their graves so that after they died, the trip to the sun would be easier.**

VOCABULARY TEST. Write **Part B** in the left margin of your paper. Then number it from 1 to 7. Write the model sentence that means the same thing as each sentence below. You have eight minutes.

1. By pausing, she lost her chance.
2. His directions were unclear and repetitive.
3. They changed their Swiss money into Canadian money.
4. The rule limited their parking.
5. Her answer was filled with irrelevant details.
6. They made up a fitting plan.
7. A strange event caused the fear that she showed.

★

Write Part C in the left margin of your paper. Then number it from 1 to 9.
     The two accounts below contradict each other on an important point. Make sure you find that contradiction when you read the accounts.

> **Passage 1.** The eclipse will take place at 2:40 P.M. on Monday, July 5. The moon will be directly between the sun and the earth, blocking the sun. This is called a total solar eclipse. The sun will actually disappear for more than two minutes. Stars will come out, and the earth will be in darkness in the middle of the afternoon. You are cautioned not to look directly at the sun during the eclipse, because this may cause blindness. The next eclipse in this area will not take place until the year 2017.

> **Passage 2.** All those wishing to view the last eclipse until the year 2017 will want to be outside at around 2:40 P.M. on Monday, July 5. The earth will be directly between the moon and the sun, causing total darkness over an area of about 2000 square miles. The eclipse will be seen in all of North America, but it will last the longest when viewed from the midwest part of the United States.

Answer each question below. Some of the questions ask where you found an answer. Write **passage 1, passage 2,** or **passages 1 and 2** for these questions.

1. These passages contradict each other on one big point. What point is that?
2. What is a solar eclipse?
3. Where did you find the answer to question 2?
4. Where will the eclipse last the longest?
5. Where did you find the answer to question 4?
6. When will the next eclipse happen?
7. Where did you find the answer to question 6?
8. What is the date of the eclipse?
9. Where did you find the answer to question 8?

Write **Part D** in the left margin of your paper. Read the passage below.

> Canadians enjoy many forms of recreation. Each year thousands of Canadians fish through the ice when the lakes and rivers freeze. Entire fishing villages seem to spring up in areas where the ice is safe. Another very popular sport in Canada is ice hockey. Each year, thousands of Canadians watch or play ice hockey. There are many professional and amateur hockey teams in Canada. Canadians also enjoy the sport of Canadian football. This game is very similar to football that is played in the United States, except Canadian football teams have twelve players instead of eleven. Another form of recreation that Canadians enjoy is sport fishing. People fish for salmon in salt water and for trout in fresh water. These are just a few of the many kinds of recreation that Canadians enjoy.

This sentence expresses the main idea: **There are many forms of recreation in Canada.** The author makes four points that fall under the main idea. Write the main idea and the four points in outline form. Label the points **A, B, C,** and **D,** and indent them under the main idea.

Here are some words that will be in some editing activities. Test yourself to make sure that you know what the words mean.

rogue—An animal that is a rogue is an animal that travels by itself and is usually mean. Here's a sentence that uses the word **rogue:**
    The elk was a rogue that avoided other animals.

sanctioned—When you sanction something, you approve of it. Here's a sentence that uses the word **sanctioned:**
    He sanctioned her decision to move to another city.

scrupulous—A person who is scrupulous is a person who pays a lot of attention to details. Here's a sentence that uses the word **scrupulous:**
    She is a scrupulous bookkeeper.

somnolent—When you are somnolent, you are sleepy. Here's a sentence that uses the word **somnolent:**
    After eating a big meal, I always feel somnolent.

Here are three main ideas:

- **Why so many people are overweight**
- **Why so many people don't walk much anymore**
- **Why so many people are lonely**

One of the main ideas fits the passage below. Read the passage.

> There have never been as many overweight people in the United States as there are today. The biggest reason is that people do not exercise as much as they used to. Machines have taken over most of the hard physical labor once done by humans. Because many people have cars, they almost never walk. In addition, people in the United States find it easier than ever to obtain all the food they want. In the past, good food was obtained only by hard physical work on the family farm or ranch. Today, it is easy to purchase more food than your body needs. Some people eat to forget their problems. Lonely, nervous, or unhappy people often eat five or six times a day simply to make themselves feel better.

Which main idea fits the passage you just read?

The author makes three points that fall under the main idea. What are those three points?

The description below tells about the city shown in one of the maps on the next page. Read the description and then answer the questions.

> This map shows a section of downtown Brownsville consisting of twelve square blocks. The colored regions represent surface area that is devoted to cars: parking lots, streets, filling stations, and garages. The heavy broken line represents the route the new elevated train will take. The light broken lines represent subway routes. Notice that more than half the surface area of this busy section of town is devoted to cars. It is also interesting to note that there is not a single park in this area.

Which map does the description tell about?

Which words in the description let you know that map B is not the one that is described?

Which words in the description let you know that map A is not the one that is described?

Which words in the description let you know that map D is not the one that is described?

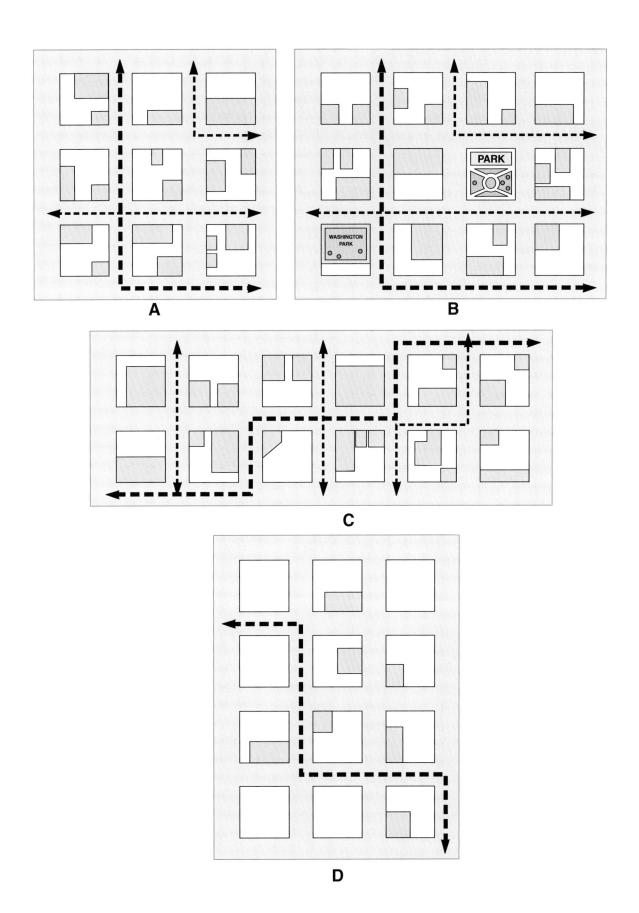

C

D

Here's a new model sentence:

The major contended that he had valid motives for concealing the data.

Read the sentence to yourself. Study the sentence until you can say it without looking at it.

Here's what the model means:

The major argued that he had sound reasons for hiding the facts.

Which word in the model means **argued?**
Which word in the model means **sound?**
Which word in the model means **reasons?**
Which word in the model means **hiding?**
Which word in the model means **facts?**

For each item, say a sentence that means the same thing.
1. The judge argued that she had sound reasons for her decision.
2. Tom was hiding the facts from his boss.

Write **Part D** in the left margin of your paper. You have two minutes to copy the paragraph below.

> **People in Canada have many forms of recreation. Some Canadians go ice fishing. Many people watch or play ice hockey. Still others like to watch or play Canadian football. Some Canadians enjoy sport fishing—both saltwater fishing and freshwater fishing.**

★

Write **Part E** in the left margin of your paper. Then number it from 1 to 11. The two accounts below contradict each other on an important point. Make sure you find that contradiction when you read the accounts.

Passage 1. An art theft was reported Sunday morning. The report was made by Count Radcliff, who owns a large collection of paintings. According to the count, the thieves broke into a skylight above the gallery and lowered themselves to the floor by rope. They stole a number of paintings and escaped through the back door. Sergeant Snorkle, who is in charge of the investigation, said that the burglar alarm had been disconnected.

Passage 2. A valuable collection of pictures painted by the Spanish artist Goya was stolen from Count Radcliff Saturday night. The chief investigating officer, Sergeant Snorkle, says that it could have been an "inside job," meaning that the burglars may have been aided by someone living inside the house. The count speculates that the burglars entered the house by breaking down the back door. The paintings were insured for ten million dollars.

Answer each question below. Some of the questions ask where you found an answer. Write **passage 1, passage 2,** or **passages 1 and 2** for these questions.

1. These passages contradict each other on one big point. What point is that?
2. What was stolen?
3. Where did you find the answer to question 2?
4. What happened to the burglar alarm?
5. Where did you find the answer to question 4?
6. What is an "inside job"?
7. Where did you find the answer to question 6?
8. When was the robbery reported?
9. Where did you find the answer to question 8?
10. Who was in charge of the investigation?
11. Where did you find the answer to question 10?

Write **Part F** in the left margin of your paper.
   Here are three main ideas:

- **Wildflowers are disappearing.**
- **Flowers are nice to smell.**
- **Most flowers have sepals, petals, stamens, and a pistil.**

One of the main ideas fits the passage below. Read the passage.

   Nearly all flowers have four basic parts. At the base of the flower, around the outside, are small, green, leaflike parts called sepals. Sepals protect the bud when the flower is still young. Above the sepals are the petals. The petals give the flower its color and odor. In many flowers, they also produce nectar, which helps attract bees. Near the center of the petals there is a ring of stamens, which produce the pollen necessary for plant reproduction. Right at the center of the flower is the pistil, a sticky shaft to which pollen adheres. The pistil is where the seeds develop.

   Write the main idea that fits the passage. List the four points that fall under the main idea in outline form. Don't forget to indent and label the four points.

Here's the latest model sentence you learned:

> **The major contended that he had valid motives for concealing the data.**

What sentence means the same thing?
What word means **argued?**
What word means **sound?**
What word means **reasons?**
What word means **hiding?**
What word means **facts?**
What's another way of saying,

> **The major argued that he had sound reasons for hiding the facts?**

The description below and one of the graphs on the next page tell about the carbon monoxide in Center City. Read the description and then answer the questions.

> Carbon monoxide is a poisonous gas found in automobile exhaust. The graph shows the amount of carbon monoxide in Center City's air during a period of twenty-four hours. Notice that the level of carbon monoxide is very high in the midmorning and late afternoon hours, when traffic through the city is heaviest. The graph also shows that three hours of rain during the night greatly reduced the level of carbon monoxide.

Which graph does the description tell about?
Which words in the description let you know that graph C is not the one that is described?
Which words in the description let you know that graph D is not the one described?
Which words in the description let you know that graph B is not the one described?

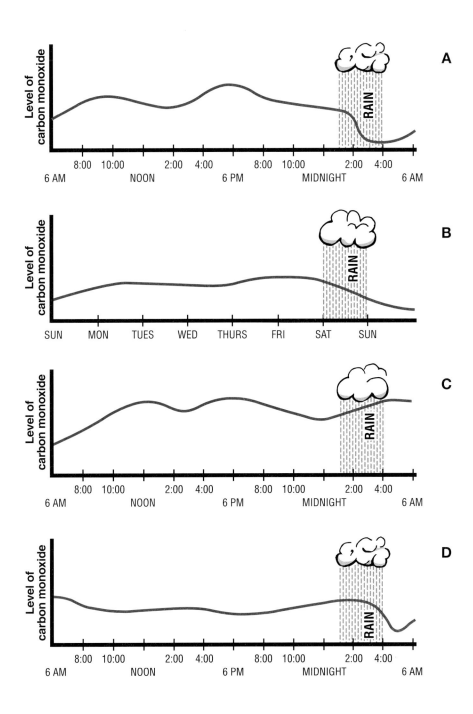

The two accounts below contradict each other on two small points. Make sure you find those contradictions when you read the accounts.

Passage 1. The circus rolled into town last night, with a long caravan of elephants bringing up the rear. The director of the circus, B. B. Barney, said that tents would be set up for business by Friday afternoon. Price of admission is $3.00 for children and $5.00 for adults. The circus features trapeze acts, lion taming, bareback riding, clowns, and a freak show. There are more animals this year than ever—zebras, lions, elephants, and even a dancing bear! Hot dogs, peanuts, and cotton candy will be sold in separate booths. Madam Sarah will read your palm and tell your fortune for $1.00.

Passage 2. The circus is back in town! All children wanting to attend the circus need $3.50 for the entry fee. There aren't as many animals as there were last year; however, there is a dancing bear from Russia that should provide a good show. The circus director, Mr. Barney, said that the circus will open on Friday. Food will be sold at the circus, and a fortuneteller will be on hand to tell your future for only $1.00. Come one, come all, to the show you won't forget!

These accounts contradict each other on two small points. What are they?

Write **Part C** in the left margin of your paper. Then number it from 1 to 8. Answer each question. Some of the questions ask where you found an answer. Write **passage 1, passage 2,** or **passages 1 and 2** for these questions.

1. What kind of bear does the circus own?
2. Where did you find the answer to question 1?
3. What does Madam Sarah do?
4. Where did you find the answer to question 3?
5. How much does it cost to get your fortune told?
6. Where did you find the answer to question 5?
7. When will the circus open?
8. Where did you find the answer to question 7?

Write **Part D** in the left margin of your paper. You have two minutes to copy the paragraph below.

Statements of ought are statements that tell what we should do or what ought to happen. Statements of ought often contain the word "ought," "should," or "shouldn't." Here is a statement of ought: You ought to go to school every day.

★ Write **Part E** in the left margin of your paper.
    Here are three main ideas:

- **A food chain involves plants, herbivores, carnivores, and decomposers.**
- **Decomposers break down dead plants and animals.**
- **Herbivores eat plants.**

One of the main ideas fits the passage below. Read the passage.

> All food chains start with plants, which make their own food from sunlight, water, carbon dioxide, and minerals in the soil. Herbivores, such as rabbits, mice, and many types of insects, are the next link in the chain. They obtain all their food from plants. Carnivores come next in the food chain. Cats, dogs, and predatory birds, such as hawks and falcons, are some of the animals that obtain food from the flesh of other animals. Decomposers, which break down dead plant and animal material, form the last link in the food chain. As plant and animal material is decomposed, minerals are returned to the soil and become food for the next generation of plants.

    Write the main idea that fits the passage. List the four points that fall under the main idea in outline form. Don't forget to indent and label the four points.

LESSON 103

A Here's the latest model sentence you learned:

> **The major contended that he had valid motives for concealing the data.**

What sentence means the same thing?
What word means **argued?**
What word means **sound?**
What word means **reasons?**
What word means **hiding?**
What word means **facts?**
What's another way of saying,

> **The major argued that he had sound reasons for hiding the facts?**

B Write **Part B** in the left margin of your paper. You have two minutes to copy the paragraph below.

> **Statements of fact tell what is or what happens. They do not tell how things ought to be. They tell how things are. Here is a statement of fact: Most of the people in Canada live along the southern border of the country.**

C Write **Part C** in the left margin of your paper. Then number it from 1 to 9. The two accounts below contradict each other on an important point. Make sure you find that contradiction when you read the accounts.

Passage 1. An accident report was filed today in the 87th Police Precinct. The report was turned in by Officer Kucharski, who was at the scene when the incident occurred. According to the report, Mrs. Bernstein was dusting her windowsill overlooking Thirteenth Avenue when she accidentally tipped over a flowerpot. The flowerpot fell two stories, and it landed on the head of Ambassador Nittnek, a visiting dignitary from eastern Siberia. The ambassador was rushed to the hospital, where doctors determined that he had a minor concussion. The ambassador contended that the incident was a plot to make him appear foolish. United States officials calmed the ambassador, and Mrs. Bernstein was fined $500.

Passage 2. Ambassador Nittnek, who is visiting the United States from eastern Siberia, suffered a slight injury today when a flowerpot fell on his head. An alert police officer spotted the incident and called an ambulance. Apparently, the flowerpot was thrown from the window of Mrs. Bernstein, a widow who lives at Thirteenth and Tulip. Officer Kucharski interviewed Mrs. Bernstein, who said that Ambassador Nittnek was responsible for the death of her husband. The ambassador was reported in good condition, with only a minor concussion.

Answer each question below. Some of the questions ask where you found an answer. Write **passage 1, passage 2,** or **passages 1 and 2** for these questions.

1. These passages contradict each other on one big point. What point is that?
2. Who reported the accident?
3. Where did you find the answer to question 2?
4. What did the ambassador say about the incident?
5. Where did you find the answer to question 4?
6. What did Mrs. Bernstein say about the incident?
7. Where did you find the answer to question 6?
8. What kind of injury does the ambassador have?
9. Where did you find the answer to question 8?

 Write **Part D** in the left margin of your paper.
    Here are three main ideas:

- **Why wilderness areas are disappearing**
- **Why wolves are disappearing**
- **How to shoot, trap, or poison a wolf**

One of the main ideas fits the passage below. Read the passage.

Wolves travel in packs of ten to fifteen members that roam over large expanses of wilderness. One pack may cover an area of almost 5000 square miles. Since there are fewer and fewer places where such large wilderness areas still exist, wolves are disappearing from our land. As the open land disappears, so does the wild game on which wolves survive. This lack of food is the second reason wolves are disappearing. Many wolves have moved up into Canada and Alaska to find more food. Finally, ranchers and farmers, in an effort to protect their livestock, have shot, trapped, and poisoned thousands of wolves. Except for those wolves in Alaska, a small population of wolves in Minnesota is the last of these animals in the United States.

Write the main idea that fits the passage. List the three points that fall under the main idea in outline form. Don't forget to indent and label the three points.

Write **Part E** in the left margin of your paper. Then number it from 1 to 3. The description below and one of the maps tell about an island. Read the description and then answer the questions.

The map shows an island in the South Pacific. Nobody lives on this island. A huge banana grove covers the southern third of the island. A small stream runs from its source, a spring at the center of the island, through the middle of the banana grove and into the ocean.

1. Which island does the description tell about?
2. Which words in the description let you know that island A is not the one that is described?
3. Which words in the description let you know that island D is not the one that is described?

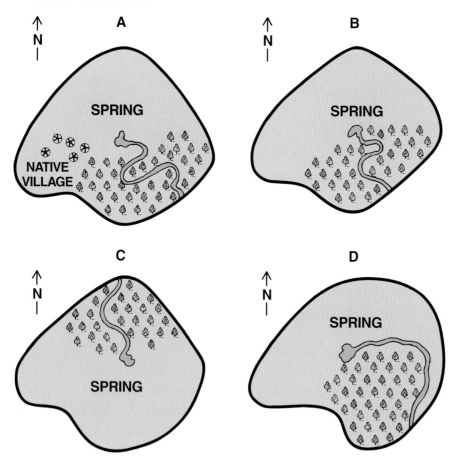

You learned a model sentence that means:
The major argued that he had sound reasons for hiding the facts.
Say that model sentence.
What word in the model sentence means **argued?**
What word in the model sentence means **sound?**
What word in the model sentence means **reasons?**
What word in the model sentence means **hiding?**
What word in the model sentence means **facts?**

The two passages below contradict each other on two important points. Make sure you find those contradictions when you read the passages.

Passage 1. The new year for all calendars has always begun in January. The Roman calendar originally had twelve months and began with January. The Egyptian calendar also had twelve months. There were some problems with the original Roman calendar, but most of these were resolved by Julius Caesar, who adjusted the length of the months so that the year was 365 days. Julius Caesar also introduced a leap year every four years. In a leap year, there is an extra day.

The names of some of the months from the early Roman calendar are with us today—September, October, November, and December. These names mean the seventh month, eighth month, ninth month, and tenth month. Julius Caesar renamed the fifth month after himself—July. The ruler who followed as his successor, Augustus Caesar, renamed the sixth month after himself—August.

Passage 2. A calendar is a way of dividing up time so that people can keep track of time in the same way. Throughout history, there have been several different calendars. For example, one day is the amount of time it takes for the earth to turn around one time. A year, which is 365 days long, is the amount of time it takes for the earth to travel around the sun one time.

Different calendars have divided up the days of the year in different ways. The original Roman calendar had ten months—January and February were added to the calendar many centuries later. The Egyptian calendar had twelve months of thirty days each, with five days tacked on to the end of the year. The Hebrew calendar has twelve months of twenty-nine or thirty days each and occasionally adds a thirteenth month to make the calendar come out evenly. The Hebrew new year is in the fall to coincide with the estimated date of Creation.

The passages contradict each other on two important points. What are those points?
Let's look up **calendar** in a dictionary or encyclopedia and find out which passage is accurate.

Each sentence below has two possible meanings. One is the meaning that the author intends. The other meaning is an unintended meaning.

- **Everybody around the racetrack cheered as the man beat the greyhound dog.**

Here's the intended meaning of the sentence:
The man ran faster than the dog.
Here's the unintended meaning of the sentence:
The man hit the dog.
The two meanings are possible because one word in the sentence can have two meanings. Which word is that?

Here's another sentence:

- **When the final buzzer sounded, the Vikings were on top of the Braves.**

What's the intended meaning of the sentence?
What's the unintended meaning?
Which words are involved in the two meanings?

Write **Part D** in the left margin of your paper. You have two minutes to copy the paragraph below.

> **Family structure varies from country to country. Most people in the United States and Canada are part of a nuclear family. This means that husband, wife, and children live together in their own living space, usually in a house or an apartment.**

★

Write **Part E** in the left margin of your paper. Then number it 1 and 2. The description below tells about one of the graphs. Read the description and then answer the questions.

The graph shows the use of electrical power in Center City. The solid line shows how much power business and industry use. The broken line shows how much power is used by private homes. Although you might expect power use to be high in the winter, the graph shows that power use is actually higher in the summer, when people use air conditioners. The graph also shows that business and industry use more power than individual homes, except during the cold winter months.

1. Which graph does the description tell about?
2. Which words in the description let you know that graph D is not the one that is described?

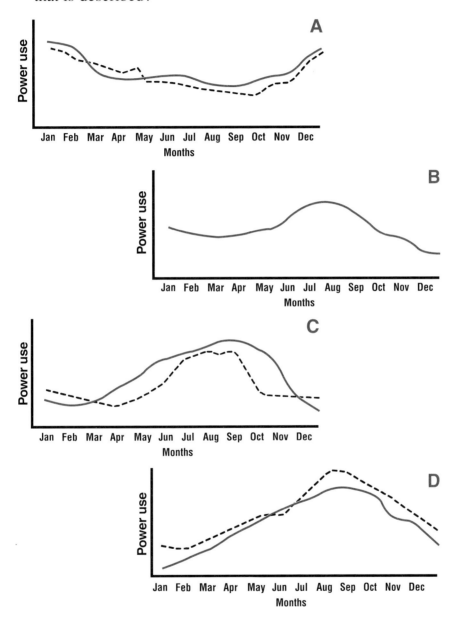

F

Write **Part F** in the left margin of your paper.
   Here are three main ideas:

- **People are vegetarians for several reasons.**
- **A vegetarian diet can decrease heart disease.**
- **Few meat eaters would kill their own meat.**

One of the main ideas fits the passage below. Read the passage.

> A vegetarian is a person who eats no meat, fish, or poultry. There are over three million vegetarians in the United States alone. They can be divided into four different groups, according to their reasons for not eating meat. Some people are vegetarians simply because they don't like the taste of meat. Other people believe that eating meat is unhealthy. The American Medical Association has published a report saying that a vegetarian diet could possibly eliminate over 90 percent of the heart disease in the United States. Some vegetarians say that killing animals is immoral. They claim that very few meat eaters would be willing to kill a cow with their own hands, skin it, bleed it, and prepare it to be eaten. A fourth group of vegetarians claims that the world food shortage makes it bad policy to eat meat. We use 75 percent of the corn, barley, oats, and soybeans we produce to feed cattle. If these grains were fed directly to humans, much less land would be wasted on livestock, more food could be produced, and fewer people would go hungry. Whatever their individual reasons, the number of vegetarians is growing rapidly.

   Write the main idea that fits the passage. List the four points that fall under the main idea in outline form. Don't forget to indent and label the four points.

A The sentence below has two possible meanings.

He said, "My new record is really groovy."

What's the intended meaning of the sentence?
What's the unintended meaning?
Which word is involved in the two meanings?

B Some statements tell about numbers or statistics. If a statement tells that most people do a certain thing, it is a statement of fact. If a statement tells that most people should do a certain thing, it is a statement of ought.

- **Everybody agreed that murder is evil.**

That statement is a statement of fact. It tells what everybody agreed about.

- **Everybody should agree that murder is evil.**

That statement is a statement of ought. It tells what everybody should agree about.

- **Almost all of the participants thought that young people should not marry when they are in high school.**

This statement is a statement of fact. It tells what most of the participants thought should happen, not what should happen.

Tell whether each statement below is a **statement of ought** or a **statement of fact.**

- **Nearly all of the members thought that the club president should go to the convention.**

What kind of statement?

- **The club president should go to the convention.**

What kind of statement?

C Write **Part C** in the left margin of your paper. You have two minutes to copy the paragraph below.

> **When the western part of the United States was first being settled, there were no cars, trains, planes, or buses. People devised other ways to haul supplies, passengers, and mail. Bull trains, the Pony Express, stagecoaches, and camels were used as transportation.**

VOCABULARY TEST. Write **Part D** in the left margin of your paper. Then number it from 1 to 8. Write the model sentence that means the same thing as each sentence below. You have nine minutes.

1. The major argued that he had sound reasons for hiding the facts.
2. A strange event caused the fear that she showed.
3. They made up a fitting plan.
4. Her answer was filled with irrelevant details.
5. The rule limited their parking.
6. They changed their Swiss money into Canadian money.
7. His directions were unclear and repetitive.
8. By pausing, she lost her chance.

★

Write **Part E** in the left margin of your paper. Then number it from 1 to 10. The two accounts below contradict each other on an important point. Make sure you find that contradiction when you read the accounts.

> **Passage 1.** Alobovia and Torania have been involved in a cold war for the last six years. The heads of these two countries have been discussing their conflicts this week at a meeting in Furgon. People all over the world are anxiously waiting for the outcome of these peace talks. At the end of today's session, the prime minister of Alobovia held a press conference. He reported that the peace talks were going very well. He is hopeful that by the end of the week, Alobovia and Torania will settle their differences. He refused to give specific details of the meetings, saying that worldwide knowledge of the details might threaten the success of the talks.

> **Passage 2.** The heads of two European countries are meeting this week in Furgon. The prime ministers of Torania and Alobovia are discussing their conflicts, which have been the basis for a cold war between the two countries for the last six years. At the end of today's session, the prime minister of Alobovia held a news conference. He denied reports that the peace talks were going well and indicated that he thought it would be some time before Alobovia and Torania would come to some agreement on their conflicts. The prime minister of Torania refused to comment on the situation.

Answer each question below. Some of the questions ask where you found an answer. Write **passage 1, passage 2,** or **passages 1 and 2** for these questions.

1. These passages contradict each other on one big point. What point is that?
2. What is a cold war?
3. How long have Alobovia and Torania been involved in a cold war?
4. Where did you find the answer to question 3?
5. Why are the prime ministers meeting?
6. Where did you find the answer to question 5?
7. What did the prime minister of Torania say about the meetings?
8. Where did you find the answer to question 7?
9. Why didn't the prime minister of Alobovia give details of the meetings?
10. Where did you find the answer to question 9?

LESSON 106

A Some arguments end with a conclusion that is a statement of ought. Here's a rule about conclusions that are statements of ought:

> **If the conclusion is a statement of ought, the rule at the beginning of the deduction must be a statement of ought.**

Here's a valid deduction:
You ought to do what your mother tells you to do.
Your mother tells you to do your homework.
Therefore, you ought to do your homework.
The conclusion is a statement of ought and the rule at the beginning of the deduction is a statement of ought. The deduction is valid.

Here's a deduction with the rule missing:
If you stay slim, you'll live longer.
Therefore, you should stay slim.
The conclusion is a statement of ought, so what do you know about the rule at the beginning of the deduction?
Here's that rule: **You should do things that let you live longer.**
Say the whole deduction.

Here's another deduction with the rule missing:
If you exercise, you'll stay in good health.
Therefore, you ought to exercise.
The conclusion is a statement of ought, so what do you know about the missing rule?
Figure out the missing rule.
Say the whole deduction.

Here's another deduction with the rule missing:
If you work hard at your studies, you'll get smart.
Therefore, you should work hard at your studies.
What kind of statement is the conclusion?
So what do you know about the missing rule?
Figure out the missing rule.
Say the whole deduction.

B The description below tells about one of the words listed below. Read the description and then answer the questions.

> The word you're looking for is made by combining two common root words. One of the root words is fact, which means **make.** (The word **factory** means **a place where you make something.**) The other common root word is man, which means **hand.** (**Manually,** meaning **by hand,** and **manicure,** which is **a beauty treatment for your hands,** both contain the root word man.)
>
> The word you're looking for, containing both fact and man, used to mean **handmade.** It means something different today.

manipulated   malefactor   manufactured   manuscript

Which word does the description tell about?
Which words in the description let you know that **manipulated** is not the word that is described?
Which words in the description let you know that **manuscript** is not the word that is described?
Which words in the description let you know that **malefactor** is not the word that is described?

 C Write **Part C** in the left margin of your paper. You have two minutes to copy the paragraph below.

> **Some statements tell about numbers or statistics. If a statement tells that most people do a certain thing, it is a statement of fact. If a statement tells that most people should do a certain thing, it is a statement of ought.**

★ **D** Write **Part D** in the left margin of your paper. Then number it from 1 to 3. Here are three main ideas:

> Main idea A. **Some children have many "parents."**
> Main idea B. **Americans live in nuclear families.**
> Main idea C. **Housing is scarce in many parts of the world.**

Each main idea fits one of the passages below. After reading all the passages, figure out which main idea goes with each passage.

Passage 1. Family structure varies from country to country. Most people in the United States and Canada are part of a "nuclear" family. This means that husband, wife, and children live together. They usually live in their own living space, such as a house or an apartment. In the nuclear family, the husband and wife provide food and shelter for their children until the children are old enough to take care of themselves.

Passage 2. Family structure varies from country to country. Some societies "share" their children. This means that the children consider any adult in the tribe as their parent. They can sleep at a different house or eat meals with a different "family" when they want to. In this way, children benefit from many different adults. A child who has a talent for art can spend lots of time with an adult who knows about art. A child who likes to build things can learn skills from an adult who also likes to build.

Passage 3. Family structure varies from country to country. In the United States and Canada, most children leave home by the time they are twenty-one. They have their own jobs and their own apartments. In much of Europe and Asia, however, housing is hard to find and very expensive. Most children keep living with their parents for a long time, even after they marry. In many countries, it is not unusual to find great-grandparents, grandparents, parents, and children all living together under one roof.

1. Main idea A is: **Some children have many "parents."** Which passage does main idea A fit best?
2. Main idea B is: **Americans live in nuclear families.** Which passage does main idea B fit best?
3. Main idea C is: **Housing is scarce in many parts of the world.** Which passage does main idea C fit best?

Write **Part E** in the left margin of your paper. Then number it from 1 to 9. The two accounts below contradict each other on an important point. Make sure you find that contradiction when you read the accounts.

> **Passage 1.** The National Forest Service today reported a wolf attack that occurred in a national park in Minnesota. "These attacks are occurring quite frequently these days," said a Forest Service employee. "The wolves have become very quick to attack because the wilderness areas where they live and feed are being destroyed." The largest population of wolves left in the United States, outside of Alaska, is in Minnesota, and consists of about 1200 wolves. The state of Minnesota has labeled wolves an endangered species and is trying to protect them.

> **Passage 2.** The National Forest Service reported that a man had been attacked by a wolf in a national park in Minnesota late last night. Ranger Thompson, who reported the attack, told reporters: "This attack is a very rare incident. Wolves have never been known to attack a human. We are afraid that the public will overreact to this event, and will start killing wolves. Since wolves are already an endangered species, any all-out attacks on wolves could wipe them from the face of the earth."

Answer each question below. Some of the questions ask where you found an answer. Write **passage 1, passage 2,** or **passages 1 and 2** for these questions.

1. These passages contradict each other on one big point. What point is that?
2. Why are wolves becoming quick to attack?
3. Where did you find the answer to question 2?
4. Name the person who reported the attack.
5. Where did you find the answer to question 4?
6. Why is it important to protect wolves?
7. Where did you find the answer to question 6?
8. In what state did the attack occur?
9. Where did you find the answer to question 8?

A   Some arguments end with a conclusion that is a statement of ought. Here's a rule about conclusions that are statements of ought:

> **If the conclusion is a statement of ought, the rule at the beginning of the deduction must be a statement of ought.**

Here's a valid deduction:
You shouldn't do things that are against the law.
Stealing things is against the law.
Therefore, you shouldn't steal things.
The conclusion is a statement of ought and the rule at the beginning of the deduction is a statement of ought. The deduction is valid.

• Here's a deduction with the rule missing:
Your mother tells you to do your homework.
Therefore, you ought to do your homework.
The conclusion is a statement of ought, so what do you know about the rule at the beginning of the deduction?
Here's that rule: **You should do what your mother tells you to do.**
Say the whole deduction.

• Here's another deduction with the rule missing:
Smoking is bad for you.
Therefore, you shouldn't smoke.
The conclusion is a statement of ought, so what do you know about the missing rule?
Figure out the missing rule.
Say the whole deduction.

• Here's another deduction with the rule missing:
If you exercise, you'll stay in good health.
Therefore, you ought to exercise.
What kind of statement is the conclusion?
So what do you know about the missing rule?
Figure out the missing rule.
Say the whole deduction.

B Some written passages give more facts about a particular subject than other passages. The two passages below tell something about the Audubon Society. Read both passages and find out which passage gives more facts about the Audubon Society.

> **Passage 1.** John James Audubon came to America in 1803. He was a talented dancer, flute player, violinist, and artist. More than anything, however, he loved the natural world of plants and animals. His biggest ambition was to paint all the species of birds in North America. Although he was poor for many years, his dedication kept him going. Within fifteen years of coming to America, he was well known and his paintings were loved in both Europe and America. It is no wonder that the Audubon Society, a society dedicated to the protection of wildlife, took the name of John James Audubon.

> **Passage 2.** Starting in 1886, many small groups devoting themselves to the appreciation and protection of birdlife sprang up in the United States. In 1905, these local societies banded together into a nationwide society that took its name from the great naturalist John James Audubon. Today, the Audubon Society is involved in many different activities. Congress gets help from the society in drafting new laws for protecting wildlife. The society publishes large amounts of information about birds, and it has a staff of lecturers who travel around the country talking about wildlife and wildlife protection.

Which passage tells more about the Audubon Society?
The other passage gives more facts about something else.
What does it tell more about?

Write **Part B** in the left margin of your paper. Then number it from 1 to 5.

- Answer each question.
- Then write whether the question is answered by **passage 1, passage 2,** or **passages 1 and 2.**

1. When did John James Audubon come to America?
2. What does the Audubon Society do?
3. When was the Audubon Society formed?
4. What was John James Audubon's biggest ambition?
5. Who is the Audubon Society named after?

Write **Part C** in the left margin of your paper. You have two minutes to copy the paragraph below.

> **During the months when there is almost no water to be found in the desert, many desert animals hibernate. Some animals can hibernate for many weeks without becoming weak. When water becomes more plentiful, they wake up and resume an active life.**

★

Write **Part D** in the left margin of your paper. Rewrite the passage below using words you have learned to replace the underlined words. Remember to start every sentence with a capital letter and to punctuate each sentence correctly.

> Bongo <u>almost never</u> exercised. <u>Most of the time</u> he sat at home and watched television. <u>Once in a while</u> he slept, but not for long. Bongo's mother thought that he should get more exercise. Bongo's greatest <u>fear</u> was that his mother would <u>limit</u> his television time. Bongo's mother <u>made up</u> a <u>plan</u> to help him exercise. She <u>changed</u> the television into an exercise machine. Now Bongo is <u>filled</u> with joy as he exercises and watches television.

Write **Part E** in the left margin of your paper. Then number it from 1 to 3.
 Here are three main ideas:

> Main idea A. **Progress creates problems.**
> Main idea B. **Progress leads to more food production.**
> Main idea C. **Progress doesn't always lead to more profits.**

Each main idea fits one of the passages that follow. After reading all the passages, figure out which main idea goes with each passage.

Passage 1. Progress in modern science has greatly changed living styles. Eating habits have changed because more food is available. New strains of wheat and corn have been developed that produce more grain per acre than ever before. Farmers are equipped with machinery that makes it possible for fewer people to do more work and also increase productivity. Improvements in the transportation and distribution systems have made vegetables of good quality available to nearly everyone.

Passage 2. Progress in modern science has greatly changed living styles. As machines have taken over the tasks once performed by the muscles of people, physical exercise has decreased. Many people spend the entire workday sitting down, and the automobile has practically eliminated walking. Unfortunately, many people who exercise very little are eating more food than ever. When people regularly eat more food than their body uses, they gradually become overweight. Excess weight, which is a cause of heart disease, diabetes, and emotional problems, is more common now than ever before in history.

Passage 3. "Progress in modern science has greatly changed the way I run my farm. Twenty years ago, I produced less than half of what I do now, and I worked nearly twice as much. New machinery has made it possible for three of us to do what would have been done by a dozen people in 1950. Unfortunately, even though we can produce a lot more, our profits are still quite small. Machinery, fertilizer, feed for the animals, and taxes are all more expensive than ever, and yet we still sell our crops at a very low price. Even with all the modern advancements, it is difficult to make a good living on a farm."

1. Main idea A is: **Progress creates problems.** Which passage does main idea A best fit?
2. Main idea B is: **Progress leads to more food production.** Which passage does main idea B best fit?
3. Main idea C is: **Progress doesn't always lead to more profits.** Which passage does main idea C best fit?

LESSON 108

 Some arguments end with a conclusion that is a statement of ought. Here's a rule about the conclusions that are statements of ought:

> **If the conclusion is a statement of ought, the rule at the beginning of the deduction must be a statement of ought.**

Here's a valid deduction:
You should do everything that lets you live longer.
If you avoid fatty foods, you'll live longer.
Therefore, you should avoid fatty foods.
The conclusion is a statement of ought, and the rule at the beginning of the deduction is a statement of ought. The deduction is valid.

Here's a deduction with the rule missing:
If you work hard at your studies, you'll get smart.
Therefore, you should work hard at your studies.
The conclusion is a statement of ought, so what do you know about the rule at the beginning of the deduction?
Here's that rule: **You should do things that will help you get smart.**
Say the whole deduction.

Here's another deduction with the rule missing:
Smoking is bad for you.
Therefore, you shouldn't smoke.
The conclusion is a statement of ought, so what do you know about the missing rule?
Figure out the missing rule.
Say the whole deduction.

Here's another deduction with the rule missing:
If you exercise, you'll stay in good health.
Therefore, you ought to exercise.
What kind of statement is the conclusion?
So what do you know about the missing rule?
Figure out the missing rule.
Say the whole deduction.

B When you combine sentences with the word **therefore,** what do you do with the period of the first sentence?

What follows the semicolon?

What follows the word **therefore?**

When you combine sentences with **who** or **which,** what punctuation do you need before **who** or **which?**

When you combine sentences with the word **however,** what do you do with the period of the first sentence?

What follows the semicolon?

What follows the word **however?**

C Some written passages give more facts about a particular subject than other passages. The two passages below tell something about Mars. Read both passages and find out which passage gives more facts about Mars.

Passage 1. In 1881, an Italian astronomer published a book of drawings that he had made during a five-year study of Mars. His drawings showed a complicated network of straight lines that he called channels. Enthusiastic observers concluded that Mars was inhabited by an advanced civilization that used the channels to distribute water around the planet's surface. As more information has been gathered, however, it has become more and more unlikely that there is any life on Mars. Martian days have temperatures as high as 80 degrees Celsius, and at night the temperature plunges to 90 degrees below zero. The Martian atmosphere is very thin and contains only a trace of oxygen, not enough to support humans. There is no water on the surface of Mars, and no living thing that we know of can survive without water.

Passage 2. For three days, Fred had roamed the rust-colored Martian desert. He was the lone survivor of a savage battle between the crew of an interplanetary ore freighter and a band of pirates from the asteroid belt. The fine red grit of the desert had worked its way into the joints of his spacesuit, so that even his smallest gestures sent squeaks through the tightly woven metallic fiber. Fred was very thirsty, and he was wandering around the desert just to keep occupied. Suddenly he spotted a large container, a 300-liter water tank that had been left by a spaceship centuries before. Fred jumped up and down and clapped his hands, his suit scraping and squeaking like a puppet with squeaky joints.

Which passage tells more about Mars?
Which of the following main ideas fits passage 2?

- Main idea A. **Fred's spacesuit squeaks.**
- Main idea B. **Fred is alone.**
- Main idea C. **Fred finds water.**

Write **Part C** in the left margin of your paper. Then number it from 1 to 5.
- Answer each question.
- Then write whether the question is answered by **passage 1, passage 2,** or **passages 1 and 2.**

1. What kind of soil is on Mars?
2. Is there any water on the surface of Mars?
3. Where did Fred's water tank come from?
4. How cold does it get on Mars at night?
5. Name three reasons why people can't live on Mars.

Write **Part D** in the left margin of your paper. You have two minutes to copy the paragraph below.

> **Progress in modern science has greatly changed our farming methods. New strains of wheat and corn have been developed that produce more grain per acre than ever before. New machinery makes it possible for fewer people to do more work.**

★

Write **Part E** in the left margin of your paper. Rewrite the passage below using words you have learned to replace the underlined words. Remember to start every sentence with a capital letter and to punctuate each sentence correctly.

> Most of the <u>time</u> Dullsville is a quiet town, but last year a spaceship flew over and dropped some American <u>money</u>. This <u>event</u> <u>changed</u> everyone into a millionaire. No one lost this <u>chance</u> to buy things. The people <u>almost</u> <u>never</u> thought about who the money belonged to. One day the spaceship returned and the people were filled with <u>fear</u>. A creature stepped out of the ship and <u>showed</u> a giant gun. As the people screamed, the creature <u>paused</u>, then shot <u>money</u> from the gun. No one screams now, and there are no <u>rules</u> to stop the creature from shooting anyone.

F

Write **Part F** in the left margin of your paper.

Here are three main ideas:

- **The Sahara Desert has lots of sandstorms.**
- **A desert can be formed in several ways.**
- **Plants need water to live.**

One of the main ideas fits the passage below. Read the passage.

One-seventh of the earth's land is covered by deserts. These hot, dry areas are usually formed in one of three ways. In some parts of the world, high air pressure makes rain an impossibility. Deserts usually result from lack of rain. Without water, few plants can live. This sets the scene for a second factor in creating a desert: erosion. With no plants to hold down the earth, the wind blows the earth away. The sandstorms of the Sahara Desert are famous. A third factor can also make a desert: humans. If there are too many people living on an area of land with too many animals, they can strip the land of all its vegetation. When they do that, erosion sets in and the area can become a wasteland. This happened in the midwestern United States in the 1930s. Certain areas became known as "dust bowls" because of the dust storms that swept the countryside. Many farmers had to give up their farms, which had turned into dry, wasted land.

Write the main idea that fits the passage. List the three points that fall under the main idea in outline form. Don't forget to indent and label the three points.

A The two passages below contradict each other on two important points. Make sure you find those contradictions when you read the passages.

Passage 1. In size, Canada is the third largest country in the world. It is a very rich country, even though large areas of its northern part are nearly impossible to live in. Canada is divided into ten provinces, the largest of which are Quebec and Ontario.

The first person from Europe to visit what is now Canada was a sailor named John Cabot, who reached Canada in 1497. Cabot returned to England with stories about the great numbers of fish that lived in the ocean off the coast of Canada. His stories tempted many British fishermen to go to Canada and begin new lives. The ancestors of about 50 percent of Canadian citizens came from Britain; the ancestors of 30 percent came from France.

Today, fishing is still the most important source of income for the coastal provinces. Since Canada has more lakes and inland waters than any other country in the world, freshwater fishing is important to Canada.

Passage 2. Most citizens of Canada live in a narrow belt along the southern border of that country, where the climate is milder. The ancestors of nearly all Canadian citizens came from Britain. The people who originally came to Canada were looking for gold because they had heard stories of great gold deposits. These stories were started by a man named John Cabot, who was the first person known to have visited Canada. Today, gold mining is still a good source of income for Canada, and many other kinds of minerals are also mined. For example, Canada mines about one-half of the world's total supply of asbestos, which is used to manufacture fireproof objects.

The passages contradict each other on two important points. What are those points?

Let's look up **Canada** in a dictionary or encyclopedia and find out which passage is accurate.

B

If the conclusion of a deduction is a statement of ought, what do you know about the rule at the beginning of the deduction?

A deduction is not valid or correct if the conclusion is an ought statement and the rule at the beginning of the deduction is not an ought statement.

Below are several deductions. Figure out whether each deduction is valid.

- Here's the first deduction:

  Nearly 90 percent of the people preferred beef.
  Beef is available at nearly every supermarket.
  Therefore, you ought to choose beef.

  What kind of statement does the deduction begin with?
  What kind of statement is the conclusion?
  Is the deduction valid?
  Explain.

- Here's another deduction:

  We should stand up for what we believe.
  John believes that the school day should be made longer.
  Therefore, John should stand up for making a longer school day.

  What kind of statement does the deduction begin with?
  Is the deduction valid?
  Explain.

- Here's another deduction:

  Suspected criminals should have fair trials.
  Jake is a suspected criminal.
  Therefore, Jake should have a fair trial.

  What kind of statement does the deduction begin with?
  Is the deduction valid?
  Explain.

- Here's another deduction:

  Aluminum can be recycled.
  Pop cans are made of aluminum.
  Therefore, pop cans should be recycled.

  What kind of statement does the deduction begin with?
  Is the deduction valid?
  Explain.

Write **Part C** in the left margin of your paper. You have two minutes to copy the paragraph below.

> **Some arguments end with a conclusion that is a statement of ought. A deduction that ends with a statement of ought is valid or correct only if the rule at the beginning of the deduction is also a statement of ought.**

★

Write **Part D** in the left margin of your paper.
Here are three main ideas:

- **Some eating plans can be dangerous.**
- **Vegetarian eating plans are very popular.**
- **There's more than one popular eating plan for staying healthy.**

One of the main ideas fits the passage below. Read the passage.

> Doctors usually recommend a balanced diet of meat, grains, vegetables, and fruit. They insist that if you eat a little bit of each of these foods daily, you will lose weight and stay healthy. Many people follow other kinds of eating plans, and they insist that they feel healthier than they ever felt before. One of these plans is a high-protein diet. On this plan, you avoid fruit, bread, potatoes, and all forms of sugar. You eat only meat, cheese, eggs, and some vegetables. This plan is less popular than it used to be, but some people still follow it. Another popular plan is a vegetarian plan. On this plan, you do not eat meat. You eat only vegetables and whole grains such as bulgur and brown rice. Some vegetarians include cheese, yogurt, and eggs in their diet. Many people claim that these foods keep them healthy. Some people claim that fasting cleans out their bodies and makes them feel better. When you fast, you eat nothing at all. Some people fast one day a week; others fast three days in a row each month. Many doctors think it is bad to fast. Although there are many other eating plans that claim to make you healthy, most people now think that a regular balanced diet is best.

Write the main idea that fits the passage. List the four points that fall under the main idea in outline form. Don't forget to indent and label the four points.

Write **Part E** in the left margin of your paper. Then number it from 1 to 7. The two passages below both tell something about coffee. Read both passages and find out which passage gives more facts about the effects of coffee.

> **Passage 1.** Coffee is one of the most popular beverages in the United States. It comes from the small beans of the coffee plant, which is grown commercially in South America. The flavor of a coffee bean depends on many things, including the time of harvest, how long the bean was roasted, and how the coffee is prepared. Coffee contains caffeine, a bitter drug that disagrees with some people. However, coffee manufacturers have discovered a way of removing the caffeine from the bean. According to some people, decaffeinated coffee has a flavor that is less bitter than regular coffee.

> **Passage 2.** Coffee is one of the most popular beverages in the United States. The mild "lift" that most coffee drinkers associate with coffee is caused by caffeine, the most widely used stimulant in the world. A normal dose of caffeine from a single cup of coffee relieves drowsiness and muscular fatigue and stimulates the thought processes. Used in large amounts (more than five cups of coffee a day), caffeine can cause insomnia, restlessness, and irritability, and may contribute to the development of ulcers and high blood pressure.

1. Which passage tells more about the effects of coffee?
2. The other passage gives more facts about something else. What does it tell more about?

- Answer each question below.
- Then write whether the question is answered by **passage 1, passage 2,** or **passages 1 and 2.**

3. What is coffee made from?
4. If you drink too much coffee, what may the caffeine do to you?
5. The flavor of coffee beans depends on several things.
   Name two.
6. What is caffeine?
7. What is decaffeinated coffee?

A Write **Part A** in the left margin of your paper. You have two minutes to copy the paragraph below.

> **Decomposers are very small plants that have no chlorophyll; therefore, they cannot convert sunlight into food. Decomposers get their food by eating the flesh or waste material of other organisms. As decomposers eat, they give off material that is high in nitrogen.**

B **VOCABULARY TEST.** Write **Part B** in the left margin of your paper. Then number it from 1 to 8. Write the model sentence that means the same thing as each sentence below. You have nine minutes.

1. His directions were <u>unclear</u> and <u>repetitive</u>.
2. Her <u>answer</u> was <u>filled</u> with <u>irrelevant</u> details.
3. The major <u>argued</u> that he had <u>sound</u> <u>reasons</u> for <u>hiding</u> the <u>facts</u>.
4. By <u>pausing</u>, she lost her <u>chance</u>.
5. The <u>rule</u> <u>limited</u> their parking.
6. A strange <u>event</u> caused the <u>fear</u> that she <u>showed</u>.
7. They <u>changed</u> their Swiss <u>money</u> into Canadian <u>money</u>.
8. They <u>made up</u> a <u>fitting</u> <u>plan</u>.

★

C Write **Part C** in the left margin of your paper.
    Here are three main ideas:

> - **Canada has several kinds of industry.**
> - **Canada is one of the largest wheat-growing areas in the world.**
> - **Much of Canada is covered by forests.**

One of the main ideas fits the passage below. Read the passage.

> Canada is a rich country, with many ways for people to earn a living. Agriculture is the primary industry. Some areas of Canada form one of the largest wheat-growing areas in the world. Other field crops include oats, barley, rye, and sugar beets. Some farms raise beef cattle; others raise dairy cattle. Still others raise chickens. Mineral mining is another important industry in Canada. Canada makes a lot of money from the minerals that are mined, which include gold, silver, copper, asbestos, and uranium. The last major industry in Canada is manufacturing. Since over one-third of Canada's land is covered by forests, most of Canada's manufactured products are forest products. Pulp and paper are the most important forest products.

Write the main idea that fits the passage. List the three points that fall under the main idea in outline form. Don't forget to indent and label the three points.

Write **Part D** in the left margin of your paper. Then number it from 1 to 6. The two passages below tell something about gardening. Read both passages and find out which passage gives more facts about how to garden.

> **Passage 1.** Having your own vegetable garden is probably easier than you think. First you should find out when the growing season in your area starts and when it ends. Some seeds can be planted early in the season (when the weather is still cold). For other seeds, you must wait for warmer weather. Generally, you can tell how good your soil is by the amount of vegetation already growing in it. If the weeds and grass are green and grow fast, the soil will probably support vegetables well. Before you plant, remove all the unwanted plants or rocks, and then break the soil up with a spade. For more information on gardening, read a book about gardening or talk to people who have good vegetable gardens.

> **Passage 2.** Gardening is a popular pastime all over the world. People everywhere grow their own fruits, vegetables, and flowers. Some people make a business of selling their flowers or produce. Others, who garden as a hobby, say that they like the good taste of fresh produce and the satisfaction of seeing things grow. Most gardeners agree that nothing matches the pleasure of seeing months of effort finally produce a harvest of tasty fruits and vegetables. In China, there is an old saying: "If you want to be happy all year long, be a gardener."

1. Which passage tells more about how to garden?
2. The other passage gives more facts about something else. What does it tell more about?

- Answer each question below.
- Then write whether the question is answered by **passage 1, passage 2,** or **passages 1 and 2.**

3. How could you get more information on gardening?
4. Name two things you should do before you plant your garden.
5. What do hobby gardeners like about gardening?
6. How can you tell whether your soil is good enough to support your garden?

Here are some words that will be in some editing activities. Test yourself to make sure that you know what the words mean.

indolent—An indolent person is a lazy person. Here's a sentence that uses the word **indolent:**
> She was fired from her job because she was so indolent.

lethal—Something that is lethal is capable of killing living things. Most bug sprays and cleaning compounds are lethal. So are guns, bombs, and many vehicles. Here's a sentence that uses the word **lethal:**
> The story told about a man who was murdered with a lethal weapon.

preceding—A preceding event is an event that happened before another event. Here's a sentence that uses the word **preceding:**
> I think that his latest strategy for traffic control is much better than his preceding one.

vital—Something that is vital is necessary. Workers are vital to the operation of a factory. Here's a sentence that uses the word **vital:**
> Food is vital for survival.

The word **especially** can often be used in place of the words **really** and **very**. Say these sentences with the word **especially:**

- She was very happy that evening.
- His hand was really sore after the game.
- The bugs were very bothersome that evening.
- Jack was really tired after the party.
- Your eyes look very green in this light.

Write **Part B** in the left margin of your paper. You have two minutes to copy the paragraph below.

> **There are several steps involved in growing a vegetable garden. First, prepare the land. Second, plant the seeds, spacing them so that the young plants will have room to grow. Next, mulch the seedlings with hay or straw. Last, water the garden.**

Write **Part C** in the left margin of your paper.
   Here are three main ideas:

- **The countries of Canada and the United States are in North America.**
- **The United States and Canada are interesting.**
- **Canada and the United States are the same in many ways.**

One of the main ideas fits the passage below. Read the passage.

> Canada is in North America. So is the United States. Canada is a large country, much larger than most of the countries in Europe. The United States is also a large country. Canada extends from the Atlantic Ocean to the Pacific Ocean. So does the United States. One of Canada's boundaries cuts through the Great Lakes. The United States shares this boundary. Part of Niagara Falls is in Canada. Part is in the United States.

Write the main idea that fits the passage. List the five points that fall under the main idea in outline form. Don't forget to indent and label the five points.

Write **Part D** in the left margin of your paper. Then number it from 1 to 11. The two accounts below contradict each other on an important point. Make sure you find that contradiction when you read the accounts.

Passage 1. The skiing industry, which is a major source of income for our state, is in trouble. For the last several years, an absence of snow has seriously affected the income of our ski resorts. We interviewed Bob Rasmussen, owner of Blue Mountain Ski Resort, to find out just how serious the situation has become.

"All I can say is that we're in trouble right now," Mr. Rasmussen told reporters. "But it's ridiculous to think that this situation will continue. I figure that next year we'll have the heaviest snowfall we've had in the last five years. That should more than make up for the money we've lost in the last few seasons."

Passage 2. Our state is in serious financial trouble. Senator Frisbee predicts some heavy taxes on the citizens if we can't solve our money problems. One of the biggest reasons for this economic slump is the dry spell we've been having. Because of the lack of snowfall, the skiing industry has not been attracting many customers. The loss of income from this industry is a serious problem for the state. When interviewed about the problem, Senator Frisbee stated: "All we can do is hope for snow. According to owners of the ski resorts, it may be several years before we have a good snowfall. In the meantime, we must tighten our belts and consent to more taxes than we are used to paying."

Answer questions 1–10. Some of the questions ask where you found an answer. Write **passage 1, passage 2,** or **passages 1 and 2** for these questions.

1. These passages contradict each other on one big point. What point is that?
2. Why is the skiing industry losing money?
3. Where did you find the answer to question 2?
4. Why does the state suffer when the skiing industry is in a slump?
5. Where did you find the answer to question 4?
6. What kind of income does Bob Rasmussen predict for the skiing industry next year?
7. Where did you find the answer to question 6?

8. What kind of income does Senator Frisbee predict for the skiing industry next year?
9. Where did you find the answer to question 8?
10. How does Senator Frisbee expect to make up for the money the state is losing?
11. Where did you find the answer to question 10?

Write **Part E** in the left margin of your paper. Then number it from 1 to 4. The description below tells about one of the organisms listed. Read the description and then answer the questions.

> This thing is an organism that you can see without a magnifying glass. The organism is a carnivore, but it does not kill. The organism lives on a host—more specifically, it lives on an animal host.

tree   lion   sheep   vulture   mistletoe   flea

1. Which organism does the description tell about?
2. Which words in the description let you know that a lion is not the organism that is described?
3. Which words in the description let you know that a vulture is not the organism that is described?
4. Which words in the description let you know that a tree is not the organism that is described?

Write **Part F** in the left margin of your paper. Then number it from 1 to 6. Assume that the map below is accurate. Examine the map carefully and then read the statements below it. Some of the statements contradict what the map shows.

- Write **contradictory** or **not contradictory** for each statement.
- If a statement contradicts the map, write what the map shows.

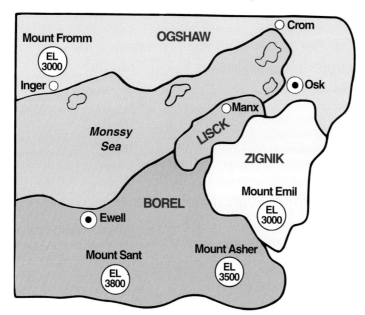

The symbol ○ means that the city has between 50,000 and 100,000 people.
The symbol ● means that the city has more than 100,000 people.
The symbol (EL 3000) means that the mountain is 3000 meters high.

The area that is shaded like this ▮ is a sea.

1. Borel, Zignik, and Lisck are all countries by the sea.
2. The city of Manx lies in Lisck and has more than 100,000 people.
3. Ogshaw and Borel are both neighbors of Zignik.
4. The islands in the Monssy Sea are near the coast of Ogshaw.
5. Zignik is larger than Lisck.
6. Mount Fromm is a mountain in Ogshaw that is 3500 meters high.

LESSON **112**

A

The word **especially** can often be used in place of the words **really** and **very.**
Say these sentences with the word **especially:**

- That math test was really hard.
- She is a very attractive woman.
- This camera is really fun to use.

B

To make a statement more general, you use the names of larger classes.
Here's a statement:
> The <u>fourteen-year-old boy</u> walked into the <u>little coffee shop.</u>

You can make the statement more general by using the name of a larger class
for each underlined part.
Here's a more general statement:
> The <u>teenager</u> walked into the <u>store.</u>

Here's a statement that is even more general:
> The <u>person</u> walked into the <u>building.</u>

- Here's a new statement:
> That <u>cocker spaniel</u> is curled up in a <u>red station wagon.</u>

Make up a more general statement by using the name of a larger class for
each underlined part.

- Here's a new statement:
> <u>Oranges</u> are often put in <u>fruit crates.</u>

Make up a more general statement by using the name of a larger class for
each underlined part.

- Here's a new statement:
> <u>Sheep, goats, cows, horses, and deer</u> on my farm like to eat <u>grass
> and bushes.</u>

Make up a more general statement by using the name of a larger class for
each underlined part.

C

Write **Part C** in the left margin of your paper. You have two minutes to copy
the paragraph below.

> **She always spoke deprecatingly about her former husband. She
> pointed out his faults and weaknesses, and she had no kind words
> about him. Her friends learned to stop asking her about him,
> because she never missed a chance to deprecate him in public.**

★ **D** Write **Part D** in the left margin of your paper. Then number it from 1 to 11. The two accounts below contradict each other on an important point. Make sure you find that contradiction when you read the accounts.

> **Passage 1.** During the lightning storm last night, some animals escaped from the circus. Falling tree limbs apparently damaged some of the cages, and several lions got out. Zebras and elephants were reported wandering around in the downtown shopping mall at about 10 P.M. last night. Bessie MacDonald, of 122 West Blakely, said that she found an upset ocelot hiding in the backseat of her car. Ms. MacDonald called the police, who gave the animal a tranquilizer and took it back to the circus grounds. Circus attendants rounded up the rest of the animals and had them safely back in cages by midnight.

> **Passage 2.** If you happen to see a lion wandering around downtown, don't panic. One escaped from the circus last night and is believed to be somewhere in the downtown area. If you see the beast, call 223-4195 and report its location.
> During the storm last night, several animals managed to escape from the circus. Circus attendants thought they had rounded up all the animals, but later discovered that one lion was still missing. Citizens are cautioned not to take walks alone and to watch their children carefully until the lion is caught. The animal won't attack unless it is teased. Circus officials hope that they can get the lion back unharmed.

Answer each question below. Some of the questions ask where you found an answer. Write **passage 1, passage 2,** or **passages 1 and 2** for these questions.

1. These passages contradict each other on one big point. What point is that?
2. When did the animals escape from the circus?
3. Where did you find the answer to question 2?
4. Where was an ocelot found?
5. Where did you find the answer to question 4?
6. How did the police calm the ocelot?
7. Where did you find the answer to question 6?
8. What are you supposed to do if you see the missing animal?
9. Where did you find the answer to question 8?
10. What caused the damaged cages?
11. Where did you find the answer to question 10?

E Write **Part E** in the left margin of your paper. Then number it from 1 to 4. The description below tells about one of the things listed. Read the description and then answer the questions.

This thing is an organism. It is a plant that grows in many places. It has chlorophyll, so it can make its own food. It produces flowers, which can be many colors. The stems of the plants have thorns, which help protect the plant from predators.

book   apple tree   horse   rosebush   decomposer   pumpkin vine

1. Which thing does the description tell about?
2. Which words in the description let you know that a book is not the thing that is described?
3. Which words in the description let you know that a decomposer is not the thing that is described?
4. Which words in the description let you know that a horse is not the thing that is described?

In the item below, the underlined sentence has two possible meanings. The sentence that follows the underlined sentence makes it clear which meaning is intended.

The boy ate the cake on the table. His mother told him to get down when she saw him there.

What are the two possible meanings of the underlined sentence?
Which is the intended meaning?

Many arguments about what we should do begin with **statements of ought.** If the argument draws a conclusion about what somebody ought to do, what do you know about the rule at the beginning of the argument?

Read the argument below.

> One of our most basic beliefs is that we should be fair to all, regardless of race, color, or creed. When we look at the courts, however, we are shocked. The courts are not fair to all. The courts have one standard for the wealthy and another standard for the poor. The courts sentence poor people for committing minor crimes. However, the courts do not treat wealthy people in the same way. If we remain consistent with our basic belief, we must conclude that we should change the courts.

What conclusion does the author draw?
Here are the last two parts of a deduction that is based on the author's argument:

The courts are not fair to all.
Therefore, we should change the courts.

The conclusion is an **ought statement.** So, what do you know about the rule at the beginning of the deduction?
Figure out the missing rule.
Say the whole deduction that summarizes the author's argument.
The argument is valid, but you may not agree with it. Do you agree with the rule that we should be fair to all?
What do you think that rule is supposed to mean?

Here's a statement:

The <u>wrench</u> is made of <u>steel</u>.

Make up a more general statement by using the name of a larger class for each underlined part.

● Here's a new statement:

The <u>woodpecker</u> jumped on the <u>recliner</u>.

Make up a more general statement by using the name of a larger class for each underlined part.

● Here's a new statement:

The <u>fat little man</u> went into the <u>bank</u> with a fistful of <u>pennies, nickels, dimes, and quarters.</u>

Make up a more general statement by using the name of a larger class for each underlined part.

Write **Part D** in the left margin of your paper. You have two minutes to copy the paragraph below.

> **He extolled her beauty in poems and songs. He extolled her to his friends by speaking of her grace, her kindness, and her wisdom. He seemed unable to say anything but good things about her. According to him, she was the best at everything.**

★ **E** Write **Part E** in the left margin of your paper. Then number it from 1 to 8. The two passages below tell something about the effects of aspirin. Read both passages and find out which passage gives more facts about the effects of aspirin.

Passage A. Doctors recommend aspirin more than any other pain reliever. In studies with cancer patients, aspirin was more reliably effective than a dozen other pain relievers, including some powerful narcotics. One side effect of aspirin is that it reduces your blood's ability to clot. People who take aspirin regularly may have trouble stopping small cuts from bleeding.

Passage B. Do you have occasional headaches or muscle pains? You know by now that doctors recommend aspirin more than any other pain reliever you can buy. But did you know that some aspirins are stronger than others? PainZip tablets have twice the amount of aspirin contained in other brands, so you get the kind of pain relief you need. Remember—for headaches, get PainZip aspirin.

Answer each question below. Some of the questions ask where you found an answer. Write **passage A, passage B,** or **passages A and B** for these questions.

1. Which passage tells more about the effects of aspirin?
2. The other passage gives more facts about something else. What does it tell more about?
3. What do doctors recommend most for pain relief?
4. Where did you find the answer to question 3?
5. What could happen if you take aspirin regularly and cut yourself?
6. Where did you find the answer to question 5?
7. What does aspirin do to your blood?
8. Where did you find the answer to question 7?

Many arguments about what we should do begin with statements of ought. If the argument draws a conclusion about what somebody ought to do, what do you know about the rule at the beginning of the argument?

Read the argument below.

> Many rules have lived with us for thousands of years. They couldn't have lived this long unless they carried a message that remains important to humans.
>
> One of these rules is: Honor your father and your mother. What this means is that you should respect your parents and do what they tell you to do.
>
> I am your father. And even though you are thirty years old and have a tough time making money, I'm telling you this: Give me a thousand dollars. That's what you should do.

What conclusion does the argument draw?

Here are the last two parts of a deduction that is based on the argument:

Your father tells you to give him a thousand dollars.
You should give your father a thousand dollars.

The conclusion is an ought statement. So, what do you know about the rule at the beginning of the deduction?

Figure out the missing rule.

Say the whole deduction that summarizes the argument.

The argument is valid, but you may not agree with it. Do you agree with the rule that we should do what our parents tell us to do?

What do you think that rule is supposed to mean?

 Write **Part B** in the left margin of your paper. You have two minutes to copy the paragraph below.

> **Doctors recommend aspirin more than any other pain reliever. In studies with cancer patients, aspirin was more reliably effective than a dozen other pain relievers, including some powerful narcotics. One side effect of aspirin is that it reduces your blood's ability to clot.**

★ Write **Part C** in the left margin of your paper. Then number it from 1 to 3.

Here are three main ideas:

Main idea A. **A balance of food exists in the desert.**

Main idea B. **Humans change a desert into farmland.**

Main idea C. **Humans make a desert.**

Each main idea fits one of the passages below. After reading all the passages, figure out which main idea goes with each passage.

Passage 1. Deserts are interesting places. Some desert areas of Australia are a good example. One hundred years ago, these desert areas didn't exist. In 1859, Australians imported twenty-four rabbits from England and released them on a ranch. Rabbits had no natural enemies in Australia, so within forty years, the rabbits had multiplied into millions. At that time, Australians raised many sheep, which eat the same plants that rabbits eat. Together, the sheep and rabbits stripped much of southern Australia of all vegetation. Without grass roots to hold down the earth, wind blew the earth away. Once green prairie grass was plentiful there, but now there is only sand and dust storms. A land that once fed sheep is now dry and empty.

Passage 2. Deserts are interesting places. Some desert plants produce as many as one and a half billion seeds per year. Most of these seeds are eaten by insects and small animals like rabbits. In turn, the rabbits and other small animals that eat seeds are eaten by larger animals, such as bobcats, eagles, and wolves. If you removed the plants that produce seeds, you would be taking food from the small animals that feed on these seeds. And if you remove the small animals, you take food from larger animals.

Passage 3. Deserts are interesting places. Often a desert can become very rich farmland. All it needs is water. That's just what's happening in Israel. The desert is being changed into green, fertile farmland. The strategy that the people of Israel use is to irrigate the land and then plant vegetation that will grip the soil with strong roots. Irrigation brings water to the land. The vegetation prevents the wind from blowing the soil away.

1. Main idea A is: **A balance of food exists in the desert.** Which passage does main idea A best fit?
2. Main idea B is: **Humans change a desert into farmland.** Which passage does main idea B best fit?
3. Main idea C is: **Humans make a desert.** Which passage does main idea C best fit?

 Write **Part D** in the left margin of your paper. Rewrite the passage that follows using the words you have learned in place of the underlined words. Use the word **especially** one time. Remember to start every sentence with a capital letter and to punctuate each sentence correctly.

Lee is worried because most of the time her dog, Sammy, is noisy. There is a very sound reason for her fear—her landlord has a rule that does not allow tenants to have dogs. She doesn't want to get evicted, so she has made up a plan: as soon as she gets a chance, she is going to have Sammy changed into a cat.

E Write **Part E** in the left margin of your paper. Then number it from 1 to 8. The two passages below tell something about rats. Read both passages and find out which passage provides more real information about a rat's ability to survive.

Passage A. Rats eat one-fifth of the world's crops each year, destroying fields as well as invading storage silos. They carry dozens of diseases to humans and other animals. Under certain conditions, rats will attack animals hundreds of times their size, including humans. Although rats cause great damage, they have been used in laboratories to study different diseases. Through laboratory experiments, rats have contributed more to curing human illness than any other animal.

Passage B. For such a small animal, the rat performs incredible feats. The average rat can climb a brick wall as if it were a ladder, swim half a mile, and tread water for three days and nights. It can survive being flushed down the toilet, gnaw through lead pipes, or fall five stories to the ground and walk away unharmed. It's no wonder that rats feel at home almost anywhere.

Answer each question below. Some of the questions ask where you found an answer. Write **passage A, passage B,** or **passages A and B** for these questions.

1. Which passage tells more about a rat's ability to survive?
2. Which of the following main ideas fits passage A?

- **Rats are strong animals.**
- **Rats are both dangerous and helpful to humans.**
- **Rats carry many diseases.**

3. Name one way that rats are helpful.
4. Where did you find the answer to question 3?
5. Name two reasons that rats are dangerous to humans.
6. Where did you find the answer to question 5?
7. Name three things rats can do that seem incredible for such a small animal.
8. Where did you find the answer to question 7?

A The two passages below contradict each other on an important point. Make sure you find the contradiction when you read the passages.

Passage 1. The gold rush began in 1849, and that's why the people who flocked to California from different parts of the world were called "forty-niners." The first great gold deposits were discovered near Sacramento, but soon others were discovered, and California was teeming with people who believed "There's gold in them there hills!" John Sutter owned the mill where the first gold was found. He was plagued by people who stole his land and mined for themselves. He even called on Congress to help him protect his claim, but it refused. While others on his property were growing rich, Sutter went bankrupt. California finally offered Sutter a small monthly pension for his help in settling the West.

Passage 2. On January 24, 1848, a worker at John Sutter's mill near Sacramento, California, discovered gold. Although Sutter tried to keep the discovery a secret, the news spread quickly. In the next year, thousands of people from all over the country packed up and headed for the hills of California. Many of them found gold, but many others found nothing at all. John Sutter successfully mined his land in the hills around Sacramento and built up one of the largest fortunes of the nineteenth century. Although many mining towns were destined to become ghost towns, Sacramento prospered and is now the capital of California.

The passages contradict each other on an important point. What is that point?

Let's look up the **gold rush** or **John Sutter** in an encyclopedia and find out which passage is accurate.

B Write **Part B** in the left margin of your paper. You have two minutes to copy the paragraph below.

> **Australia imported some live rabbits from England. These rabbits soon multiplied into millions. The rabbits helped strip the vegetation from part of Australia. Without grass roots to hold down the earth, wind blew the earth away, and the area became a desert.**

VOCABULARY TEST. Write **Part C** in the left margin of your paper. Then number it from 1 to 8. Write the model sentence that means the same thing as each sentence below. You have nine minutes.

1. The <u>rule</u> <u>limited</u> their parking.
2. They <u>made up</u> a <u>fitting</u> <u>plan</u>.
3. By <u>pausing</u>, she lost her <u>chance</u>.
4. His directions were <u>unclear</u> and <u>repetitive</u>.
5. Her <u>answer</u> was <u>filled</u> with <u>irrelevant</u> details.
6. The <u>major</u> <u>argued</u> that he had <u>sound</u> reasons for <u>hiding</u> the <u>facts</u>.
7. A strange <u>event</u> caused the <u>fear</u> that she <u>showed</u>.
8. They <u>changed</u> their Swiss <u>money</u> into Canadian <u>money</u>.

★

Write **Part D** in the left margin of your paper. In the passage below, the underlined words can be replaced with words you have learned. Rewrite the passage using the words you have learned. Use the word **especially** one time. Remember to start every sentence with a capital letter and to punctuate each sentence correctly.

> Kevin <u>argued</u> that girls should not be allowed to join the rowing team. He <u>said</u> that they are <u>almost never</u> strong enough. Everyone laughed at him, because his argument was not based on <u>sound</u> <u>facts</u>. He kept arguing, however, and the girls got tired of his <u>repetitive</u> nonsense. They <u>made up</u> a <u>really</u> <u>fitting</u> <u>plan</u> to <u>show</u> their strength. They picked him up and dunked him in the river.

Write **Part E** in the left margin of your paper. Then number it 1 and 2.
Here are two main ideas:

Main idea A. **Schools are responsible for a student's education.**
Main idea B. **Students are responsible for their own education.**

Each main idea fits one of the passages below. After reading both passages, figure out which main idea goes with each passage.

Passage 1. The school is being sued for damages, because when Albert graduated, he couldn't read well enough to fill out a job application. But it's not the school's fault that Albert can't read. Albert was one of those students who are incapable of learning. The school gave Albert every opportunity to learn—the same opportunities it gave to other students. Albert didn't take advantage of those opportunities. That doesn't mean that the school is responsible.

Passage 2. The school is being sued for damages because when Albert graduated, he couldn't read well enough to fill out a job application. The school's responsibility is to teach students how to read, write, and do arithmetic. We don't build schools and hire teachers to babysit kids until they are eighteen. If the schools aren't responsible for the education of children, then let's get rid of the schools.

1. Main idea A is: **Schools are responsible for a student's education.**
   Which passage does main idea A best fit?
2. Main idea B is: **Students are responsible for their own education.**
   Which passage does main idea B best fit?

The word **particularly** can often be used instead of the words **very, really,** and **especially.**

Say these sentences with the word **particularly:**

- She was especially sad at dinnertime.
- His leg was very sunburned.
- He liked to cook, especially for large groups.
- She runs a lot, especially on Sundays.
- They were really glad to be home.
- Her shoes were especially dirty after the rain.
- His hair is very long.

How do you make up statements that are more general?
To make up a statement that is more specific, you use the name of a smaller class.

Here's a picture:

Here's a statement about the picture:
> **They went into a building.**

Here's a more specific statement that uses the name of a smaller class for each underlined part:
> **A woman and a man went into a restaurant.**

Here's a statement that is even more specific:
> **A curly-haired woman and a large man went into Harry's Restaurant.**

• Here's a different statement about the picture:

He carried underline{something}.

Make up a more specific statement by using the name of a smaller class for each underlined part.

• Here's a different statement about the picture:

She was wearing something.

Make up a more specific statement by using the name of a smaller class for each underlined part.

Write **Part C** in the left margin of your paper. You have two minutes to copy the paragraph below.

> **Rats eat one-fifth of the world's crops each year, destroying fields as well as invading storage silos. They carry dozens of diseases to humans and other animals. Under certain conditions, rats will attack animals hundreds of times their size, including humans.**

★ Write **Part D** in the left margin of your paper. Then number it from 1 to 12.

The two passages below tell something about mouthwash. Read both passages and find out which passage gives more facts about mouthwash.

> **Passage A.** Mouthwashes that claim to stop bad breath by killing bacteria are useless. No amount of gargling could kill even one-tenth of the bacteria in the human mouth. Bad breath from eating garlic and onion does not come from your mouth at all. The digested garlic gets into your bloodstream, then your lungs, and finally comes out with each breath. Mouthwash cannot help this problem. Some kinds of bad breath come from throat infections that develop when the throat is too dry. Unfortunately, many mouthwashes contain alcohol, which actually dries the throat even more, making infection and bad breath more likely.

> **Passage B.** Most sore throats are due to virus infections, which cannot be stopped with mouthwash. Some sore throats are caused by bacteria alone, and they should be treated with antibiotics. The only way to determine what kind of organisms are causing a throat infection is to take a few drops from the infected area and examine them under a microscope. If the doctor prescribes an antibiotic for you when you have a sore throat, be sure to use all the pills prescribed. If you stop taking the pills in the middle of the treatment, a much more powerful infection may result. Treating a sore throat with mouthwash may provide temporary relief from pain, but it cannot cure serious throat infections.

Answer each question below. Some ask where you found an answer. Write **passage A, passage B,** or **passages A and B** for these questions.

1. Which passage tells more about mouthwash?
2. The other passage gives more facts about something other than mouthwash. What does this passage tell more about?
3. Why doesn't mouthwash help bad breath that results from eating garlic?
4. Where did you find the answer to question 3?
5. How can mouthwash make a throat infection worse?
6. Where did you find the answer to question 5?
7. How can mouthwash help a sore throat?
8. Where did you find the answer to question 7?
9. Can mouthwashes kill all the bacteria in your mouth?
10. Where did you find the answer to question 9?
11. Why should you take all the antibiotic pills that a doctor prescribes for a throat infection?
12. Where did you find the answer to question 11?

E Write **Part E** in the left margin of your paper. Then number it from 1 to 3. Each item below tells about the picture. For each item, write a statement that is more specific by using the name of a smaller class for each underlined part.

1. The <u>vehicle</u> stopped to let the <u>animal</u> out.
2. The <u>woman</u> was playing a <u>musical instrument</u>.
3. The <u>ape</u> was wearing a <u>tie</u>.

The word **particularly** can often be used instead of the words **very, really,** and **especially.** Say these sentences with the word **particularly:**
- She likes to play tennis, especially with Mary.
- The air smelled really clean after the storm.
- Ray plays the guitar very well.

Sometimes the rule at the beginning of an argument is not stated in the argument. You have to figure it out.

Here's an argument that has an ought statement for a conclusion.

> Nancy was teasing Brad and trying to get him to do silly things.
> "I'll bet you're too scared to jump out of that tree," Nancy said, pointing to a large oak tree in the yard.
> "I am not," replied Brad. He climbed the tree and then jumped.
> "I'll bet you wouldn't ride your bike blindfolded," Nancy said.
> "Riding a bicycle blindfolded is too dangerous," Brad replied. "Therefore, I shouldn't do it."

What conclusion does the author draw?
What evidence is used to support this conclusion?

Here's the last part of the argument:
Riding a bicycle blindfolded is too dangerous.
Therefore, you shouldn't ride a bicycle blindfolded.
Figure out the missing rule.
Say the whole deduction.

Here's another argument that has an ought statement for a conclusion.

> When Janet came home from the park, her father asked her to come into his study. "Janet," he said, "I'm concerned about your behavior lately. I know that it's spring, and the weather is getting warmer, but I don't think that's a good reason to abandon your responsibilities. Your mother told you to do your homework and you left for the park. When your mother tells you to do your homework, you should do it."

What conclusion does the author draw?
What evidence is used to support this conclusion?

Here's the last part of the argument:
Your mother told you to do your homework.
Therefore, you should do your homework.
Figure out the missing rule.
Say the whole deduction.

Do you agree with the rule that people should do what their mothers tell them to do?

Can you think of any situations that would be unfair if people did what their mothers told them to do?

 How do you make up statements that are more general?

To make up a statement that is more specific, you use the name of a smaller class.

Here's a picture:

• Here's a statement about the picture:

The <u>man</u> was sitting on a <u>chair</u>.

Make up a more specific statement by using the name of a smaller class for each underlined part.

• Here's a different statement about the picture:

The <u>children</u> walked out of the <u>store</u>.

Make up a more specific statement by using the name of a smaller class for each underlined part.

• Here's a different statement about the picture:

He was playing a <u>musical instrument</u>.

Make up a more specific statement by using the name of a smaller class for each underlined part.

Write **Part D** in the left margin of your paper. You have two minutes to copy the paragraph below.

> **Most sore throats are due to virus infections, which cannot be cured with mouthwash. Some sore throats are caused by bacteria and should be treated with antibiotics. If a doctor prescribes an antibiotic for your sore throat, be sure to take all the pills.**

★

Write **Part E** in the left margin of your paper. Then number it from 1 to 14.
    The two passages below tell something about alfalfa. Read both passages and find out which passage gives more facts about the characteristics of alfalfa.

> **Passage A.** Alfalfa is one of the first crops that people grew to provide food for domestic animals such as horses or cows. Although alfalfa originally was grown in Asia, alfalfa is now an important source of hay throughout the world. Farmers often plant alfalfa in fields that have been overworked in previous years, because the alfalfa nourishes the soil with nitrogen. Although it is usually harvested before it flowers, farmers usually let one field bloom to provide nectar for honeybees. Alfalfa is sometimes added to ready-made foods to increase the vitamin content of those foods.

> **Passage B.** Alfalfa is one of the first crops that people grew to provide food for domestic animals. Alfalfa produces sweet hay, and the word **alfalfa** means **the best fodder.** Alfalfa grows quickly, and it grows in many types of soil. It endures well in hot, dry spells because its taproot extends two or three meters down into the ground, where it reaches moist soil. The plant smells sweet like clover, and it has yellow, blue, or purple flowers.

    Answer each question that follows. Some of the questions ask where you found an answer. Write **passage A, passage B,** or **passages A and B** for these questions.

 1. Which passage tells more about the characteristics of alfalfa?
 2. Which of the following main ideas fits passage A?

• **Alfalfa is grown to feed domestic animals.**
• **Alfalfa has several uses.**
• **Alfalfa contains nitrogen.**

3. Why do farmers plant alfalfa in overworked fields?
4. Where did you find the answer to question 3?
5. Why can alfalfa survive in dry climates?
6. Where did you find the answer to question 5?
7. Where was alfalfa originally grown?
8. Where did you find the answer to question 7?
9. Name one of the first crops that people grew to provide food for their animals.
10. Where did you find the answer to question 9?
11. What does the word **alfalfa** mean?
12. Where did you find the answer to question 11?
13. Why do farmers sometimes let alfalfa fields bloom?
14. Where did you find the answer to question 13?

 Write **Part F** in the left margin of your paper. Then number it from 1 to 3. Each item tells about the picture. For each item, write a statement that is more specific by using the name of a smaller class for each underlined part.

1. The container had money scattered around it.
2. The dog had something in its mouth.
3. She was juggling some balls.

Write **Part G** in the left margin of your paper. Rewrite the passage below in three or four sentences. Combine consistent sentences with **and** or **therefore.** Combine inconsistent sentences with **but** or **however.** Combine some sentences with **who** or **which.**

> I took a train trip out to Washington state this summer. Trains are usually late. The train I rode was right on time. The conductor took our tickets. The tickets were purchased in the station. My brother hit his head on the top of the observation car. He wouldn't go in that car anymore.

Write **Part H** in the left margin of your paper.
　　Here are three main ideas:

- **Animals communicate in different ways.**
- **Communication among dogs or rattlesnakes is simpler than human communication.**
- **Prairie dogs kiss.**

One of the main ideas fits the passage below. Read the passage.

> The whir of the rattlesnake, the bark of a dog, and thousands of other sounds and actions are used by animals to communicate. In order to live together, animals must be able to communicate. Compared with human speech, the language of most animals is simple, but these animals do communicate with each other. When prairie dogs want to be recognized, they exchange kisses. Dolphins, whales, and porpoises speak to each other in high-pitched whistles and clicks. When a male fiddler crab sees a female, he waves his claws to signal that he is ready to mate. The cichlid, which is a freshwater fish, has several ways of communicating. Cichlids will change their color and the position of their fins when they want to express their feelings.

Write the main idea that fits the passage. List the four points that fall under the main idea in outline form. Don't forget to indent and label the four points.

LESSON 118

A You've learned two words that can be used instead of the words **really** and **very.** What are those words?

Make up a sentence that uses the word **especially.**

Make up a different sentence that uses the word **particularly.**

B Sometimes the rule at the beginning of an argument is not stated in the argument. You have to figure it out.

Here's an argument that has an ought statement for a conclusion.

> "I understand your problem," his mother said. "You're interested in some things that are not taught at your school. I had a similar problem when I was in school. I was interested in astronomy. There was no way to study astronomy in my classes, so I studied on my own. You're interested in photography, so you should study photography on your own. Maybe you can enroll in a class at the Community Center."
>
> "You're right," Brian said. "I'll do that."

What conclusion does the author draw?

What evidence is used to support this conclusion?

Here's the last part of the argument:

Brian is interested in photography.

Therefore, Brian should study photography on his own.

Figure out the missing rule.

Say the whole deduction.

Here's another argument that has an ought statement for a conclusion.

> "Alvin, your sister tells me that you've been spending your lunch money on chocolate bars. You're not giving your body the nutrition it needs. If you eat the right kinds of foods, you'll be healthier. So you ought to eat the right kinds of foods."

What conclusion does the author draw?

What evidence is used to support this conclusion?

Here's the last part of the argument:

Eating the right kinds of foods will make you healthier.

Therefore, you ought to eat the right kinds of foods.

Figure out the missing rule.

Say the whole deduction.

Do you agree that people should do things that will make them healthier?

Can you think of any situations where people shouldn't do things that would make them healthier?

Write **Part C** in the left margin of your paper. You have two minutes to copy the paragraph below.

> **Alfalfa is one of the first crops that people grew to provide food for domestic animals. Alfalfa produces sweet hay, and the word "alfalfa" means "the best fodder." Alfalfa grows quickly, and it grows in many types of soil and many types of climate.**

★

Write **Part D** in the left margin of your paper. Then number it from 1 to 3. Each item below tells about the picture. For each item, write a statement that is more specific by using the name of a smaller class for each underlined part.

1. The <u>vehicle</u> landed <u>on the ground</u>.
2. <u>They</u> were playing <u>a game</u>.
3. The <u>animals</u> ran away.

A When you combine sentences with the word **so,** what do you do with the period of the first sentence?
What word follows the comma?

When you combine sentences with the word **but,** what do you do with the period of the first sentence?
What word follows the comma?

When you combine sentences with the word **and,** what do you do with the period of the first sentence?
What word follows the comma?

B Write **Part B** in the left margin of your paper. You have two minutes to copy the paragraph below.

> The fecundity of this soil is amazing. You can scatter corn seeds on top of the ground, and two months later you'll have cornstalks taller than you are. This ground grows everything from watermelons to strawberries as big as your fist.

Write **Part C** in the left margin of your paper. Then number it from 1 to 3. Each item below tells about the picture. For each item, write a statement that is more specific by using the name of a smaller class for each underlined part.

1. He was pounding with a <u>tool</u>.
2. <u>She</u> was carrying some <u>building materials</u> as she moved up an <u>object</u>.
3. <u>They</u> were working on a <u>building</u>.

LESSON 120

A Write **Part A** in the left margin of your paper. You have two minutes to copy the paragraph below.

> **In Africa, there is a special partnership between tickbirds and large land animals such as the rhinoceros. The rhino provides the tickbird with food and with transportation. The tickbird frees the rhino of parasites and signals when danger is approaching.**

B **VOCABULARY TEST.** Write **Part B** in the left margin of your paper. Then number it from 1 to 8. Write the model sentence that means the same thing as each sentence below. You have nine minutes.

1. By pausing, she lost her chance.
2. His directions were unclear and repetitive.
3. They changed their Swiss money into Canadian money.
4. The rule limited their parking.
5. Her answer was filled with irrelevant details.
6. They made up a fitting plan.
7. A strange event caused the fear that she showed.
8. The major argued that he had sound reasons for hiding the facts.

★   Write **Part C** in the left margin of your paper. In the passage below, the underlined words can be replaced with words you have learned. Rewrite the passage using the words you have learned. Use the word **particularly** at least one time. Use the word **especially** at least one time. Remember to start every sentence with a capital letter and to punctuate each sentence correctly.

> My roommate Jan is really honest, so I was surprised when she showed signs of hiding something from me. I had asked her who was coming to dinner, and she paused for a very long time. Then she gave me a really unclear answer. That night I found out that she had a sound reason for keeping the facts a secret: she was having a surprise birthday party for me!

Write **Part D** in the left margin of your paper. Then number it from 1 to 3. One of the graphs is described below. Read the description and then answer the questions.

The graph below shows how the average American family spends its income. As you can see, almost half of an average income is spent on food. Another large part of the income goes to taxes. The remaining money is spent on entertainment, house payments, clothes, and gasoline.

A	B	C	D
food	food	food	food
taxes	taxes	taxes	taxes
entertainment	entertainment	entertainment	entertainment
gasoline	gasoline	gasoline	gasoline
clothes	clothes	clothes	clothes
house payments	house payments	house payments	house payments

1. Which graph does the description tell about?
2. How do you know that the description does not tell about graph A?
3. How do you know that the description does not tell about graph D?

E

Write **Part E** in the left margin of your paper. Then number it from 1 to 3. Each item below tells about the picture. For each item, write a statement that is more specific by using the name of a smaller class for each underlined part.

1. <u>She</u> was washing clothes in an <u>appliance</u>.
2. <u>She</u> was licking <u>something sweet</u>.
3. <u>They</u> were in a <u>building</u>.

F

Here are some words that will be in some editing activities. Test yourself to make sure that you know what the words mean.

extrovert—An extrovert is an outgoing person who likes to be with people and gets along well with people. Here's a sentence that uses the word **extrovert:**

      She is popular at school because she is such an extrovert.

genius—A genius is an extremely intelligent person. Here's a sentence that uses the word **genius:**

      She is a genius at arithmetic, but she has no plans to go to college.

miser—A miser is a person who is very stingy. Here's a sentence that uses the word **miser:**

      He is such a miser that he washes his used paper plates.

subsequent—A subsequent event is an event that follows another event. Here's a sentence that uses the word **subsequent:**

      The first act of the play is less boring than the subsequent act.

A The two passages below contradict each other on an important point. Make sure you find the contradiction when you read the passages.

Passage 1. Honeybees seem to have a language, but their language is not much like human language. One very simple reason that the honeybee's language can't be like ours is that the brain of a honeybee is little more than a speck. It doesn't contain very many nerve cells. Honeybees don't actually learn language the way humans do. Honeybees are born with some sort of understanding and some types of responses. The first time they see another honeybee perform a particular dance, they respond and go to the place signaled by the dance. Honeybees also do other things they haven't been taught. If honeybees are raised in a place where they never see a beehive or see another bee build a beehive, the honeybees will still build a perfect hive the first time they try. Every cell inside the beehive will have six sides, even though the bees have never seen such cells before. Honeybees are like tiny computers that have been designed to do some very complicated things.

Passage 2. One of the most notable characteristics of honeybees is their ability to build a hive that is complete with places to store food and nurseries for raising young bees. The honeybees in the hive each have their own tasks to perform. Some collect pollen, others work on building the nest, and still others are responsible for looking after the helpless larvae. The complex organization of a beehive is all the more remarkable because honeybees have no way of communicating with each other. Each bee seems to know what it is supposed to do, or where it is supposed to go to gather nectar, without ever exchanging information with other honeybees. Honeybees seem to be born with a highly developed set of instincts that direct their activities during their entire lives.

The passages contradict each other on an important point. What is that point?

Let's look up **bee** or **honeybee** in an encyclopedia and find out which passage is accurate.

B Some passages present a main idea that is called a moral. When a passage presents a moral, the passage presents specific events. The moral is a general statement about those events.

The passage below presents this moral:

If you try, you'll succeed.

> Irma started out as the poorest high jumper on the track team. Her best jump was slightly more than three feet. But Irma wanted to be a star high jumper. So she practiced, listened, and talked to herself. She watched the better jumpers—watched the way they approached the bar, how they tossed their arms when they started over the bar, and how they moved their legs. She listened to the coach when he explained jumping techniques to other jumpers. She arrived at practice early every day, and she worked and worked. At the end of her first season, she was better. She approached the bar faster, she had a better takeoff, and she tossed her arms with more force. She could now clear one and one-half meters, which isn't bad. But, by the end of the second season, Irma could clear six feet. She placed second in the state. You might say that she had the ability all along, but Irma also worked very hard.

Name the specific events in the story that show Irma tried.
Name the specific events in the story that show Irma succeeded.

 C Write **Part C** in the left margin of your paper. You have two minutes to copy the paragraph below.

> **She tenaciously held on to her position in the argument. Everybody tried to attack what she said, but she would not give an inch. She was so tenacious that the people who tried to attack her argument finally got tired and gave up.**

★ Write **Part D** in the left margin of your paper. Then number it 1 and 2. One of the graphs is described below. Read the description and then answer the questions.

The graph shows how Bernard spends his allowance. He puts 20 percent of it into his savings account. He divides half of it equally among clothes, entertainment, and food. A quarter of his allowance gets invested in his hobby, which is model-car racing.

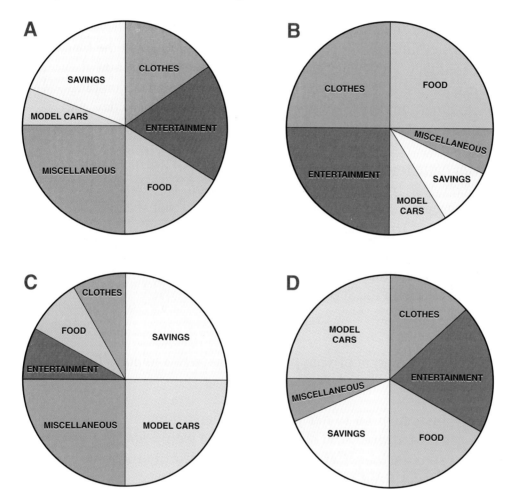

1. Which graph does the description tell about?
2. How do you know that the description does not tell about graph A?

Write **Part E** in the left margin of your paper. Then number it from 1 to 4. Look at the picture. Then rewrite each sentence.

1. There was a <u>container</u> on the <u>table</u> with some <u>fruit</u> in it.
   Write a more specific statement.
2. The <u>big hairy ape</u> was breaking a <u>dining-room chair</u>.
   Write a more general statement.
3. The <u>boy</u> was crouching beside a <u>chair</u>.
   Write a more general statement.
4. The <u>boy</u> was crouching beside a <u>chair</u>.
   Write a more specific statement.

Write **Part F** in the left margin of your paper. In the following passage, the underlined words can be replaced with words you have learned. Rewrite the passage using the words you have learned. Use the word **particularly** at least one time. Use the word **especially** at least one time. Remember to start every sentence with a capital letter and to punctuate each sentence correctly.

> When a <u>really</u> nasty dog appeared on the bike path, she <u>showed fear</u>. <u>Once in a while</u> she panics in a frightening situation, and this time, by <u>pausing</u>, she lost her first <u>chance</u> to escape. Then she <u>made up</u> a <u>very fitting plan</u> and got away. Later, when she retold the story, some of the <u>facts</u> seemed <u>unclear</u>. But she was <u>really</u> glad to be safe.

A Some passages present a main idea that is called a moral. When a passage presents a moral, the passage presents specific events. The moral is a general statement about those events.

The passage below presents this moral:

If you do things right the first time, you can save time.

> Sid was trying to put up the jib sail on his boat when he noticed that there was a small tear in the sail. Sid was in a great hurry, so instead of taking time to sew the rip, he used a large safety pin to hold the sides of the rip together. The wind wasn't very stiff anyhow. Sid put up the sails and started across the lake. Suddenly, a great gust of wind hit the sails and tore the jib from top to bottom. Repairing the jib required three hours of sewing. It also caused two large blisters on Sid's fingers.

How could Sid have saved time by doing things right the first time?

B The argument below is faulty because it breaks this rule:

> **Just because events have happened in the past doesn't mean they'll always happen.**

Read the rule over to yourself and get ready to say it.

Here's an argument:

> **I don't think we should hire Mr. Smith. Ten years ago, he was fired from his job because he was so lazy. We don't want to hire a lazy person.**

What does the writer want us to conclude?

What evidence does the writer use to support this conclusion?

Say the rule the argument breaks.

Here's how you could show that Mr. Smith may not be a lazy person anymore. Find out who Mr. Smith has worked for recently. Ask those employers if Mr. Smith is still lazy.

C Write **Part C** in the left margin of your paper. You have two minutes to copy the paragraph below.

> **Some passages present a moral. When a passage presents a moral, the passage presents specific events. The moral is a general statement about those events. Here is a moral that you may have heard: Don't count your chickens before they're hatched.**

★ **D** Write **Part D** in the left margin of your paper. Then number it from 1 to 4. Look at the picture. Then rewrite each sentence.

1. A <u>girl</u> was flying a <u>kite</u>.
   Write a more specific statement.
2. <u>They</u> were running toward a <u>tree</u>.
   Write a more specific statement.
3. A <u>spotted dog</u> was chasing after the <u>little girl</u>.
   Write a more general statement.
4. A <u>girl</u> was flying a <u>kite</u>.
   Write a more general statement.

Write **Part E** in the left margin of your paper. Then number it 1 and 2. Here's an argument for why you should use White and Bright Toothpaste. Part of the argument is contradicted by the graph.

　　The graph shows the percentage of cavities that our test group had before and after using White and Bright Toothpaste. In 1990, when we started examining our test group, about 12 percent of their teeth had cavities. By 1993, when our test group started using White and Bright, about 18 percent of their teeth had cavities. After the group used White and Bright, the percentage of cavities dropped. If you are tired of going to the dentist, consider White and Bright Toothpaste.

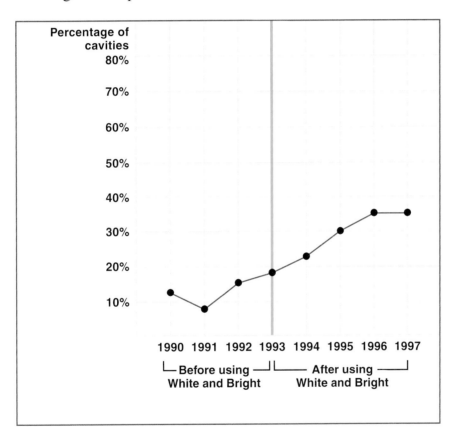

1. Part of the argument is contradicted by the graph.
   Which part is contradicted?
2. What does the graph show?

Write **Part F** in the left margin of your paper. Then number it 1 and 2. Here's a fact: **St. Louis is located near the junction of three rivers.**

1. In what kind of reference book would you look to find evidence to support this fact?
2. Look at the map below. Then write the names of the three rivers that join near St. Louis.

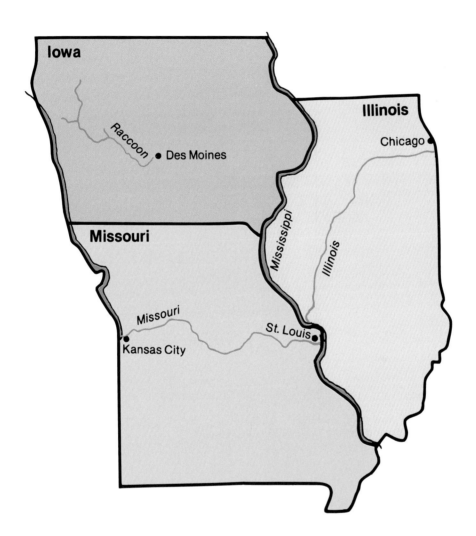

Write **Part G** in the left margin of your paper. Then number it from 1 to 3. The description below tells about one of the words shown below. Read the description and answer the questions.

> One root of this word is <u>dict</u>, which means say. A machine that records what you say is a <u>dict</u>aphone. If you say something is going to happen before it happens, you pre<u>dict</u> it.
>
> The other root of this word is <u>mal</u>, which means **evil** or **bad.** <u>Mal</u>nutrition is **bad nutrition.** <u>Mal</u>odorous means **evil-smelling.** The word made up of <u>dict</u> and <u>mal</u> means **an evil saying,** or **a curse.**

malicious   contradiction   malefactor   malediction

1. Which word does the description tell about?
2. How do you know that the description does not tell about the word **contradiction?**
3. How do you know that the description does not tell about the word **malicious?**

Write **Part H** in the left margin of your paper. In the passage below, the underlined words can be replaced with words you have learned. Rewrite the passage using the words you have learned. Remember to start every sentence with a capital letter and to punctuate each sentence correctly.

> <u>Once in a while</u>, a <u>really</u> strange <u>event</u> happens in our town. Last week all the <u>money</u> in town was suddenly <u>changed</u> into fruit, and all the fruit was <u>changed</u> into <u>money</u>. Tourists <u>showed</u> a lot of confusion when they saw our bank <u>filled</u> with apples and plums. The tourists were <u>very</u> glad, however, to have a <u>chance</u> to pick from our <u>money</u> trees.

LESSON 123

 A The argument below is faulty because it breaks this rule:

> **Just because events have happened in the past**
> **doesn't mean they'll always happen.**

Read the rule over to yourself and get ready to say it.

Here's an argument:

> **I don't think the United States should help support Japan's**
> **economy. The Japanese did bomb Pearl Harbor in 1941. As soon as**
> **they have the money, they'll do it again.**

What does the writer want us to conclude?

What evidence does the writer use to support this conclusion?

Say the rule the argument breaks.

Here's how you could show that the Japanese may not bomb Pearl Harbor again as soon as they have the money. Find out if the Japanese have had enough money to bomb Pearl Harbor since 1941 and if they have bombed it again.

B A passage that presents a moral tells about what kind of events?

The moral is a statement about those events that is more _____.

The passage below presents this moral:

Don't judge the whole by its parts.

> It was the first time Tammy had been to the Girls' Club on Fifth Street, and it wasn't a very good introduction to the club. Tammy was fourteen at the time. A tall girl named Jo, who was sixteen and very tough, blocked Tammy's way as she tried to enter the club. "Hey, do you want me to punch you out?"
>
> At first Tammy didn't believe that Jo was talking to her. "Me?" she asked. "What did I do?"
>
> "I'm going to flatten you, you hear me?" Jo said and gave Tammy a little push.
>
> "Wait a minute," Tammy said. "I don't want to fight."
>
> "Well, if you stick around here, you will fight, and you'll fight me."
>
> Tammy went home and she never went back to the club. Three years later, Tammy was playing tennis with Linda Becker. Linda was terrific, and she easily beat Tammy. After the game, Tammy said, "I thought I could play pretty well, but you're the best I've seen."
>
> "Oh, I'm not very good," Linda said. "You should see some of the other girls at the club."

"Which club is that?"

"The Girls' Club on Fifth," Linda said. She went on to explain about the tennis program and the swimming program and all the outings that the club sponsored. After talking for about five minutes, Linda concluded, "It's the best club in the world."

Tammy said, "I never would have thought that. I tried going there once but it seemed like nothing but a place for bullies."

"I'll bet you met Jo. We kicked her out just about three years ago. She is one bad apple!"

Tammy said, "Gee, maybe I should give the club another try."

Name the specific whole that is referred to in the story.
Name the specific part that is referred to in the story.
Tell what somebody said when she judged the whole by the part.

Write **Part C** in the left margin of your paper. You have two minutes to copy the paragraph below.

> **Here's a rule that is sometimes broken in faulty arguments: Just because events have happened in the past doesn't mean they'll always happen. Some people never have a chance to escape the mistakes they've made because other people break this rule.**

★ **D** Write **Part D** in the left margin of your paper. Then number it from 1 to 4. Look at the picture. Then rewrite each sentence.

1. She was riding a <u>horse</u>.
   Write a more specific statement.
2. <u>It</u> was jumping through a <u>hoop</u>.
   Write a more specific statement.
3. <u>A short clown in dotted pants</u> was <u>tossing three empty bottles into the air and catching them</u>.
   Write a more general statement.
4. He balanced on <u>something that is narrow</u>.
   Write a more specific statement.

Write **Part E** in the left margin of your paper. In the passage below, the underlined words can be replaced with words you have learned. Rewrite the passage using the words you have learned. Remember to start every sentence with a capital letter and to punctuate each sentence correctly.

> Rafael <u>almost never</u> <u>pauses</u> before doing the <u>fitting</u> thing. When he found a box full of <u>money</u> in the woods, he called up the man whose name was on the box. The man's <u>answer</u> was <u>very</u> <u>unclear</u>. He <u>argued</u> that he had a <u>very</u> <u>sound</u> <u>reason</u> for <u>hiding</u> it, but he thanked Rafael anyway and gave him a reward. Rafael was glad to be helpful, and <u>really</u> glad to have some extra <u>money</u>.

Write **Part F** in the left margin of your paper. Then number it from 1 to 11. The two accounts below contradict each other on an important point. Make sure you find that contradiction when you read the accounts.

Passage 1. A fire broke out in the Northside Apartments this morning. The fire was reported by Mr. James Monroe of 143 North Shore Road. Firefighters rushed to the six-story apartment building, where the fire was spreading rapidly. Thanks to some brave and prompt action by Fireman Foley, all the tenants escaped unharmed. Mrs. Fran Goode was trapped in a bedroom, and Fireman Foley dashed in and carried the unconscious woman to safety. Fire Chief Hanrahan says there is evidence to support the theory that the fire was set purposely. He is working with the firefighters on the investigation.

Passage 2. Fireman Foley became a hero this morning when he rescued an unconscious woman from a smoke-filled room. The room collapsed in flames behind him as he emerged carrying Mrs. Fran Goode. The fire occurred in the Northside Apartments. The six-story building was already blazing when firefighters reached it. Fireman Foley suffered smoke inhalation and some burns on his hands. Mrs. Goode is reported in good condition. Fire Chief Hanrahan says that the fire started on the first floor, where a tenant had fallen asleep while smoking a cigar.

Answer each question below. Some of the questions ask where you found an answer. Write **passage 1, passage 2,** or **passages 1 and 2** for these questions.

1. These passages contradict each other on one big point. What point is that?
2. Where did the fire occur?
3. Where did you find the answer to question 2?
4. What kind of injuries did Fireman Foley have?
5. Where did you find the answer to question 4?
6. Who is investigating the cause of the fire?
7. Where did you find the answer to question 6?
8. Who rescued Mrs. Fran Goode?
9. Where did you find the answer to question 8?
10. Who reported the fire?
11. Where did you find the answer to question 10?

When you wish to find out information on a subject, you may consult a book or a person. You are using the book or the person you consult as a **source of information.**

Some sources of information are better than others. A doctor is a good source of information about medical and health problems. A doctor is not necessarily a good source of information about plumbing, raising corn, or building houses.

A car mechanic is a good source of information for answering some kinds of questions. Name some questions that could be answered best by a car mechanic.

A car mechanic is not necessarily a good source of information for answering other kinds of questions. Name some questions that could not be answered best by a car mechanic.

A lawyer is a good source of information for answering some kinds of questions. Name some questions that could be answered best by a lawyer.

A lawyer is not necessarily a good source of information for answering other kinds of questions. Name some questions that could not be answered best by a lawyer.

B A passage that presents a moral tells about what kind of events?
The moral is a statement about those events that is more _____.

The passage below presents this moral:
Never buy something you haven't seen.

> Tom received a phone call from Doris on Saturday morning. Doris said, "Tom, I just talked to Marie, and she told me that there's a red bike down at the police station that you can buy for forty dollars. She says it's in really good shape and it has eighteen speeds and everything. I knew you'd been looking for a bike, so I thought I'd let you know about this one."
>
> "Wow," Tom said. "It's in good shape, huh?"
>
> "Oh yeah. Marie says it's spotless."
>
> "Well, I can't get down to the police station until this afternoon because I've got an appointment with the dentist."
>
> "That will be too late. They'll sell it this morning," Doris said. "Tell you what. Marie said she was going by that way. If I give her a call right now, she can buy it for you. Then all you have to do is pay her back."
>
> "Good deal," Tom said. "Call her back and tell her to buy it."
>
> So Marie bought the bike and later that day Tom went to the police station to get it. He looked around where the bikes were, but he couldn't locate a red eighteen-speed in spotless condition. The only red eighteen-speed was a complete mess, with bent wheels, a shift lever that didn't work, bald tires, bent handlebars, and a crooked frame. When Tom finally realized that the junky bike was the one that he had purchased, he said, "What have I done?"

Name what someone in the story bought without seeing.
Tell what was wrong with the thing.

 C Write **Part C** in the left margin of your paper. You have two minutes to copy the paragraph below.

> **There are over forty types of cleaner fish. These fish provide a special service to larger ocean animals by cleaning parasites and wounded flesh from the animals. Sometimes animals may actually wait in line while the cleaner fish work on other animals.**

★ D Write **Part D** in the left margin of your paper. Then number it from 1 to 4. Look at the picture. Then rewrite each sentence.

1. A boy was running toward the boat.
   Write a more specific statement.
2. A boy with a monkey on his shoulder was sitting in a rubber raft.
   Write a more general statement.
3. A volcano was erupting on the tropical island.
   Write a more general statement.
4. A bird was following the boy.
   Write a more specific statement.

Write **Part E** in the left margin of your paper. Then number it from 1 to 3. Here are three main ideas:

> Main idea A. **One kind of penguin mates during antarctic winters.**
> Main idea B. **Penguins have been around for millions of years.**
> Main idea C. **Penguins had to adapt to cold weather to survive.**

Each main idea fits one of the passages that follow. After reading all the passages, figure out which main idea goes with each passage.

> **Passage 1.** Penguins are one of the oldest kinds of birds. They have been on Earth for at least fifty million years. Some of the ancient penguins were more than five feet—taller than many people—and weighed about two hundred pounds. The tallest penguin today is the emperor penguin, which is only about three feet tall. Other kinds of penguins range from about a foot and a half to just less than three feet tall.

> **Passage 2.** Penguins have always made their home in Antarctica, which is a cold, ice-covered land. But Antarctica wasn't always cold. Millions of years ago, it was a green and pleasant land. Penguins thrived there because they had no predators. But Antarctica's climate slowly changed to one of icy winds and snow. Penguins had to find food in the sea. The strongest penguins learned to swim and survive the cold. Weak penguins died. Today, there are seventeen known kinds of penguins, and they all live in cold waters.

> **Passage 3.** The emperor penguin is the tallest and oddest of all penguins. It is the only animal that breeds in Antarctica during the winter. It mates and hatches its eggs in the coldest place on Earth! The emperor penguin sings to attract a mate. The female lays a large green egg that weighs about a pound. Then the male sits on the egg until it hatches several weeks later. The male is proud of the egg, and sings while he sits on it. Meanwhile, the female is off fishing. When the egg hatches, the female comes back. The parents take turns feeding the chick and sheltering it from the antarctic cold by sitting on it.

1. Which passage does main idea A best fit?
2. Which passage does main idea B best fit?
3. Which passage does main idea C best fit?

A
When you wish to find out information on a subject, you may consult a book or a person. You are using the book or the person you consult as a **source of information.**

> Some sources of information are better than others. A doctor is a good source of information about medical and health problems. A doctor is not necessarily a good source of information about plumbing, raising corn, or building houses.
>
> A secretary is a good source of information for answering some kinds of questions. Name some questions that could best be answered by a secretary.
>
> A secretary is not necessarily a good source of information for answering other kinds of questions. Name some questions that could not be answered best by a secretary.
>
> A dentist is a good source of information for answering some kinds of questions. Name some questions that could be answered best by a dentist.
>
> A dentist is not necessarily a good source of information for answering other kinds of questions. Name some questions that could not be answered best by a dentist.

B
The passage below presents one of these morals:

- **What you have is better than a promise of something that you might get.**
- **You should always take advantage of opportunities that sound good.**
- **You should never listen to a man who talks about gold mines.**

Read the passage and figure out which moral fits.

> Jack had an office job that paid well. He liked his work, but he had been working there for seven years, and the routine had been getting on his nerves. Every day, five days a week, he got up at 7 A.M. After drinking his coffee, he drove to the office. He worked at the office for eight hours, then went home and watched television. He thought that life could be a bit more exciting than it was. Unfortunately, he owed around $5000 to various department stores, and couldn't just quit his job. So Jack kept working.
>
> One day, a man came to the door when Jack was watching television. The man said that he represented a firm from Chicago. The firm owned gold mines in Africa and had just uncovered a big vein of

gold. The man said that it was a sure bet. The man told Jack that he would be a millionaire overnight if he bought shares in the gold mine. It seemed a fine opportunity to make some money without even working for it. So Jack gave the man all his savings, which amounted to about $2000. The next day, he resigned from his job because he knew that soon he would be rich.

Unfortunately, Jack never heard from the man again. There was no gold mine. Jack's bills piled up, but he had no income. Finding another job was hard. He finally got hired at another office, but for much lower pay than what he had received before.

Which moral fits the passage?

 Write **Part C** in the left margin of your paper. You have two minutes to copy the paragraph below.

> **Penguins have always made their home in Antarctica, which is a cold, ice-covered land. But Antarctica hasn't always been cold. Millions of years ago, it was a warm, green, pleasant land. Penguins thrived in that land because they had no predators.**

 VOCABULARY TEST. Write **Part D** in the left margin of your paper. Then number it from 1 to 8. Write the model sentence that means the same thing as each sentence below. You have nine minutes.

1. The major argued that he had sound reasons for hiding the facts.
2. A strange event caused the fear that she showed.
3. They made up a fitting plan.
4. Her answer was filled with irrelevant details.
5. The rule limited their parking.
6. They changed their Swiss money into Canadian money.
7. His directions were unclear and repetitive.
8. By pausing, she lost her chance.

★ **E**

Write **Part E** in the left margin of your paper.

Here are three main ideas:

> - **Many marble games have interesting names.**
> - **Many people enjoy playing marbles.**
> - **Fatty Box is a marble game.**

One of the main ideas fits the passage below. Read the passage.

> There are many popular marble games with interesting names. One popular marble game is called Ringer. Ringer is played with thirteen marbles. It is the game that is played each year in the National Marbles Tournament. Another game with an interesting name is Old Bowler. Old Bowler involves a square shooting area and requires players to shoot marbles off the corners of the square. Variations of Old Bowler are played throughout the world. A game that is very similar to Old Bowler is a game called Fatty Box. Fatty Box is very popular in the Boston area.

Write the main idea that fits the passage. List the three points that fall under the main idea in outline form. Don't forget to indent and label the three points.

LESSON 126

A The two passages below contradict each other on two important points. Make sure you find those contradictions when you read the passages.

Passage 1. Suffrage means the right to vote. In the past, many countries, including the United States, allowed only men, landowners, or people from rich families to vote. Most countries today have laws that give all citizens over a certain age the right to vote. In the United States, women didn't have the right to vote until 1940. Suffrage was an issue for nearly fifty years, and the women who fought for the right to vote were called suffragettes. One of the most famous of these women was Susan B. Anthony. Ms. Anthony once tried to vote in a presidential election, but when a judge told her that she couldn't vote, she decided she didn't want to get in trouble and went home. She devoted the rest of her life to fighting for women's rights. She published her own newspaper, lectured around the United States, and wrote many magazine articles and a book.

Passage 2. Susan B. Anthony, who was born in 1820, taught school for fifteen years. She became a part of the antislavery movement and eventually began to struggle for women's rights. Today, we take for granted that the Constitution applies to all American citizens. In the 1800s, women were deprived of many constitutional rights, including the right to vote. In the election of 1872, Susan B. Anthony set out to change that. She turned up at the polls and voted. Later, she was arrested and sent to trial. The judge fined her $100, which she refused to pay. In 1920, fourteen years after Ms. Anthony's death, the Nineteenth Amendment was passed, granting women the right to vote.

The passages contradict each other on two important points. What are those points?

Let's look up **suffrage** or **Susan B. Anthony** in an encyclopedia and find out which passage is accurate.

B | **A biased argument is an argument that tells the truth, but it tells only part of the truth.**

Study the graph below. Then read the biased argument that is based on the graph.

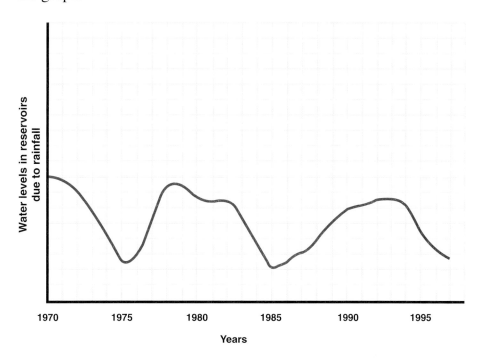

We are having a water shortage in 1997 because the water commissioner that we elected last year is irresponsible. Our reservoirs are at their lowest levels in ten years. Not since the droughts of 1975 and 1985 have we been so dry. It's time for a new water commissioner. Impeach Nad Honker!

This argument is biased because it doesn't take into account some important information. What information is that?

Let's say you wanted to attack the argument above. What would you say?

Write **Part C** in the left margin of your paper. You have two minutes to copy the paragraph below.

> **When you wish to find out information on a subject, you may consult a book or a person. You are using the book or the person you consult as a source of information. Some sources of information are better than others.**

★

Write **Part D** in the left margin of your paper. Then number it 1 and 2.

One of the graphs on the next page is described below. Read the description and answer the questions.

> The graph shows the amount of money spent on the United States space program during the years from 1960 to 1973. These were the early years of the space program. More money was spent in 1966 than in any other year. The graph also shows that the United States never spent more than six billion dollars on the space program in a single year during that time. Spending for the space program in the 1990s has been at least thirteen billion dollars each year.

1. Which graph does the description tell about?
2. How do you know that the description does not tell about graph B?

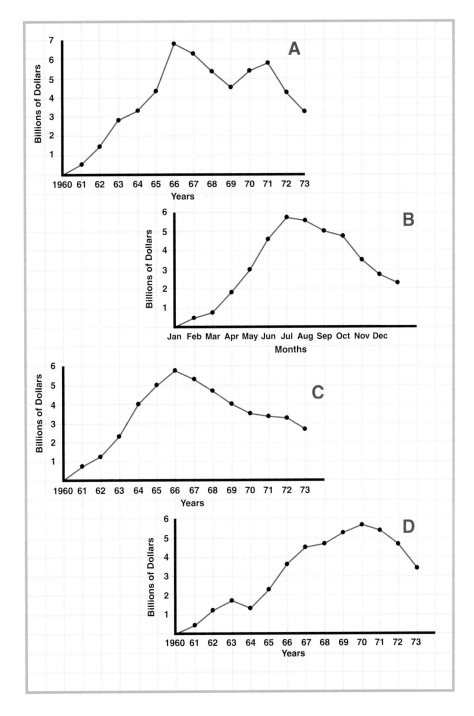

Write **Part E** in the left margin of your paper. The passage below presents one of these morals:

> - **You should never learn anything new.**
> - **Sailing a boat can be dangerous.**
> - **A little knowledge can be a dangerous thing.**

Read the passage and figure out which moral fits.

Carmen had been sailing a couple times with her brother. She loved the water, and she loved sailboats. Her brother, Francisco, let her hold the tiller when they sailed. Carmen loved to steer the boat so that it leaned over, low in the water. A couple times she even helped Francisco put up the sail. Carmen felt that she was beginning to know quite a bit about sailing. One sunny Saturday, when Francisco was in town, Carmen decided she wanted to go sailing. The sailboat was tied up to the dock by their summer cabin. She untied the ropes and got into the boat, put up the sail, and drifted away from the dock. Just then a very strong wind came up. When Carmen tried to steer into it, the boat tipped all the way over on its side, and she fell into the water. She grabbed the side of the boat and held on for what seemed like hours. Finally a boat came by, and a woman helped Carmen out of the water.

Write the moral that fits the passage.

Write **Part F** in the left margin of your paper. Then number it from 1 to 10. The two passages below tell something about desert plants. Read both passages and find out which passage gives more facts about desert plants.

> **Passage A.** In the desert, rain comes only occasionally. The rain may either soak deep into the sand, or it may run off where there is a hard layer just below the surface of the desert. There may be no more rain for a whole year. Desert plants must have methods of storing water or reaching it. Some desert plants have deep roots that go down to where the sand is moist. Other desert plants, such as palm trees, have almost no roots at all. They store water in their trunks. Still other desert plants, such as cactus plants, are one big water-storage tank. If you slice open a cactus plant and squeeze the pulp that is inside, you will get large amounts of water.

> **Passage B.** Desert plants store moisture for use in the driest part of the year. Some plants store water in their leaves; others store water in their stems. Because the desert plants store water, they are ideal sources of water for animals that live in the desert. And people who are lost in the desert can often obtain enough water simply by cutting open particular desert plants.

Answer each question below. Some of the questions ask where you found an answer. Write **passage A, passage B,** or **passages A and B** for these questions.

1. Which passage tells more about desert plants?
2. The other passage gives more facts about something other than desert plants. What does it tell more about?
3. Why do many desert plants store water?
4. Where did you find the answer to question 3?
5. How do desert animals sometimes use desert plants?
6. Where did you find the answer to question 5?
7. How do some desert plants reach water?
8. Where did you find the answer to question 7?
9. In which parts of some desert plants can you find water?
10. Where did you find the answer to question 9?

LESSON 127

A

A biased argument is an argument that tells the truth, but it tells only part of the truth.

Study the graph below. Then read the biased argument that is based on the graph.

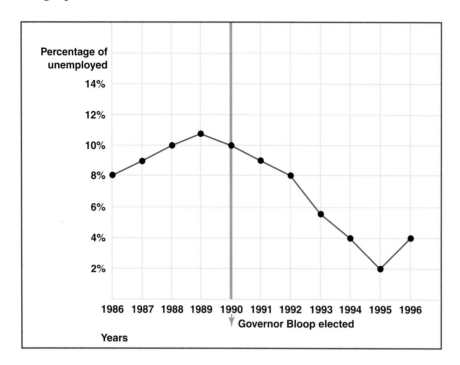

When Governor Bloop was elected in 1990, he promised the people of this state that he would reduce the unemployment rate. I don't see how we could possibly elect him to another term in office. Why, in the last year alone, the unemployment rate has **doubled** from 2 percent in 1995 to the current figure of 4 percent. We can't have this sloppy kind of economic management in our state. "Say no to Bloop, vote for Bleep."

This argument is biased because it doesn't take into account some important information. What information is that?

Let's say that you wanted to attack the argument above. What would you say?

B

Some arguments are faulty because they do not use good sources of information. They use people who are experts in one field to talk about another field.

Read this argument: Professor Deedee has been with the university for twelve years. He is the chairperson of the English department. He has received four awards for his work. All of us who have worked with him have marveled over how intelligent he is. So, when he tells us that our new storm sewers should be routed near the freeway, we should follow his suggestion.

324 LESSON 127

The argument uses Professor Deedee as a source for what kind of information?

Is Professor Deedee a good source for this information?

For what kind of information would Professor Deedee be a good source?

Write **Part C** in the left margin of your paper. You have two minutes to copy the paragraph below.

> **Desert plants store moisture for use in the driest part of the year. Some plants store water in their leaves; others store water in their stems. This water storage makes desert plants ideal sources of water for animals that live in the desert.**

★

Write **Part D** in the left margin of your paper. The passage below presents one of these morals:

* **When you stay very close to something, you may not see it plainly.**
* **When you work like mad, you will certainly fail.**
* **When you shoot 50 percent on a twenty-foot jump shot, you're doing great.**

Read the passage and figure out which moral fits.

> John worked like crazy at basketball. He was weak on moving left and on his fadeaway jump shot. So hour after hour, he dribbled left, jumped, faded, and released the ball; however, he didn't hit many of those shots. But he kept trying and trying. After about two months of daily practice, he still wasn't hitting the shot every time. In fact, he was still missing it about half the time. John was discouraged.
>
> One day, John got into a game of one-on-one with Greg, the best player in the school. To John's surprise, he actually beat Greg in one of the three games they played and almost beat him in the other two. After the game, Greg said, "Man, you are something else. Where did you get that shot moving to the left?"
>
> "But I miss that shot nearly half the time I take it," John said, shaking his head.
>
> "Man," Greg said, "if you make that shot half the time, you're shooting 50 percent. That's a great percentage for a twenty-foot jump shot."

Write the moral that fits the passage.

LESSON 128

A Some arguments are faulty because they do not use good sources of information. They use people who are experts in one field to talk about another field.

> Read this argument: Mr. Leo Frank is a graduate of the University of Indiana School of Agriculture. He has done a number of field studies for leading seed and fertilizer manufacturers. Currently, he owns and manages over 6000 acres of farmland in central Illinois and Indiana. He has served on the Agricultural Advisory Board for three presidents. Mr. Frank is considered a leader in scientific farming, and here's what he says about Fliggo Steer Fertilizer: "It is the best fertilizer on the market. It goes farther and produces more, particularly on row crops. I don't think there's another fertilizer that can match it for performance or for cost."

The argument uses Mr. Frank as a source for what kind of information? Is Mr. Frank a good source for this information?

B The ads below tell the truth. But they don't actually say what they may seem to say.

Read this ad:

> Four out of five doctors that we surveyed recommended the pain reliever found in Brand A aspirin.

Does the ad actually say that the doctors recommended Brand A aspirin?
How would the ad be written if it said that the doctors recommended Brand A aspirin?

Read this ad:

> Use Knock-Em-Dead Bug Killer. It has the chemical that professional exterminators use. It kills bugs instantly, no matter where they are hiding.

Does the ad actually say that Knock-Em-Dead Bug Killer is used by professional exterminators?
How would the ad be written if it said that professional exterminators used Knock-Em-Dead Bug Killer?

Write **Part C** in the left margin of your paper. You have two minutes to copy the paragraph below.

> **Some arguments are faulty because they do not use good sources of information. They use people who are experts in one field to talk about another field. Many television commercials use this trick. Don't be fooled by these kinds of commercials.**

★

Write **Part D** in the left margin of your paper. Then number it from 1 to 3. The description below tells about one of the words shown below. Read the description and answer the questions.

> One root of this word is vor, which means **eat.** An animal that eats plants is called an herbivore. Someone who eats a lot is voracious.
>
> The other root of this word is omni, which means **all.** A collection of all kinds of writing is an omnibus. Something that is all-powerful is omnipotent. This word, containing both roots, describes animals that will eat all things—meat and plants.

omniscient   carnivore   omnivorous   omnifarious

1. Which word does the description tell about?
2. How do you know that the description does not tell about the word **omnifarious?**
3. How do you know that the description does not tell about the word **omniscient?**

E Write **Part E** in the left margin of your paper. The passage below presents one of these morals:

- **Rich people get richer.**
- **Don't question good luck when it comes your way.**
- **A person with $4.56 in his pocket should not turn down a gift of $1000.**

Read the passage and figure out which moral fits.

> George Tiller was a perfect failure, and he was very poor. He had $4.56 in his pocket, and that was all the money he had in the world. He had almost no food in his shabby apartment, and he hadn't worked for nearly three weeks.
>
> He stuffed some bubble gum into his mouth and walked from the apartment, not quite knowing where he would go. He had no way of knowing that he was on his way to a very strange encounter. On the other side of town was a rich man who had decided on his sixtieth birthday to give some money to a needy person. That rich man, Arnold Glib, was driving toward George Tiller's neighborhood when George walked down the front steps of his apartment building.
>
> About ten minutes later, Arnold Glib parked his car near Tiller's apartment building and began looking for a needy person.
>
> George was just walking, not going anywhere in particular. He noticed a fancy car parked at the curb. The car was black and so expensive that George couldn't even afford the key to it. Then George noticed a man in a black coat. The man was standing by the car, and he was speaking to George. "Say there, I would like to talk to you for a moment."
>
> George noticed that the man was holding a pile of money. The man said, "Please take this money," and handed George $1000.
>
> "Why should I?" George asked, staring at the pile of bills. "What kind of sucker do you think I am?"
>
> "You don't understand. I want to help you." Arnold smiled and shrugged. "Oh, forget it." Arnold put the money back into his pockets and walked away.
>
> George shook his head and reached into his own pocket, where he kept all his money: $4.56. As he stood there, he wondered if the money that Arnold had offered him was real.

Write the moral that fits the passage.

The ads below tell the truth. But they don't actually say what they may seem to say.

Read this ad:

> Together, the people at Rammel's Real Estate Company have over 100 years of experience. Experience is the key word in real estate. See one of the people at Rammel's to help you buy or sell any kind of property.

Does the ad actually say that each person at Rammel's has a lot of experience?

How would the ad be written if it said that each person at Rammel's has a lot of experience?

Read this ad:

> We have tested Blinko Car Batteries in cars entered in a demolition derby. After over forty hours of the most horrible abuse in head-on collisions, not one battery failed. If our batteries can stand up under this kind of abuse, you can imagine what they would do in your car.

Does the ad actually say that Blinko Batteries are better for your car?

How would the ad be written if it said that Blinko Batteries are better for your car?

 The passage below presents a moral. Read the passage. Then make up a moral that fits the passage.

Coro was a monkey who lived in New Guinea. Like all monkeys, Coro loved rice. One day Coro was in the jungle when he noticed a woman walk up to the tree in which he was perched. The woman put a heavy wooden box on the ground. Then she tossed several handfuls of rice on the ground. The rice formed a trail to the box.

As soon as the woman left, Coro scampered down the tree and began to eat the rice. He ate and ate, following the trail to the box. As he popped grains of rice into his mouth, he noticed that there was a hole in the box, just large enough for his hand to squeeze through. And inside the box was a huge pile of rice.

Coro reached in and grabbed the biggest fistful of rice his hand could hold. And then he tried to pull his hand out of the box. But the opening in the box was too small for his fist to go through. If Coro had tried to take a tiny handful, he probably could have forced his hand through the opening, but with his fist bulging with rice, there was no chance.

As he tugged and jerked, never letting go of the rice, he noticed that the woman was running toward him. But did Coro let go of the rice and escape? No. Coro just pulled harder, and before he realized what had happened, the woman had a rope around his neck. Coro had been tricked.

Make up a moral for the passage. Start the moral with the words, "If you _____."

 Write **Part C** in the left margin of your paper. You have two minutes to copy the paragraph below.

> **Crabs live in the oceans. A crab's shell is hard, and its armor is solid except for one small tender spot on the underside of the crab's shell. If a predator could reach that soft spot, the predator could easily kill the crab.**

★ Write **Part D** in the left margin of your paper. The passage below presents a moral. Read the passage. Then make up a moral that fits the passage.

> There once was a man who decided to build a house. Winter was approaching, so the man said to himself, "I'll do this house the fast way," and he did. He slapped up boards here and there. He didn't take the time to measure and fit. He pounded and slapped things together. Soon—very soon—his house was completed. "Not bad," he said to himself, until somebody came over to his house and slammed the front door, and down came the walls. In the end, the man had to rebuild his house the right way. It took him much longer this time, however, because he had to work in the cold, and he had to clear away the wreck of the old house.

Write a moral for the passage. Start the moral with the words, "If you _____."

Write **Part A** in the left margin of your paper. You have two minutes to copy the paragraph below.

Tolerant trees do not need much sunlight to survive. They are usually slow growers. Tolerant trees can survive in the shade; therefore, they don't have to grow fast and be the first to reach for sunlight. A white oak is a tolerant tree.

VOCABULARY TEST. Write **Part B** in the left margin of your paper. Then number it from 1 to 8. Write the model sentence that means the same thing as each sentence below. You have nine minutes.

1. His directions were unclear and repetitive.
2. The rule limited their parking.
3. They made up a fitting plan.
4. The major argued that he had sound reasons for hiding the facts.
5. By pausing, she lost her chance.
6. They changed their Swiss money into Canadian money.
7. Her answer was filled with irrelevant details.
8. A strange event caused the fear that she showed.

Write **Part C** in the left margin of your paper. Then number it 1 and 2. One of the graphs is described below. Read the description and then answer the questions.

The circle graph is divided into seven sections, showing seven different sources of air pollution in the United States. The single largest cause of air pollution is road vehicles. The total pollution caused by power plants and by industry is about the same as pollution caused by road vehicles. Some people think that waste disposal is the major cause of air pollution. The graph shows that waste disposal causes only a small part of the problem.

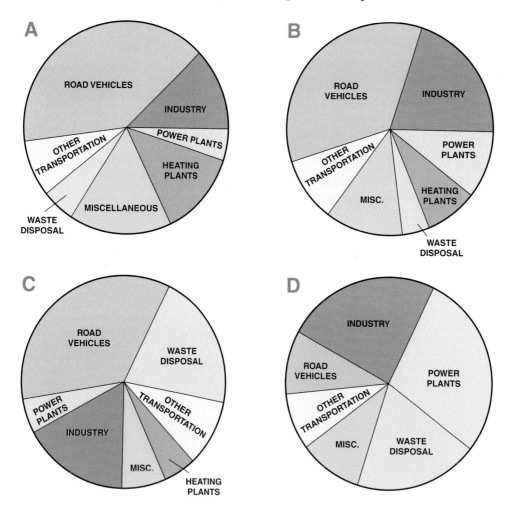

1. Which graph does the description tell about?
2. How do you know that the description does not tell about graph A?

Write **Part D** in the left margin of your paper. The passage below presents a moral. Read the passage. Then make up a moral that fits the passage.

> The Swedish exchange student called Rose for a date, and she turned him down. She just didn't think she'd like Gunnar. He wore funny clothes and had a strange way of talking. She didn't think they would have much in common.
>
> Sunday, when she took her clothes to the laundromat, Gunnar was there. She said hello and sat down to read the paper while her clothes were being washed. Gunnar came over and sat down beside her. "Do you come here often?" he said. He meant it as a joke. "Only to wash clothes," Rose said seriously. He laughed. Rose looked at him, and then she laughed too. Then they talked about baseball, which both of them liked a lot. By the time the clothes were washed, they had discovered that they liked a lot of the same things. This time, when Gunnar asked Rose if she'd like to see a movie, Rose accepted. She realized that Gunnar was fun to be with, and that she wanted to get to know him better.

Write a moral for the passage. Start the moral with the words, "If you ＿＿＿＿＿＿＿＿."

Here are some words that will be in some editing activities. Test yourself to make sure that you know what the words mean.

emphatically—When you say something emphatically, you say it as if you really mean it. Here's a sentence that uses the word **emphatically:**
   His mother spoke emphatically when she told him to clean his plate.

independent—An independent activity is an activity that you do on your own. Here's a sentence that uses the word **independent:**
   The teacher assigned an independent project to each student.

proximity—The proximity of an object is how close the object is to something. Here's a sentence that uses the word **proximity:**
   He was in such proximity to the fire that his boots started smoking.

LESSON 131

A

A biased argument is an argument that tells the truth, but it tells only part of the truth.

Study the description below. Then read the biased argument that is based on the description.

> Name: Lisa Bennett
> Age: 26
> Height: 6 feet 3 inches
> Weight: 150 pounds
> Occupation: Model
> Experience in occupation: Five years of modeling
> Education: High school graduate, two years of college
> Marital status: Married, one child
> Hobbies: Skiing, photography
>
> I'll grant you that most of her qualifications are very good—in fact, they're probably better than any of the other candidates that we're considering for the job. However, I would like to point out one fact. Mrs. Bennett is not a good candidate because she weighs 150 pounds. We all know that women who weigh 150 are far too heavy to model. Let's face it; they're fat. So I vote against hiring Mrs. Bennett.

This argument is biased because it doesn't take into account some important information. What information is that?

Let's say that you wanted to attack the argument above. What would you say?

B

Read the paragraph below.

> The people of Sipple had gone to the lake outside their city ever since the city was formed. They swam, fished, and canoed. Then, in 1979, a large factory was built near the lake. After 1979, nobody went to the lake.

The paragraph gives a clue about what caused the people to stop going to the lake. What caused them to stop?

Name two ways that it could cause people to stop going to the lake.

Write **Part C** in the left margin of your paper. You have two minutes to copy the paragraph below.

> **Intolerant trees cannot survive in the shade. They usually try to shade everything beneath them by putting out lots of leaves on top. If there is no sunlight beneath the tree, no competing vegetation can spring up next to the tree.**

★

Write **Part D** in the left margin of your paper. The passage below presents a moral. Read the passage. Then make up a moral that fits the passage.

> When Fran was eleven, she collected pennies. She loved to skateboard. Almost every day after school, she played with Dizzy and Deb. She did great imitations of her teachers, particularly Mr. Briggs. And she was starting to learn to play the guitar.
>
> Then she entered the gymnastics program at the Academy for Perfection. Her daily schedule called for her to be at the academy every day—even Sundays—at 7:30 A.M. On all days except Sundays, she worked on the parallel bars for two hours, the vaulting horse for two hours, the balance beam for two hours, and the floor exercises for two hours. Later in the day, she had a one-hour dancing lesson. On Sundays she had a light workout for about three hours. In addition to the gymnastic work, Fran did schoolwork—reading, arithmetic, science, social studies, writing, and special projects. For some subjects, she attended regular classes. For other subjects, she was taught by teachers at the academy between the periods of work in various areas of gymnastics.
>
> Fran is now seventeen, and they say that she may make the Olympic team. She's obviously a good gymnast, but she's not much fun anymore. She never talks about anything but gymnastics. I don't think she collects pennies, goes skateboarding, or does any of the other things she used to do. She spends most of her time doing gymnastics.

Write a moral for the passage. Start the moral with the words, "If you _____."

A

A biased argument is an argument that tells the truth, but it tells only part of the truth.

Study the graphs below. Then read the biased argument that is based on the graphs.

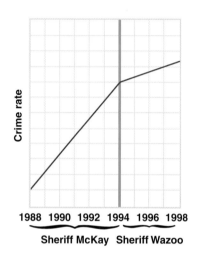

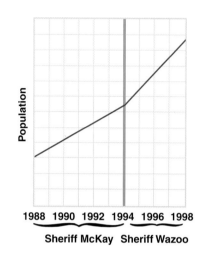

Sheriff Wazoo was elected in 1994. At that time, the crime rate in the county was forty crimes per day. These included crimes against property, murders, other violent crimes, and other forms of disorder. When we look at the crime rate now, four years later, we see that the rate has risen to over forty-seven crimes per day. Imagine that! Although Sheriff Wazoo has spent more money than his predecessor, Sheriff McKay, the crime rate has gone up by more than seven crimes per day. If this is the best Sheriff Wazoo can do, I say let's get somebody in the office who can do the job. Let's put McKay back in office and put a stop to this rising crime rate.

This argument is biased because it doesn't take into account some important information. What information is that?

Let's say that you wanted to attack the argument above. What would you say?

B

Read the paragraph below.

I lived on a farm in Pennsylvania and worked in a nearby town. I had four goats, a horse, two dogs, and three kittens. Two weeks ago I got a new job. I don't have any animals now.

The paragraph gives a clue about why the writer doesn't have animals anymore. Why doesn't the writer have animals anymore?
Name two ways that it could cause the writer not to have animals anymore.

Write **Part C** in the left margin of your paper. You have two minutes to copy the paragraph below.

> **The captain made an innuendo at dinner. He hinted that he might quit his job. What he actually said was, "I won't be here much longer." But I'm fairly sure that his innuendo meant that he was quitting his job.**

★ Write **Part D** in the left margin of your paper. Then number it from 1 to 5. Assume that the picture below is accurate. Examine the picture carefully. Then read the statements below the picture. Some of the statements contradict what the picture shows.

- Write **contradictory** or **not contradictory** for each statement.
- If a statement contradicts the picture, write what the picture shows.

1. The man is leaning over the speaker's stand as he delivers his speech.
2. A pitcher of water is on the table beside the speaker.
3. The man is wearing a suit and a hat.
4. The man has his left hand on the speaker's stand, and he is reaching for a glass of water with his right hand.
5. The curtain behind the speaker is concealing him from the crowd.

LESSON 133

A Read the paragraph below.

> Before August, Ted had a lot of friends. Whenever you would see Ted, you would almost always see a group of people around him, talking and laughing. In August, Ted began working for High Saddle Riding School. Now, whenever Ted is in public, there aren't any people around him. Sometimes a person will come up and say a few words to Ted, but that person will quickly leave.

The paragraph gives a clue about what caused people to stop being around Ted. What caused them to stop?

Name two causes for Ted's not having lots of friends anymore.

B Write **Part B** in the left margin of your paper. You have two minutes to copy the paragraph below.

> **In early civilizations, people used to celebrate when the shortest day of the year passed and the days started getting longer again. In the Northern Hemisphere, the shortest day comes late in December, which is when the celebration would occur.**

★

C Write **Part C** in the left margin of your paper. In the passage below, the underlined words can be replaced with words you have learned. Rewrite the passage using the words you have learned. Remember to start every sentence with a capital letter and to punctuate each sentence correctly.

> "Your <u>answer</u> is <u>unclear</u> and filled with <u>very</u> <u>irrelevant</u> facts. You know that <u>the</u> <u>rules</u> forbid the sort of thing you did. I'm not at all sure you had <u>really</u> <u>sound</u> <u>reasons</u> for <u>hiding</u> your action, but we will give you one more <u>chance</u> to prove yourself here. You should be <u>very</u> careful about acting in a <u>fitting</u> manner in the future."

When you combine sentences with the word **but,** what do you do with the period of the first sentence?

What word follows the comma?

When you combine sentences with the word **therefore,** what do you do with the period of the first sentence?

What follows the semicolon?

What follows the word **therefore?**

When you combine sentences with **who** or **which,** what punctuation comes before **who** or **which?**

Write **Part B** in the left margin of your paper. You have two minutes to copy the paragraph below.

> **He was exonerated from the charge of speeding through the city. At the trial, his lawyer pointed out that he was the only doctor who could help a patient at County Hospital; the patient would have died unless he was operated on within an hour.**

Write **Part C** in the left margin of your paper. Then number it 1 and 2. Read the argument below and study the map. Part of the argument is contradicted by the map.

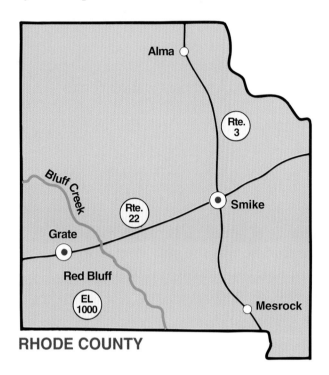

RHODE COUNTY

The symbol ○ means that the city has between 5000 and 10,000 people.
The symbol ◉ means that the city has between 10,000 and 20,000 people.

The symbol (Rte. 22) means that the name of the road is Route 22.

The symbol (EL 1000) means that the mountain is 1000 meters high.

There are several good reasons for routing the new interstate highway through Alma, Smike, and Mesrock.

- Smike is one of the larger towns in Rhode County.
- There are no mountains in the way.
- Right now, there is no road that connects these three towns.
- The new interstate would cross Route 22.
- There are no rivers or creeks to build bridges over.

1. Part of the argument is contradicted by the map. Which part is contradicted?
2. What does the map show?

D Write **Part D** in the left margin of your paper. Rewrite the passage below in three or four sentences. Combine consistent sentences with **and** or **therefore.** Combine inconsistent sentences with **but** or **however.** Combine some sentences with **who** or **which.**

Charges were brought against Mr. Jones by the FTC. FTC stands for Federal Trade Commission. Mr. Jones had advertised that his product contained lots of vitamins and minerals. It really contained only chemicals. Many people had spent money on food that was nutritionally worthless. These people were angry. Mr. Jones knew he was in big trouble if he got Judge Lawson. Judge Lawson gave stiff penalties for false advertising.

LESSON 135

A | **A biased argument is an argument that tells the truth, but it tells only part of the truth.**

Study the graph below. Then read the biased argument that is based on the graph.

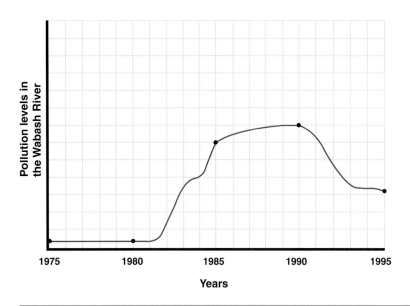

> Over the last five years, the Dino factory has cut pollution in the Wabash River to half of what it was in 1990. The environmentalists are being unfair when they conclude in their report, "The Dino plant is the biggest problem for the river." Actually, the Dino factory is part of the solution! Ever since the plant opened in 1980, management has done everything possible to be a constructive, helpful part of this community. The recent program to cut waste levels in half is just one example of Dino's good will toward its neighbors and the river.

This argument is biased because it doesn't take into account some important information. What information is that?

Let's say that you wanted to attack the argument above. What would you say?

B | Write **Part B** in the left margin of your paper. You have two minutes to copy the paragraph below.

> **The population of animals depends on the food supply. When the supply goes up, more animals can eat. If too many animals eat, they will reduce the food supply. When the food supply goes down, the population of the animals will go down also.**

VOCABULARY TEST. Write **Part C** in the left margin of your paper. Then number it from 1 to 8. Write the model sentence that means the same thing as each sentence below. You have nine minutes.

1. By pausing, she lost her chance.
2. They changed their Swiss money into Canadian money.
3. Her answer was filled with irrelevant details.
4. A strange event caused the fear that she showed.
5. The major argued that he had sound reasons for hiding the facts.
6. They made up a fitting plan.
7. The rule limited their parking.
8. His directions were unclear and repetitive.

★

Write **Part D** in the left margin of your paper. The passage below presents a moral. Read the passage. Then make up a moral that fits the passage.

> Glenda visited her friend Carla, who lived in a town in southern Texas. Most of the families who lived in this town were Mexican, like Carla's family. Carla and her father met Glenda at the bus station and drove her home. They arrived just before supper. Carla's mother explained that she had fixed beef enchiladas for dinner. "I have two kinds—one for Glenda and one for us."
>
> "What's the difference?" Glenda asked.
>
> Carla's mother laughed and then said, "How hot it is. We like things hot—probably too hot for you."
>
> "I don't know," Glenda said. "I've had hot chili and I like it."
>
> "The hot enchiladas are quite hot," Carla said. "If you're not used to really hot food, you should try the mild one."
>
> "Oh, come on," Glenda said. "Let me take a taste of a hot one." She took her fork and cut off a piece from one end of an enchilada. The piece was mostly tortilla, which is not very hot.
>
> Glenda ate it and said, "Oh, that's nothing." She cut a large piece from the center of the enchilada and popped it into her mouth. A moment later, her eyes filled with tears and she gasped, "Oh, oh!" She drank a lot of water and walked around with ice cubes in her mouth for the rest of the evening, but her tongue was still sore.

Write a moral for the passage. Start the moral with the words,
"If you _____."

A   **A biased argument is an argument that tells the truth, but it tells only part of the truth.**

Study the graph below. Then read the biased argument that is based on the graph.

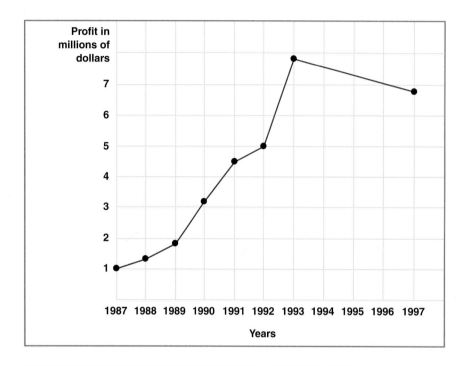

To our customers:

No one likes to see the price of our products go up. You end up paying more, and we always end up losing some customers. But, as this graph shows, our profits have been declining steadily over the last four years. There's no way for us to continue operating this way. Every business has to make a profit. That's why we are announcing this price increase for our products.

This argument is biased because it doesn't take into account some important information. What information is that?

Let's say that you wanted to attack the argument above. What would you say?

B Write **Part B** in the left margin of your paper. You have two minutes to copy the paragraph below.

> **The soldiers were camped in ice and snow for weeks at a time without warm clothes and with little food. They exhibited a great deal of fortitude. Although they were cold and hungry, no one complained. Some even joked about the weather.**

★ **C** Write **Part C** in the left margin of your paper. Then number it from 1 to 11. The two accounts below contradict each other on an important point. Make sure you find that contradiction when you read the accounts.

Passage 1. The small country of Murk has reportedly attacked its neighbor, the kingdom of Smoo. According to reports wired in by Dave Finch, our foreign reporter, Murkian jets bombed Smoo last night, and Murkian soldiers moved into the city of Gona, capital of Smoo. All the details of this attack are not yet known. Over 100 Smoo citizens have been killed. Our president said last night that we will not get involved.

Passage 2. The age-old war between Murk and Smoo flared up again yesterday when Murk launched a full-scale attack on Gona, capital of Smoo. Without warning, Murkian bombers flew over Gona and dropped bombs at about 8 P.M. About 200 Smoos are believed to be dead. The Smoo army is still fighting Murkian soldiers in the streets. The king of Murk has made no comments about the attack. Our president told reporters that this could mean world war and that he was ready to give Smoo whatever help it needs.

Answer each question. Some questions ask where you found an answer. Write **passage 1, passage 2,** or **passages 1 and 2** for these questions.

1. These passages contradict each other on one big point. What is that?
2. Which country was attacked?
3. Where did you find the answer to question 2?
4. What is the capital of Smoo?
5. Where did you find the answer to question 4?
6. At what time did Murk attack Gona?
7. Where did you find the answer to question 6?
8. Who sent in the reports of the attack?
9. Where did you find the answer to question 8?
10. What reasons does the king of Murk give for this attack?
11. Where did you find the answer to question 10?

Write **Part D** in the left margin of your paper. Then number it from 1 to 3.
Here are three main ideas:

> Main idea A. **You pay for more than you eat.**
> Main idea B. **There are ways to make your food dollar go further.**
> Main idea C. **Inflation is eating into the American dollar.**

Each main idea fits one of the passages below. After reading all the passages, figure out which main idea goes with each passage.

Passage 1. Inflation is a serious problem in many countries of the world. Inflation means that prices keep going up. Ever since you were born, prices have been increasing. Every year, food costs more. In the United States, over one-third of the average wage is spent on food. If inflation continues in the United States, close to one-half of the average wage will be spent on food!

Passage 2. Because of rising food costs, people have become interested in stretching their food money. Some ways of saving on food are: use powdered milk for baking; mix hamburger with cereal for a bigger meat loaf; buy the cheaper cuts of meat and tenderize them yourself by cooking them longer or marinating them. Eggs are still one of the cheapest forms of protein and can be made into many interesting dishes.

Passage 3. With food prices soaring, you might think that the farmers in the United States are making a big profit. That is not true. In fact, many farmers are going broke and are selling out to big companies. Who, then, is making the money? Shipping food by truck costs a lot. Processing food—such as canning or freezing—costs a lot. You also pay for the colorful packaging of a box of breakfast cereal and for television advertisements of a product. Actually, most of the money you pay for a can of tuna or a can of beans goes to the "middle men"— the ones who ship and process the food before it reaches your table.

1. Main idea A is: **You pay for more than you eat.** Which passage does main idea A best fit?
2. Main idea B is: **There are ways to make your food dollar go further.** Which passage does main idea B best fit?
3. Main idea C is: **Inflation is eating into the American dollar.** Which passage does main idea C best fit?

Read the paragraph below.

> Five people went into that house over there. A woman met each of them at the door. Then she took them into the living room. They have been very quiet, but every now and then I see one of them peeking out the front window.

The paragraph gives a clue about what the people are doing inside the house. What is the clue?
Name two things they could be doing.

Write **Part B** in the left margin of your paper. You have two minutes to copy the paragraph below.

> **With food prices soaring, you might think that farmers are making big profits. That is not true. In fact, many farmers are going broke. Most of the money that you pay for food goes to the people who ship and process the food.**

★ Write **Part C** in the left margin of your paper.

Here are three main ideas:

> • **The world is covered by large amounts of water.**
> • **Exploration of the ocean depths is a fairly recent phenomenon.**
> • **Sir John Ross and William Beebe explored the ocean.**

One of the main ideas fits the passage below. Read the passage.

Exploring deep in the oceans presents several problems: for example, the lack of light and the severe water pressure. These problems prevented deep-sea exploration for many years. Finally, in 1818, Sir John Ross brought up samples of mud from the ocean floor. He discovered worms in this mud, which had come from over 6000 feet below. Other explorers searched for life below the sea. In 1872, a vessel used strictly for exploring the ocean used nets to investigate the depths of the ocean. The organisms hauled up in these nets had never been seen by people before. This proved that life existed in spite of the darkness and the tremendous pressure. In 1934, William Beebe and Otis Barton actually went down to a depth of 3027 feet. These people used a deep-sea diving vessel called a bathysphere. They had the opportunity to observe many kinds of sea creatures.

Write the main idea that fits the passage. List the three points that fall under the main idea in outline form. Don't forget to indent and label the three points.

A Read the paragraph below.

> Tom was one of the strongest boys in school. He was very active and happy. His parents took out their old wood stove and installed a new gas furnace last year. Since that time, he has become weaker, unhappy, and less active.

The paragraph gives a clue about what caused Tom to become weaker and less active. What caused him to get weaker and less active?
Name two ways that it could cause him to get weaker and less active.

B Write **Part B** in the left margin of your paper. You have two minutes to copy the paragraph below.

> **The Norwegian lemming has a strange way of handling overpopulation. About every five years, the lemming population increases greatly. The lemmings then march out of the mountains where they usually live. They keep marching until some die, which reduces the population.**

★ **C** Write **Part C** in the left margin of your paper. In the passage below, the underlined words can be replaced with words you have learned. Rewrite the passage using the words you have learned. Remember to start every sentence with a capital letter and to punctuate each sentence correctly.

> The writer's article was <u>unclear</u> and <u>repetitive</u>, filled with <u>very</u> boring jokes and <u>irrelevant</u> <u>facts</u>. When he showed it to his editor, she <u>argued</u> that he would have to <u>make up</u> a different <u>plan</u> for the article. Then she told him, "<u>Most of the time</u> your articles are <u>very</u> well written. I think you can <u>change</u> this poorly written article into one that people will <u>really</u> want to read."

D Write **Part D** in the left margin of your paper. Then number it from 1 to 14. The two passages on the next page tell something about hailstorms. Read both passages and find out which passage gives more facts about the damage that hailstorms cause.

Passage A. Hailstorms can cause more property damage than tornadoes. The falling ice destroys crops and kills livestock. Animals as large as horses are occasionally killed in hailstorms. Leaves and fruit are knocked off trees in orchards. Fields of grain, such as wheat or corn, suffer the most. A hailstorm can flatten a ripe field of wheat or corn in a few minutes.

Passage B. Hail is formed in clouds that have strong air currents going up and down. These clouds may be seven or eight kilometers from top to bottom. The air at the top of the clouds is very cold, while the air near the bottom is warm. Rain starts falling in these clouds. But air currents take the raindrops up to the top of the cloud, where they freeze into tiny balls. Then they drop down inside the cloud, and as they do, they are covered with water. Again, the air currents take them up to the top, where the water freezes. Again, they drop down, gathering another coating of water. This process goes on until the hailstone becomes so heavy that it drops from the clouds. Sometimes, these stones are as big as baseballs. If you want to see how many times a hailstone has gone up and down through a cloud, break it open and count the layers, or rings. Every time the stone went up through the cloud, it gathered one layer.

Answer each question below. Some of the questions ask where you found the answer. Write **passage A, passage B,** or **passages A and B** for these questions.

1. Which passage tells more about the damage that hailstorms cause?
2. The other passage gives more facts about something else. What does it tell more about?
3. How can you figure out how many times a hailstone has gone up and down through a cloud?
4. Where did you find the answer to question 3?
5. When does a hailstone finally fall from a cloud?
6. Where did you find the answer to question 5?
7. What is the temperature like at the top of a cloud?
8. Where did you find the answer to question 7?
9. What is the temperature like at the bottom of a cloud?
10. Where did you find the answer to question 9?
11. Name two reasons that farmers don't like hailstorms.
12. Where did you find the answer to question 11?
13. What carries a hailstone up and down in a cloud?
14. Where did you find the answer to question 13?

A biased argument is an argument that tells the truth, but it tells only part of the truth.

Study the graph below. Then read the biased argument that is based on the graph.

> Since 1990, there has been a constant rise in the number of war toys that have been purchased for children. I think we should enlarge the war-toy department in our store. After all, more and more people are buying war toys.

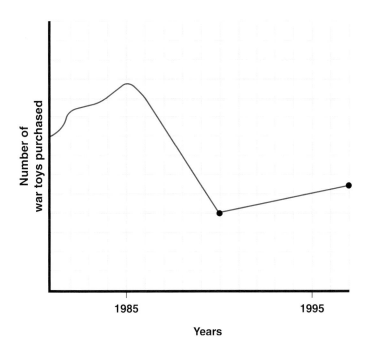

This argument is biased because it doesn't take into account some important information. What information is that?

Let's say that you wanted to attack the argument above. What would you say?

Write **Part B** in the left margin of your paper. You have two minutes to copy the paragraph below.

> **Hailstorms can cause more property damage than tornadoes. Animals as large as horses are occasionally killed in hailstorms. Leaves and fruit are knocked off trees in orchards. A hailstorm can flatten a ripe field of wheat or corn in a few minutes.**

Write **Part C** in the left margin of your paper. Then number it from 1 to 5. The graph below shows the divorce rate for some years between 1945 and 1980. Assume that the graph is accurate. Examine the graph carefully and then read the statements below it. Some of the statements contradict what the graph shows.

- Write **contradictory** or **not contradictory** for each statement.
- If a statement contradicts the graph, write what the graph shows.

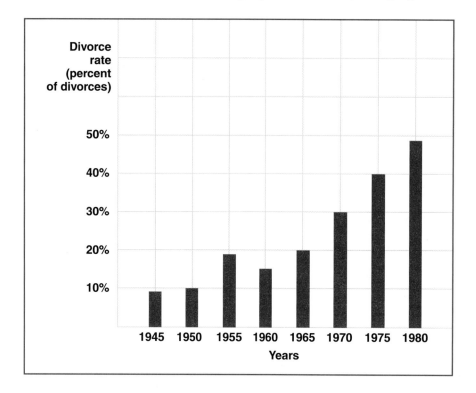

1. Of the years shown on the graph, 1945 had the lowest divorce rate.
2. Between 1950 and 1970, the divorce rate doubled.
3. The divorce rate in 1955 was lower than the divorce rate in 1960.
4. The divorce rate has been increasing since 1965.
5. The divorce rate in 1980 was almost 40 percent.

Write **Part A** in the left margin of your paper. You have two minutes to copy the paragraph below.

> **Last Christmas I got a job decorating windows for the department store downtown. My boss criticized me for putting too many details in the decorations. Finally I devised a strategy for some window scenes that she liked: Santa Claus stuffing stockings with gifts.**

 VOCABULARY TEST. Write **Part B** in the left margin of your paper. Then number it from 1 to 8. Write the model sentence that means the same thing as each sentence below. You have nine minutes.

1. A strange event caused the fear that she showed.
2. Her answer was filled with irrelevant details.
3. They changed their Swiss money into Canadian money.
4. By pausing, she lost her chance.
5. His directions were unclear and repetitive.
6. The rule limited their parking.
7. They made up a fitting plan.
8. The major argued that hc had sound reasons for hiding the facts.

Write **Part C** in the left margin of your paper.
Here are three main ideas:

> - **Many people enjoy mountain climbing.**
> - **There are many dangers in mountain climbing.**
> - **Climbers have to be careful when they cross glaciers.**

Mountain climbers face many dangers. Rockfall is a common danger in mountain climbing. Rockfall is often caused when water enters the fine cracks in rocks and then freezes. When the water freezes in cracks, it expands and often causes the rocks to crack open and fall on climbers below. Climbers also have to be careful when they cross glaciers. The movement of ice can cause giant cracks called crevasses. These cracks may be covered with fresh snow, and a climber who is unroped may fall into one. Bad weather can also be dangerous to climbers. Mist or blowing snow can prevent climbers from seeing their route. Even a little mist or blowing snow may cause climbers to become lost. Winds can become so strong in mountains that climbers may be blown off ridges. Many climbers have been killed in avalanches. Avalanches are sudden snow or rock slides that bury everything in their path.

Write the main idea that fits the passage. List the four points that fall under the main idea in outline form. Don't forget to indent and label the four points.

GLOSSARY

aesthetic A building that has aesthetic value is one that has artistic value.

affirm When you affirm something, you agree with it.

ambiguous An ambiguous statement is an unclear statement.

appropriate An appropriate idea is a fitting idea.

Arabian horse An Arabian horse is a light, fast horse that is bred to produce more intelligent horses.

atlas An atlas is a reference book that has maps and gives facts about places. It shows the size of cities and countries, how far it is from one place to another, and the number of people who live in different places.

audibly When you say something audibly, you say it loud enough for people to hear you.

boar A boar is a wild pig with large tusks.

boycott A boycott takes place when people stop buying from a business or selling to a business. When a business is successfully boycotted, it can either change its practices or go out of business.

Braille Braille is the system of reading and writing that blind people use. Braille is read by running your fingers across patterns of bumps.

carnivorous Carnivorous animals eat other animals. If there were no herbivorous animals, carnivorous animals would become extinct. The teeth and the eyes of carnivorous animals are well designed for hunting. The teeth of carnivorous mammals are pointed. Their right eyes and their left eyes see nearly the same things.

catastrophe A catastrophe is a terrible event that results in death and destruction. Earthquakes, fires, and floods are catastrophes.

cautious When you are cautious, you are very careful.

clarity Something that has clarity is very clear. A diamond with great clarity is a very clear diamond.

cleaner fish Cleaner fish eat parasites from larger ocean animals. Sharks allow cleaner fish to eat things inside their mouths.

clewe In Middle English, **clewe** was the word for thread.

clue A clue is a hint that helps you find your way out of a puzzle.

coast-to-coast railroad The first coast-to-coast railroad in the United States was completed in 1869.

cold war A cold war happens when two countries are close to being in a shooting war with each other.

conceal When you conceal something, you hide it.

consistent Things that are consistent are things that you expect to happen together.

contend When you contend that something is true, you argue that it is true.

convert When you convert something, you change it.

cow A cow is an herbivorous animal that has several stomachs. In a cow's first stomach, organisms digest the cellulose contained in plants. In the second stomach, the organisms are digested.

crab A crab is an animal that has a hard shell. Crabs have different ways to protect themselves from predators: crabs have strong pincers; some crabs live inside hard objects; some crabs carry sea anemones; some crabs disguise themselves with plants and other animals.

currency Currency is money.

data Data are facts.

decomposers Plants that do not have chlorophyll are decomposers.

deprecate When you deprecate someone, you express disapproval of that person.

devise When you devise something, you make it up.

dictionary A dictionary is a reference book that gives facts about words. It shows how to spell a word and how to pronounce it. It tells which part of speech a word is and what the word means. A dictionary also tells the history of words.

diligent A diligent person is a careful person.

donkey A donkey is an animal that descended from equus. Two other names for a donkey are a burro and an ass.

ebullient An ebullient person is a joyful person.

ecology The word **ecology** comes from a Greek word that means **house.** The study of ecology is the study of living things in the world and how they affect each other.

emphatically When you say something emphatically, you say it as if you really mean it.

encyclopedia An encyclopedia is a reference book that gives facts about nearly everything. It tells about planets and plants, about animals and buildings, and about history and famous people.

endangered species An endangered species is one that is nearly extinct. There are more than 1000 species of animals that are currently endangered.

eohippus Eohippus was the earliest-known close relative of the modern horse. We know that eohippus was related to the horse because its skeleton resembles that of a modern horse. Eohippus defended itself by outrunning its enemies. The feet of eohippus changed over the centuries to make it a better runner.

equus Modern horses and other similar animals belong to a group called equus. Some types of equus became large and others became slender, depending on what climate they lived in.

excruciating An excruciating pain is an unbearable pain.

exonerate When you exonerate someone, you free that person of blame.

extinct A type of animal becomes extinct when there are no more animals of that type. A hundred years ago, people were not concerned with ecology because they believed there was no end to different types of wildlife.

extol When you extol something, you praise it.

extraneous An extraneous comment is an irrelevant comment.

extrovert An extrovert is an outgoing person who likes to be with people and gets along well with people.

fallacious A fallacious argument is an argument that is full of error.

fecund Fecund soil is fertile soil.

fenestration The fenestration of a room is the arrangement of windows in the room.

financial aid When people receive financial aid for their schooling, they get the money they need to pay their tuition or living expenses.

fortitude Someone who has fortitude has courage.

fubsy A fubsy person is a fat person.

genius A genius is an extremely intelligent person.

haze When you haze people, you torment them.

herbivorous Herbivorous animals eat plants. If there were no plants, herbivorous animals would become extinct. The teeth and the eyes of many herbivorous mammals are well designed for grazing. The teeth of a herbivorous mammal are flat. Many herbivorous mammals can eat and watch out for enemies at the same time. Their right eye and their left eye don't see the same things.

hesitate When you hesitate, you pause.

hibernate When an animal hibernates, it curls up in a safe place and sleeps for a long period of time.

Houston, Texas Houston is a large city in the southern part of the United States. The two things that stimulated Houston's growth were a railroad and a canal.

ignominious An ignominious person is a disgraceful person.

illusion An illusion is something that doesn't exist.

imitation Something that is fake is an imitation.

inconsistent Things that are inconsistent are things that you don't expect to happen together.

independent An independent activity is an activity that you do on your own.

indolent An indolent person is a lazy person.

inflation Inflation means that prices keep going up.

innuendo An innuendo is something that is said as a hint.

inquiries Inquiries are questions.

interrogation An interrogation session is a questioning session.

intolerant trees Intolerant trees cannot survive in the shade.

irrelevant   Information that does not help explain a fact is irrelevant to the fact.

lease   A lease is an agreement to pay for an apartment or house for a set period of time.

lemming   A Norwegian lemming is a furry, ratlike animal that normally lives in the mountains. The lemming population sometimes gets too big because there aren't many predators in the mountains. The lemmings reduce their population by marching to the sea.

Leonardo da Vinci   Leonardo da Vinci was an inventor, a painter, a musician, and a scientist. He was an Italian, and he lived from 1452 to 1519.

lethal   Something that is lethal is capable of killing living things.

loquacious   A loquacious person is a talkative person.

magnanimous   A magnanimous person is a generous person.

main-idea sentence   The main-idea sentence of a paragraph is the sentence that tells what the paragraph is about. The main idea of a paragraph is the most important idea.

malaise   A malaise is a feeling of depression.

malapropos   A malapropos comment is an inappropriate comment.

malign   When you malign someone, you speak badly about that person.

marital status   Your marital status tells whether you are married, single, widowed, or divorced.

maverick   A maverick can be a person who isn't a part of the group.

Millard Fillmore   Millard Fillmore was moderate in his views, which means he didn't take a strong stand on anything. He became president of the United States when President Taylor died.

miser   A miser is a person who is very stingy.

monthly expenses   Your monthly expenses are how much you pay out each month for things such as rent, food, and car maintenance.

monthly income   Your monthly income is how much money you make each month.

motive   When you have a motive for doing something, you have a reason for doing it.

niggling   Niggling details are petty or small details.

nook   A nook is a small place.

notorious   A notorious person is a well-known person. A notorious person usually has become famous as a result of having done something bad.

obliterated   When something is obliterated, it is destroyed.

opportunity   An opportunity is a chance.

organism   Any living thing is an organism.

overpopulated   When a place is overpopulated, too many things are living there.

panache   When you have panache, you have a dashing charm.

paragraphos   The Greek word **paragraphos** means **by the side of writing.**

parasite   A parasite is one kind of carnivore that does not kill. It gets its nourishment from animal hosts. Fleas, ticks, mosquitoes, and leeches are parasites that live on animals.

penurious   A penurious person is a stingy person.

plants   Green plants are the only living things that manufacture their own food. For plants to manufacture food, they must have sunlight, water, and carbon dioxide. Plants are different from animals in several ways. Plants "breathe in" carbon dioxide, they "exhale" oxygen, and they make their own food.

Pony Express   The Pony Express delivered mail from St. Joseph, Missouri, to Sacramento, California, in eight days instead of the twenty days that mail delivery had taken before. The Pony Express was faster because fresh horses were stationed along the route.

preceding   A preceding event is an event that happened before another event.

predator   A predator is a carnivorous animal that kills.

proximity   Proximity to an object is how close the object is to something.

qualifications for a job   Your qualifications for a job are the things that you have done that would make you good at the job.

redundant   A redundant sentence is a repetitive sentence.

reference for a job   When you name somebody as a reference, that person is supposed to give evidence about what kind of worker you are and how reliable you are.

regulation   A regulation is a rule.

relevant   Information that helps explain a fact is relevant to that fact.

remote   A remote area is an area that is far from towns or cities. Very few people live in remote areas.

replete   A speech that is replete with jokes is filled with jokes.

response   A response is an answer.

restrict   When you restrict something, you limit it.

robot   A robot is a machine that looks and does some things like a human.

rogue   An animal that is a rogue is an animal that travels by itself and is usually mean.

roots   The roots of plants help prevent the formation of a desert by holding down the soil.

sanction   When you sanction something, you approve of it.

scavenger   A scavenger is one kind of carnivore that does not kill. It eats the remains of animals that are already dead. Bears, porcupines, crows, and vultures are scavengers.

scrupulous   A person who is scrupulous is a person who pays a lot of attention to details.

siblings   Siblings are people who have at least one parent in common.

somnolent   When you are somnolent, you are sleepy.

sorrow   Sorrow is sadness. When you are filled with sorrow, you are very sad.

spoonerism   A spoonerism is made by exchanging the first parts of words.

statement of fact   A statement of fact tells what is or what happens.

statement of ought   A statement of ought tells what we should do or what ought to happen.

strategy   A strategy is a plan.

subsequent   A subsequent event is an event that follows another event.

tantalize   When you tantalize someone, you tease that person by putting something just out of reach.

temporary   Situations that are temporary do not last forever. They change.

tenacious   A tenacious person is a stubborn person.

tickbird   A tickbird removes parasites from a rhinoceros and signals danger. The rhinoceros provides food and transportation for the tickbird.

title for property   A title is a piece of paper that tells who owns something.

tolerant trees   Tolerant trees do not need much sunlight to survive.

tuition   Tuition is the fee that people pay to attend a school.

uncouth   An uncouth remark is a vulgar remark.

unctuous   An unctuous liquid is an oily liquid.

valid   A valid excuse is a sound excuse.

vital   Something that is vital is necessary.

wildlife   Wildlife is made up of plants and animals that are wild.